D0993862

José Mourinho:
The Rise of the Translator

by Ciaran Kelly

BENNION KEARNY

NORWICH CITY COLLEGE		
Stock No.	251 880	
Class	796.334 KEL	
Cat.	B2	Proc	3wc

251 880

Published in 2013 by Bennion Kearny Limited.

Copyright ©Bennion Kearny Ltd 2013

Ciaran Kelly has asserted his right under the Copyright, Designs and Patents Act, 1988 to be identified as the author of this book.

ISBN: 978-1-909125-37-7

All Rights Reserved. No part of this publication may be reproduced, stored in a retrieval system, or transmitted in any form or by any means, electronic, mechanical, photocopying, recording or otherwise, without the prior permission of the publisher.

This book is sold subject to the condition that it shall not, by way of trade or otherwise, be lent, re-sold, hired out or otherwise circulated without the publisher's prior consent in any form of binding or cover other than that it which it is published and without a similar condition including this condition being imposed on the subsequent purchaser.

Bennion Kearny has endeavoured to provide trademark information about all the companies and products mentioned in this book by the appropriate use of capitals. However, Bennion Kearny cannot guarantee the accuracy of this information.

Published by Bennion Kearny Limited
6 Woodside, Churnet View Road
Oakamoor, ST10 3AE

www.BennionKearny.com

Cover image and inside images: ©Lee Bullen [LeeBullen.com]

Acknowledgements

This project would never have been possible without the support and assistance of so many people.

Firstly, I'd like to thank each of the interviewees - Damià Abella, Tal Ben Haim, Khalid Boulahrouz, Lauren Cochrane, Jorge Castelo, Jerzy Dudek, Ben Greenhalgh, Jiří Jarošík, Rene Krhin, Russell Latapy, David Mateos, Philippe Montanier, Carlos Neto, Samuel Okunowo, César Peixoto, Nelson Rivas, Craig Rocastle, Mario Rosenstock, Lawrie Sanchez, Knut Tørum, Ernesto Valverde, Steven Watt, and Nigel Worthington - for generously giving me their time.

None of the above-mentioned had shared their Mourinho musings exclusively and in such depth before, so it was an absolute privilege. While some of these names are not synonymous with the traditional Mourinho narrative, that was part of their charm: new insights, fresh anecdotes, and some surprising revelations.

Still, these interviews would not have been possible without those who helped to arrange them so special thanks to Paulo Amorim, Lisa Charlton, Claudio Cioffi, Patxi Xabier Fernandez, Eric Forest, Kristine Fraser, Viktor Kolář, Rodger Linse, Pierre Locht, Wayne Mandeville, Rolf Olstad, Emanuel Roşu, Wojciech Szaniawski, Edit Tóth, and Morgane Zeli for putting up with my incessant emails and calls.

Without a professional and enthusiastic publisher, this book would never have hit the shelves so a massive thank you to Bennion Kearny and my incredibly attentive publisher, James Lumsden-Cook, for believing in this book as much as I have.

Special thanks, also, to Lee Bullen for the fantastic cover and illustrations.

A huge thank you, too, to those who have encouraged and harnessed my passion for writing over the past few years, particularly my former tutors at St Mary's College, Twickenham and News Associates, London.

Then, there are those closest to me. Ironically, I found this the most difficult part of the book to write; in this instance, words cannot tell the full story.

Whether it was my brother, Seán, bringing down his Merlin Premier League sticker book in 1997 to kick this all off; or my sister, Laura, loaning me my first Roald Dahl book, I owe a lot to my siblings' continued support.

My folks, John and Angela, have been the enthusiastic pillars in my journey up until this point. They have never pushed me into any career path and I will be forever grateful for that. I hope this book has gone some way to repaying their faith.

Finally, there are those dozen or so special crew supporters, who have always shown a keen interest in my escapades. Here's to many more hilarious adventures in Galway and beyond; I guess the next round's on me…

About the Author

Ciaran Kelly is a fledgling football writer from Galway, Ireland. He completed an NCTJ-accredited Masters in Sports Journalism at St Mary's College, Twickenham in 2013. Ciaran also holds a Bachelor of Arts in English and History from NUI Galway. The author of Johan Cruyff: The Total Voetballer, Ciaran has contributed to FourFourTwo, the Southwestlondoner newspaper, and cfcuk fanzine. He has also written a popular weekly feature with backpagefootball since 2011. Ciaran has interviewed a range of high-profile figures, including Bertie Ahern, Eamon Dunphy, and Brian Barwick.

Table of Contents

"A man of genius makes no mistakes. His errors are volitional and are the portals of discovery."

James Joyce, Scylla and Charybdis, *Ulysses*

Preface: Birth and Rebirth

The 26th of January, 1963 began like any other Saturday morning for Félix Mourinho. In Setúbal - a small town 45 kilometres south-east of Lisbon - the 24-year-old polished his boots, soaked his goalkeeping gloves in warm water, and ironed his pre-match suit in preparation for another Primeira Divisão match as Vitória Setúbal's number one. Shortly afterwards, the goalkeeper was to set off for Vitória's newly-opened Estádio Bonfim to stake yet another claim for a Portuguese cap. Among those watching would be his four-year-old daughter, Teresa.

Then, the contractions started.

* * *

It was an intriguing era for the birth of José Mário dos Santos Mourinho Félix, with the first 11 years of his life falling under António de Oliveira Salazar's dictatorial rule.

Salazar's Portugal clung on to the three Fs: Football, Fado (song) and Fátima (religion), and the 1960s were a landmark era for all three. Portugal qualified for its first World Cup in 1966. The success of singers such as Amália Rodrigues, Alfredo Marceneiro and Fernando Maurício brought Lisbon Fado to a television audience. And the legacy of the reputed apparition of the Virgin Mary at Fátima in 1911 lived on, with speculation over the remaining Third Secret of Lúcia Santos - which predicted persecution for Christians in the 20th century - drawing worldwide attention.

In 1974, Salazar's party, Estado Novo (New State), lost power following the so-called Carnation Revolution when the Armed Forces Movement staged a bloodless military coup. The young Mourinho witnessed a different Portugal: the Third Republic under the presidencies of António de Spínola, Francisco da Costa Gomes and, particularly, the elected António Ramalho Eanes. Finally, there was the encouragement of the freedoms of speech, the vote, and educational advancement. The thuggish International State and Defence Police agency was abolished, and there was a broadening of women's horizons in the work place.

And, at last, there was a movement away from inhumane African colonisation, Salazar's controversial pet project that instigated the costly and unpopular Portuguese Colonial War in Angola, Portuguese Guinea, and Mozambique from 1961. The latter would have a particular effect on Mourinho - with the Mozambique-born Eusébio a childhood idol - and it must be noted that Mourinho's eventual marriage to the Angolan-born Matilde Faria, in 1989, would have been condemned by Salazar.

Preface

However, Portugal's return to democracy - for the first time since 1926 - was not going to be a seamless, joyous transition for the upper-class Mourinho family.

Chapter 1: The Dream is Over

While the Carnation Revolution certainly broadened Mourinho's horizons, the family, as a whole, were to suffer somewhat and Félix even considered uprooting to a club in Spain. For a centre-right family like the Mourinhos, it was a disconcerting period.

Mourinho's mother, Maria dos Santos, a popular primary school teacher in Setúbal, came from privileged stock. Her uncle, Mário Ledo, was one of Portugal's leading providers of the Portuguese staple of sardines – with bases in Setúbal, Oporto, and the Algarve. Thriving under the immense patriotism and self-sufficiency ideal of the Salazar regime, Ledo was one of Setúbal's wealthiest men. He even provided land for, and funded the building of, the Estádio Bonfim, Setúbal's multi-purpose stadium, in 1962. In an era before excessive wages for footballers, there was no understating just how important the financial security provided by Ledo was for the Mourinho family.

However, in 1972, Uncle Ledo died, of natural causes, and his business was expropriated by the state. In tandem with the unprecedented event of a Communist mayor coming to power in Setúbal, the Mourinhos were rocked. The family lost their holiday homes, complete with maids and servants, scattered across the coast and were forced to move into a smaller house. For Mourinho, though, this has to be put into context: "From my childhood, I had friends at the top of the social classes and friends who lived with great difficulties. This made me be prepared for everything in life and to know how to co-exist, to live and get along with everyone. It was a time of change in Portugal and for me, a very positive life experience that prepared me for a lifetime."

* * *

Rather than the playground or the school yard, the classroom was to play a major role in shaping Mourinho - which came as little surprise given Maria's influence in enrolling her son in a private school. As young as three years of age, Mourinho had been intrigued by the morning routine of his seven-year-old sister, Teresa, readying her uniform and lunch. In fact, the school environment bred Mourinho's early thirst for perfectionism and as early as five years of age, he would have all of his pens, crayons and rulers perfectly ordered and cased in his satchel. While this may not seem terribly revealing or prophetic, few five-year-olds are capable of consistently exhibiting these kinds of organisational and management skills.

Still, given Mourinho's love of football, it was Félix – despite often being on away trips with Vitória and later, another club, Belenenses – who had the most profound effect on Mourinho. The young Mourinho would absorb all things football from his father and, remarkably, the result of this was a three-year-old Mourinho being inconsolable after England knocked Portugal and his beloved Eusébio out of the 1966 World Cup quarter-finals.

As early as four years of age, Mourinho acted as a training ground ball-boy behind Félix's goal during Vitória's training sessions. Buoyed, Félix believed Mourinho could follow in his footsteps and continue the Mourinho legacy in Portuguese football. The goalkeeper stressed the importance of following the national game, but with the influx of Western culture post-Salazar, Mourinho was soon to begin his love affair with the English First Division as a childhood supporter of Liverpool and an idoliser of Kevin Keegan and Kenny Dalglish. This was to coincide with Félix winning his only cap for Portugal, as a 34-year-old against Ireland in the Independence Cup in 1972.

The broadening of Mourinho's horizons, as he grew up, only increased his obsession with football and while Félix soon realised that Mourinho would not play at the highest level, he found other uses for his son outside his ballboy duties. Mourinho began to accompany Félix on away trips as his father's playing career neared its end and, as a result, it was inevitable that Félix would utilise José when his management career took off at Rio Ave in 1981. Having graduated into management as head coach of Estrela Portalegre in 1976, Félix would spend many Monday evenings with the teenage Mourinho talking through the importance and justification of substitutions. It is a tradition that has carried on with Mourinho and his own son, José Mário Jr, in recent years.

At Rio Ave, Félix asked the 19-year-old Mourinho to compile scouting dossiers, manage the Under-16s, and pass on messages to players during matches. Even though Félix rarely selected Mourinho as a player, Mourinho certainly played his part in Félix's ground-breaking success. Rio Ave recorded a then club-record fifth place in 1981-82, and Mourinho was a popular figure in the dressing room. This was testament to Mourinho's affable personality, with few dressing room concerns over favouritism regarding team selection. Baltemar Brtio, a commanding 30-year-old Brazilian defender, was among those who closely bonded with Mourinho.

However, Rio Ave's then president, José Maria Pinho, believed nepotism was in the offing and even prohibited Mourinho from being picked for an end-of-the-season clash against the champions-elect, Sporting Lisbon, in 1981–82. Rio Ave went on to lose the game 7-0 and this episode was to play a massive part in Félix's decision to leave for Belenenses that summer.

So, while Mourinho was to follow Félix, again, to Belenenses as a contracted player, his contribution behind the scenes was more note-worthy. It set the tone for Mourinho's playing career: making just 94 appearances as a dogged midfielder in seven seasons for Rio Ave, Belenenses, Sesimbra, and Comércio e Indústria. Ironically, though, as Mourinho's playing career seemingly stagnated in the lower leagues, he was to enjoy the most memorable period of his career – away from his father's shadow.

At Sesimbra in Division Three, for example, Mourinho stood out as one of the team's leaders. Known as Zé to his team-mates, Mourinho had a penchant for incessantly interacting with the referee on the field. However, boardroom strife and a demotivated squad, due to seriously delayed wage payments, inhibited any chance Mourinho had of tasting nominal success in what should have been his pivotal, burgeoning years between 1983 and 1985.

With Mourinho's final club, Comércio e Indústria in Setúbal's Division 1, the Portuguese had the strongest bond with his team-mates. It was the club, at 22 years of age, where Mourinho realised his level. So, despite the fact he received no wage and had to pay for his own equipment, Mourinho relished the shackles being lifted. From enjoying feasts of boar to all-night drinking sessions – paid for by the club's Arab president – Mourinho thrived in amateur football. According to one of his then team-mates, Luis Filipe, Mourinho even had a fondness for soaking his coaches by hanging water buckets on top of the dressing room door in a crude practical joke.

Unsurprisingly, therefore, these antics meant that Mourinho was an immensely-popular player at Indústria but there was another reason for this heroic status. Following one of their daily training sessions, Mourinho and his team-mate, Dé, were the only players left in the dressing room of the Plaza de Toro. Mourinho was the last to leave and lock-up, with Dé heading to the car park to drive home in his 10-year-old FIAT. As Dé turned the ignition, the car's engine caught fire and he banged his head after being bumped into the driver's door. The heat, as well as Dé's dazed state, meant that the driver's door would not open. With the passenger's door close to a wall and unable to open - Dé was trapped. Screaming, and near-asphyxiated, things were looking grim until an alerted Mourinho burst out of the dressing room and rescued his team-mate.

If ever an episode was to illustrate the selfless, all-for-one mentality Mourinho was to breed as a manager with his players in the proceeding decades, this was it.

Chapter 2: The Mister

Having realised that his wageless efforts with Comércio e Indústria were no longer sustainable enough to survive, Mourinho looked to another career path. However, while it may have seemed that retirement as a footballer at 24 spelt the end of Mourinho's association with football, in 1987, it was clear that it was only with regards to playing football. As a result - having previously ignored his mother's attempts to enrol him into a business school in 1982 - Mourinho opted to study a five-year sport science course at Instituto Superior de Educacao Fisica in Lisbon to keep his coaching prospects alive.

Professors Jorge Castelo and Carlos Neto were two of Mourinho's tutors at the Instituto, between 1982 and 1987, and they told me about the Mourinho years.

JC: "At the time, Mourinho was part of a group of students who were confronted with a strategic change at the university. Students were able to choose between a degree in physical education or sports training. 15/16 students opted for sports training, with a specialisation in football. This group of students was highly motivated because they were able to fully devote themselves to the study of football observation, analysis, planning, and training. We had good conditions for these students to be able to fulfil their potential.

"At that time, we looked at the study of football under three essential topics: the logic of how the player develops, the strategic and tactical logic of football, and the training methods for combining the logic of learning with the internal logic of the game. Out of these three logics, we devoted the most time to the internal logic of the game, with tactical analysis and re-analysis of competitions involving clubs and national teams... The VCR had just appeared on the market, which allowed us to observe games at different speeds and angles, and allowed us to replay pivotal moments to understand, categorise, and regularly check playing routines. Clearly, we can see the university's influence in Mourinho's methodology."

CN: "I taught the Fundamentals of Physical Education and I have a very positive memory of Mourinho as a person, with a strong personality and a great conviction in his opinions about Sports and Physical Education. He also had an accurate critical sense, good observational skills for movement tasks, and a good knowledge about the sports' context. Mourinho was also successful in many disciplines that required some mathematical knowledge (Biomechanics, Statistics of Physical Education, Methods of Assessment in Physical Education, Kinanthropometry). He had a nice relationship with his peers, and had a good rational capability for thinking about problems in a philosophical, technical, and scientific manner… There was no tension between Mourinho and any of his teachers. I recall a good dynamic and a great enthusiasm in the football department."

JC: "Mourinho was popular with his classmates. He was one of the prominent members of this group who had the motivation, the will, and the ability to become a coach of excellence. I can't say that Mourinho, as a student, knew more than others in the context of analysis, planning, and training of the game, but he had some elements that stood out. He was quicker to think, solve problems, adapt to situations, and influence the group.

"Mourinho only wanted to work in football for his future, no doubt about it. He didn't make it as a professional player, so here was another route that was just as important: coaching… Other members of the same group have gone on to have good professional careers, but there is quite a difference between what Mourinho has achieved and what *all* of his other classmates have done. The key was that he had a father who played and coached: Mourinho, during his childhood and adolescence, experienced more of the game's situations, emotions, and dramas. He was closer than anyone to the specifics of the game."

CN: "His father won many titles in his football career as a goalkeeper and José never achieved such a successful career as a player. However, he showed an early innate ability to organise and prepare reports and files for his father's teams. So, I believe that his family environment was also very important for his future career…. From his enrolment, Mourinho showed an interest in football training. In his final year at the Institute, he chose football as his option in the Methodology of Sports Training discipline. In addition, his research seminar was about the Observation and Analysis of Modern Football. He graduated with good grades and became a Physical Education teacher in a secondary school in Setúbal, his home town, showing his aptitude to prepare, organise, and manage people."

JC: "I must admit, I didn't witness anything that was a concrete indication that Mourinho would go on to become the best coach in the world. I knew Mourinho would always go on to be a coach, but that he would go on to be *the* best was very difficult to predict… Nothing is impossible in football. A high level player can have multiple paths and directions in the future. The same goes for coaches: they may spring from different cultures, journeys, and experiences that do not necessarily come from being a top professional player. In fact, for everything, you need determination, motivation, willingness and commitment. These are the factors that make us more capable and competent."

CN: "His personal characteristics (personality, character, persistence, and work capacity) were already noticeable when he was a student. It is not difficult to understand that these traits could pre-empt the future success that he ended up having in his career. His experience as a football player, as his father's assistant, and the scientific, pedagogical and technical background that he acquired during his course reveal his ambition to become a great football coach…We need to reinforce that he had a great team of football teachers in this school. This team helped to create a new paradigm of Portuguese football. Mourinho was part of this process as a student."

Intriguingly, in gaining entry to the institute, Mourinho had to re-take his final entrance exams after failing honours maths. Over 27 years later, though, he would go on to receive an honorary degree from the same university for his accomplishments in professional football. Surprisingly, it was not a popular decision, according to Castelo and Neto.

JC: "I was part of the FMH's [Technical University of Lisbon] sport science department who decided on the award of an honorary degree to José Mourinho. Not all were in agreement, even if football is *the* most appreciated sport in Portugal. The 'elites' consider the study of football as a minor 'God', but a lot of these 'elites' were pure opportunists. As we say in Portugal, 'God writes straight with crooked lines…'"

CN: "These criticisms tend to occur in the assignment of an honorary PhD degree. In Mourinho's case, this degree was legal. It started by a proposal from the Scientific Council of FMH, which was approved by the Senate of the Technical University of Lisbon with only one abstention. It was a day of great pride and joy for me and for my colleagues, because it was proof of the recognition of one of our former students as an excellent professional. In fact, it is now unquestionable that Mourinho is a person of great quality in the world of football; he is *the Special One*."

* * *

Mourinho's time at university was not only momentous for his professional career but also for the consummation of his personal life. Having met his childhood sweetheart, Matilde 'Tami' Faria, at a teenage disco in Setúbal in 1980, the couple kept in touch at university. Tami was born to a ship chandler in Angola, who had been left disabled after being shot when he fought in the Angolan War of Independence. It saw the family, like thousands of others, being airlifted and relocated to Lisbon in 1975.

Tami was studying philosophy at the Catholic University of Lisbon and is sure to have influenced Mourinho's growing appreciation of deeper thinking as his life has progressed.

Chapter 2

The couple would go on to marry in 1989, after Mourinho began climbing the coaching ladder as a youth coach at Vitória Setúbal.

* * *

With his perfect hybrid of sporting intellectual astuteness and immense hunger, Mourinho quickly grasped the teachings of his tutors at university, including football coaches such as Carlos Queiroz and Jesualdo Ferreira. Interestingly, there was little evidence of the tense relationship Mourinho and Ferreira would share in the future, with Mourinho eventually going on to remark that Ferreira was a "donkey who worked for 30 years, but never became a horse".

Utilising the teachings that the likes of Neto, Castelo, and Ferreira passed on to him, Mourinho spent two years as a 'freelance' PE teacher in various primary schools - in Arangues, Alhos Vedos, and Bela Vista - between 1987 and 1989. One student of Mourinho's at the time remarked how, before he arrived, no girls wanted to do PE but once the alluring Mourinho started teaching, the sign-up sheets were full. Mourinho certainly enjoyed the job and cited working with children with learning and physical disabilities as a personal highlight.

So, while it was clear that Mourinho had not left a lasting legacy as a full-time professional footballer, he vowed to make his father proud by doing the next best thing: becoming a ground-breaking football manager. The early signs of this innovativeness were Mourinho's attention to detail and eccentric quirks, many of which are still evident today. Mourinho always arrives one hour early for training; takes his seat in the dugout five minutes before the players emerge; only scribbles down notes in the first-half; and makes sure he is the first to enter the dressing room before his players or staff post-match.

Mourinho, though, did not have the most glamorous beginning to his coaching career. Portugal did not subscribe to the UEFA coaching curiculum and Mourinho started the first part of his UEFA coaching course in Largs, Scotland as a shy and introverted individual in 1988. Aside from his obsession with transitions of play, Mourinho was not, initially, remembered by the likes of Gordon Strachan and Andy Roxburgh – who were among the 150 students on the course – or lecturers such as Paul Sturrock and Ross Mathie. Also, reflecting just how far Mourinho had to go, one of the first things he learnt on the course was the need to have players with their backs to the sun when giving them instructions during a huddle in training.

Still, owing much to his drive and determination, Mourinho became a youth coach at Vitória in 1989 and was able to support his wife, Tami, by doing something he loved. Also, given his experience as a PE teacher, it was a relatively seamless transition into coaching teenage footballers with the first part of his UEFA coaching course already completed.

It was not just Mourinho who was making an impression as a young member of staff. Manuel Fernandes, the prolific Portuguese striker who netted 189 goals in 326 games for Sporting Lisbon, spent his final playing season at Vitória in 1987-88 under Malcolm Allison. Despite being just 37 years of age, the star striker was given the opportunity to replace Allison in the summer of 1988.

Fernandes greatly impressed in his two seasons managing Vitória: finishing fifth in his first season and seventh in his second. Eager for a new challenge – a continuing theme in the nomadic career of Fernandes – the Portuguese took over at Estrela da Amadora in 1990. Tellingly, after accepting the position, the only member of staff Fernandes took with him from Vitória was Mourinho. Why? Well, aside from glowing reports from youth players, the 27-year-old greatly impressed Fernandes with his modern outlook and enthusiasm.

Still, it was to prove a disappointing campaign for Fernandes and Mourinho as Amadora finished in 18th place and were relegated to the Segunda Divisão. Meanwhile, the duo's former club, Vitória de Setúbal, dropped an incredible 10 places and were also relegated.

The nomadic Fernandes then left for Ovarense in the Segunda Divisão after just a season at Amadora and, again, planned to take Mourinho with him. Mourinho, though, was wanted as a fitness coach by his former tutor and Fernandes' replacement, Ferreira, at Amadora. While, admittedly, a difficult decision, Mourinho began to resent having to rely on the inconsistent Fernandes and stayed another year at Amadora. However, by the end of the 1991-92 campaign, Ferreira was dismissed after a dismal 13th place finish in the Segunda Divisão. Clearly, Mourinho needed a more stable introduction to the world of football. In Sir Bobby Robson, he had that man.

Despite his roaming tendencies, the importance of Fernandes in Mourinho's early coaching career cannot be understated and he proved crucial to Mourinho meeting Robson. The Englishman - in his first real foreign job, following a two-year spell with the predominantly English-speaking PSV Eindhoven - had sought a translator at Sporting Lisbon. With Sporting's president, Sousa Cintra, appointing Fernandes as Robson's official assistant when the Englishman took over at Sporting in 1992, Mourinho was the perfect fit. After all, English, Spanish and, obviously, Portuguese were among Mourinho's arsenal of languages. In that one moment, growing up in a post-Salazar era had paid dividends, with the democratic Portuguese government advocating the teaching of, at least, one foreign language for students. So, while, initially, the role of translator may have seemed a step back, Mourinho would soon be shadowing the *Mister*, Robson, to such a degree that he was soon consulted over tactics and coaching methods. Having learnt so much previously from his father and his tutors at the Instituto, the genesis of Mourinho, the coach, had firmly begun.

Robson first met Mourinho at his unveiling, with the Portuguese standing alongside Sintra to greet the Englishman at Lisbon Airport. The first impressions were warm, with the slick Mourinho already a striking figure in Robson's eyes: "The president brought along a bright young lad called José Mourinho, who said that he was to be my interpreter. A good looking guy; told him not to stand next to me too many times! I knew he was keen and I knew, at one time, he would leave me."

Despite a 30-year age gap, the duo soon struck up an unlikely friendship – centred on a distaste for the tempestuous Sintra. For example, while the transfers of Paulo Sousa and António Pacheco to Sporting from Benfica greatly weakened Sporting's bitter rival and boosted attendances, Robson was never consulted by Sintra about signing them. Additionally, when Sporting were to play Benfica on 17 October, Sintra forbade Robson from scouting Benfica at their stadium, the Estádio da Luz, yet, on the flipside, offered him and the squad quadruple bonuses for victories against Benfica and Porto.

Mourinho and Robson, though, flourished and once Mourinho gained Robson's trust – including compiling a dossier of simple Portuguese football phrases for Robson to learn – the Englishman would involve Mourinho on the training pitch. Joining Robson and Fernandes on the training field, Mourinho had numerous roles – despite the fact that Robson always liked to be in full control. He acted as a goalkeeping coach, took part in training matches if numbers needed to be made up, stood alongside Robson in his every dealing with the press, and attended backroom and boardroom meetings. Subsequently, Mourinho, in his own words, began the 15-year trek to becoming "an overnight success".

Robson quickly learnt of the merits of Mourinho's soon to be trademark fearless nature with national stars. With the likes of Luís Figo and Jorge Cadete among Sporting's playing staff, Robson was struck by Mourinho's composure: "When I'd indicate and say to José 'tell him this, tell him that', I always had the feeling José was saying it in the way and manner I would have… He told me what the players were saying when they thought I couldn't understand." Obviously, Mourinho would also benefit - not least with Robson's famed, old-school, simple instructions and his mastery of the art of team building. Mourinho, too, would quickly be struck by Robson's habit of arriving just ten minutes before a training session began, and the

Englishman's focus on shooting and finishing drills. Also, regarding methodology, Mourinho learnt a lot from Roger Spry, Robson's acclaimed fitness coach at Sporting at the time.

Still, owed to Robson's reputation as one of football's great gentlemen, it should come as little surprise to think that Robson's early fostering of Mourinho would prove the basis for the Portuguese's ardent refusal to ever rest on his laurels: "One of the most important things I learnt from Bobby Robson is that when you win, you shouldn't assume you are *the* team and when you lose, you shouldn't think you are rubbish." However, despite being top in the Primeira Liga, their relationship was, seemingly, about to come to an end in arctic conditions in Salzburg on 7 December, 1993.

Robson's work had been paying off domestically, but the erratic Sintra was desperate to deliver Sporting's first European trophy since the UEFA Cup Winners' Cup in 1964. Robson valued the league more but having defeated Salzburg 2-0 in the first-leg of the third-round of the UEFA Cup, confidence was high going into the return leg a week later. It should have been straightforward but the conditions were desperate; Sousa even wrapped brown bags around his feet for extra warmth. The Iberian-dominated Lisbon were shocked by the temperatures and were defeated 3-0 after extra time in front of the onlooking Sintra.

On the flight home, an incensed Sintra took the pilot's intercom and informed Robson, in Portuguese, that he was to be dismissed. Summing up the unexpected absurdity of the situation for Robson, it was, naturally, not until Mourinho told him in English that he understood the enormity of the situation. It was to prove the first time Robson was sacked in what was, at that stage, a glittering 26-year managerial career. However, despite the sacking coming just four-and-a-half years after nearly being hounded out of the England job by the English media, Robson was undeterred.

In fact, the Sporting experience actually inspired the 60-year-old further – particularly in the aftermath of his farewell dinner with the players. Among the attendees was Serhiy Scherbakov, who had been signed by Robson from Shakhtar Donetsk just months previously. Robson believed the 22-year-old Ukranian had the potential to become one of the greatest midfielders in the world. After the surprisingly merry dinner, though, Scherbakov drove home over the alcohol limit and jumped a red light – leading to a horrific car crash.

Scherbakov was left paralysed - fracturing his skull and spinal column in three places - and never regained the use of his legs. Robson and Mourinho were rocked by the crash, with both men feeling immense guilt for Scherbakhov's career-ending accident coming in the immediate aftermath of their farewell dinner.

Chapter 2

It was not to prove the last time that Robson and Mourinho were to share an immense emotional connection and experience.

Chapter 3: El Traductor

Having left Sporting holding top spot in the Primeira Liga when he departed, Sir Bobby Robson could hold his head up high and was snapped up by Porto in the summer of 1994. The Englishman had not seen the offer coming and had originally planned to follow the final leg of England's cricket tour of the West Indies in April. With the Porto deal in place, the dedicated Robson cancelled his trip to the Caribbean and, tellingly, rather than bringing Manuel Fernandes with him to the Estádio das Antas as his assistant, he took Mourinho. Tami, meanwhile, was to stay in Setúbal and was soon to expect the couple's first child, Matilde Jr.

There was still confusion about Mourinho's exact role amongst those inside the club, with rumours of Mourinho being the most expensive interpreter in Portuguese football on £35,000 per year. However, the scouting dossiers Mourinho compiled were invaluable and Robson – who had worked with the eyes and ears of the likes of Dave Sexton and Howard Wilkinson previously – rated them as the best he had ever seen.

Mourinho was to take the art of compiling scouting dossiers to a whole new level and to put this into context, Nigel Worthington – who played under Wilkinson for six years at Sheffield Wednesday and Leeds – told me about the preparation of a typical Wilkinson report: "Howard Wilkinson's scouting dossiers had everything planned to the most minute detail. Whether he was looking at an opposition player or planning pre-match tactical reports, he probably covered both instances a minimum of four or five times both home and away. This was to make sure of the performance by both the player and the team, and to see if there were any discrepancies."

Russell Latapy, who played under Robson and Mourinho at Porto between 1994 and 1996, gave me a breakdown of Mourinho's scouting dossiers: "We always, and I mean *always*, had all the information to win the game against the other team. We knew, for example, if there was a right-footed player playing left-back; if the centre forward had a tendency to go in behind or drop deep; and what was the player's strongest foot. We knew exactly how the other team played and that made it a lot easier, in terms of one v one battles on the field."

* * *

Without the medium of Manuel Fernandes, Mourinho and Robson's complimentary styles began to blossom and, as a result, their bond strengthened in Robson's eyes: "The more time we spent together, the more we liked each other. Somehow, our talents and personalities interlocked." This was partly why Robson signed the then 16-year-old upstart, André

Chapter 3

Villas-Boas, to Porto's observation department as he saw the same enthusiasm, attention to detail, and daring that Mourinho had displayed. After all, Villas-Boas, infamously, had the audacity to question Robson's persistence with the misfiring Sergei Yuran, instead of Domingos Paciência, after realising that the Englishman lived in his apartment block at Rua Tenente Valadim.

It was not just Mourinho and Villas-Boas who were feeling Robson's influence and under the Englishman's guidance, Porto were to enjoy landmark success. As well as hoisting the 1994 Taça de Portugal, Porto won the 1994–95 and 1995–96 Primeira Liga titles. With Robson's free-flowing football and the all-out attacking trident of Domingos, António Folha and Edmilson, it came as little surprise that the Englishman's reputation as one of the continent's greatest managers was restored. The Portuguese press even awarded him a double-meaning nickname, *Bobby 5-0*. As well as this being a reference to the numerous high-scoring results Robson achieved with Porto, it was also a jibe at Robson's cautious predecessor, Tomaslav Ivić, who often played with five defenders.

Latapy gave his take on the success of the Robson/Mourinho partnership at Porto: "It was a fantastic time. At the time, you were talking about one of the real legends of world football. I really learnt a lot from Sir Bobby. Just the simple things in the games, you know: control, passing, maintaining a really high concentration level, and the will to win. Every day in training he was focused on that desire to do well and to win. More importantly, for me, it was the values he gave to the team: to respect the game and everything that comes along with it.

"We played on a Saturday, so on a Thursday, for example, we would only train for 75 minutes. Then, Bobby would take all the balls off the pitch and get all the players off the pitch. I don't know if it was because we had so many games to play; we were playing in so many competitions: the Champions League, the cup, and the league. Maybe he wanted to keep us fresh for matchday, but the players, actually, wanted to do more – he was holding us back!

"It was in the early days of Mourinho's career that I met him. At that time, I didn't speak Portuguese too well and Mourinho was the link between the coaching staff and players. That was the thing that really caught my eye at the time. It was really easy for him to intermingle between the two sets… He was on the training pitch and close to Bobby, passing on the messages that Bobby wanted to relay. He was always there, hands-on, on the pitch and getting involved. It was really easy to speak to him and to get my point across and, also, for the coaches to get their view across. He got on really well with the players. He would even go out with our families for meals; the players trusted in him.

"This is my take on his translations, especially since I speak Portuguese a lot better now. There are certain things that get lost in translation. Sir Bobby wanted to get a certain message across and it's difficult, at times, to translate word-for-word. Mourinho understood the message that Bobby was trying to get over and he was able to explain this message perfectly to get the desired message over.

"It would be difficult to say that I saw something in him that would put him up there with the world's greatest coaches. In all honesty, at the time, you couldn't see it. What I would say, though, is that you could tell, straightaway, that he was a very organised and very good coach. He wanted to get things done. He had a way of getting his philosophy over to the players, and the players were really close to him and liked working for him. But, becoming one of the best coaches in the world, obviously, is a lot of hard work and you need that element of luck – which he has had along the way. In saying that, you need also time and he's had that too, in most of the jobs he has taken."

* * *

Tragedy was to overshadow every club Robson and Mourinho were to work together at. On 28 August, 1994, 26-year-old central midfielder Rui Filipe was killed in a car accident. Filipe was a Portuguese international and was one of the team's most influential playmakers. Having barely recovered from his guilt over Serhiy Scherbakov's paralysis, Robson was inconsolable for days and the Englishman played a pivotal role in Porto's immediate decision to erect a bust memorial of Filipe outside the Estádio das Antas. Poignantly, each day from then on in, Robson was to place his hand on the head of the bust on his way to work.

Latapy reflected on that early period of both his, and Robson's, career at Porto: "I remember it perfectly, because I had just arrived at the club. Rui Filipe, at the time, was an established player at the club and these were the players you had to compete with if you wanted to play in the team. Obviously, as a young player, you paid particular attention to what guys like him did on the pitch. You needed to learn from the established players if you wanted to become an established player yourself. But, yes, it did have a great effect – not only the technical staff but all the players as well… One of the strengths of Porto is the camaraderie, the teamwork – they fight for each other. The players are not only colleagues on the pitch, they are friends off the field too. The players live as a family."

* * *

Chapter 3

Amid his renewed popularity, Arsenal were the first to approach Robson, to replace George Graham in February 1995. However, Porto's affable president, Pinto da Costa, begged the Englishman to stay. Robson remained, but after establishing Porto as one of the most attractive football teams on the continent, he was headhunted by Barcelona to replace Johan Cruyff in the spring of 1996. Such was Mourinho's importance to Robson, the Portuguese became heavily involved in the discussions and even travelled to Barcelona to discuss terms. Having driven Robson to Barcelona and then back to Porto at 2am in his Suzuki Vitara, Mourinho planned to continue the extra 350km to reach the heavily-pregnant Tami in Setúbal. The journey provided a lucky escape for Mourinho, with the Portuguese falling asleep at the wheel but only splitting his head open in the resulting crash.

Again, Mourinho followed Robson and such was his understanding of the delicate culture of Barcelona and the importance of their *cantera*, he even learnt Catalan in preparation. Still, replacing an icon like Johan Cruyff was never going to be easy for Robson, with the Englishman even acknowledging Cruyff's standing as Barcelona's most groundbreaking manager of all-time in his opening speech to the squad. Ernesto Valverde, who played under Cruyff at Barcelona between 1988 and 1990, told me about the scale of the challenge that awaited Robson: "Apart from pre-season, we always trained with the ball in reduced spaces. Cruyff also restored our threat in set plays and we constantly practiced them until we dominated them completely. He was so dedicated: [his assistant] Charly Rexach and him participated in ball possession drills and even in short matches. That was a problem because even though they weren't as strong as us physically, they played better than we did on some occasions!

"In the beginning it was difficult to adjust to his philosophy, because he was very daring and the players were not used to playing with three defenders and lots of space at the back. It demanded absolute game control and sometimes this was not possible. With time, everything was far better as everybody knows.

"Cruyff was always very demanding with his players. He wanted absolute perfection in all the training sessions, in each and every pass; he didn't allow mistakes. He forced us to be at our best in every match… Football training methods have not been the same since he arrived and we owe him a great deal for the evolution of football in Spain. I consider myself quite lucky to have been there at that moment. I learned what it meant to play for a great team such as Barça, whose only objective is winning match after match and relishing the pressure that entails."

So, even though Cruyff's son, Jordi, assured Robson that there would be no hard feelings and that he would be happy to play for him, Mourinho felt otherwise. Despite the Dutchman's placidness, Mourinho advised Robson to sell Cruyff to Manchester United and curb any danger of a mole or a dressing room mutiny. Mourinho would even attend negotiations with Sir Alex Ferguson, Martin Edwards, and Maurice Watkins when Manchester United's delegation visited Barcelona.

Robson was later thankful for Mourinho's gut instinct: "Jordi would have gone back home and his Dad would have asked him what happened at the club… and if a story had leaked from the dressing room, he would have been seen, unfairly or not, as the prime suspect. It would have been a no-win situation, for if I hadn't picked him, it would have been seen as me getting back at his father and I couldn't let people think that way. Even though it wouldn't have been true, it would have been manna from heaven for the anti-Robson, anti-Barcelona brigade."

So, although Robson certainly took Mourinho with him for professional reasons – with the duo spending hour upon hour honing a hybrid of Robson's trademark attacking instincts with Mourinho's blossoming defensive nous – there was a clear affinity between the pair as well. Regardless of a 30-year age gap, it was, after all, Robson who taught Mourinho that there was more to life than winning: "I always remember with a little smile that after I was upset after a defeat, he said, 'Don't be sad because in the other dressing room, someone is bouncing around with happiness.'" Also, both the Mourinhos and the Robsons lived in the same apartment complex in Sitges, which was the perfect seaside getaway from the intense pressures of life at the Nou Camp. The couples would spend many an evening at the Mourinhos' apartment, with Tami bonding over cooking with Robson's wife, Elsie, and Mourinho and Robson sharing a passion for Anthony Hopkins' films.

Mourinho's role and influence was growing and during pre-season in 1996, he took centre stage as *El Traductor* (the translator). Mourinho gave eloquence and nuance to Robson's trademark short answers, and a clear shift had taken place since 1992. Santi Giménez of AS newspaper remarked that, "It was immediately obvious that Mourinho couldn't translate because he had such strong opinions of his own." Realising that Mourinho had worked with Robson before and was far from an agency-hired translator, Giménez mischievously asked Robson in broken English if Mourinho was his boyfriend. In a remarkably similar precedent to Zlatan Ibrahimović facing the same question regarding Gerard Piqué at Barcelona in 2010, a markedly confident Mourinho's reply was: "Bring your sister along and we can find out if that's true." Remarkably, though, in contrast to some 15 years later,

Chapter 3

Mourinho enjoyed a positive relationship with the Spanish press and even liaised with them during social occasions.

Still, around the corner, yet another tragedy was to strengthen Robson and Mourinho's friendship even further. Mourinho's cherished, and only, sibling, Teresa, died from diabetic septicaemia in 1997 – epitomising the circle of life, just under a year after the birth of Mourinho's first child, Matilde Jr. Having his family and Robson so close, somehow, helped to carve Mourinho's incredible, and now trademark, mental strength and focus on the task at hand.

So, while the Barcelona hero, José Ramón Alexanko, was Robson's official assistant, the Englishman fought desperately for Mourinho's appointment; in the words of Barcelona's then vice-president, Joan Gaspart: "[President] Núñez told Robson that in no way would he hire a translator, when he [Robson] already had a home aide, and at his insistence, Núñez offered Mourinho only 10,000 pesetas a month. He [Mourinho] stayed for free at my hotel room, the Arenas, because he barely had enough money to live. When he proved that he was more than a translator, Núñez raised the salary and searched for an apartment for him."

Reflecting his newly-appreciated skills, Mourinho was put on a whopping £300,000 annual salary as Robson's *El Traductor*. With a greater platform and budget – which was clearly evident in Robson's world-record signing of Ronaldo for $17 million – Mourinho, too, benefited: compiling then revolutionary and carefully edited individual video dossiers on opponents for each member of the squad. Samuel Okunowo, who would go on to join Barcelona in 1998, told me about a typical Mourinho report: "The reports were great. Mourinho would tell us about individual players and how they played. So, when we played, he didn't have to point things out - it was second-nature. We knew multiple things about the player: what he can do and how to get at him. That's what he was always after."

These incredibly modern methods complimented Robson's old-school coaching – which included writing tactics in chalk on the dressing room floor and being known as Grandad Miquel by his players – brilliantly. Laurent Blanc, then entering the peak of his career at 30 years of age, was among those to appreciate Mourinho's homework and Mourinho was unfazed when dealing with such illustrious names. After all, rather than lecturing these stars, Mourinho preferred the guided discovery method, whereby the said player would make a suggestion about a given drill and his observations would be compared to Mourinho's. The duo would then 'discover' a compromise.

In fact, the Portuguese even quibbled with Ronaldo on one occasion: "It's no good scoring a wonder goal and then spending the other 89 minutes sleeping." This would offer a telling precedent ahead of Mourinho's coaching of flair players years later and, according to Robson, the Portuguese went down well with the players: "Ronaldo, among others, took to José quite quickly. So, if a player was left out, he [the player] blamed me, not José. I had to keep a distance from the players, as a manager does. José could cross over that line and come back again." One of those players was Pep Guardiola, the former Nou Camp ballboy, who graduated from La Masia under Cruyff in 1990.

A fans' favourite, as a Catalan icon and one of the world's best deep-lying midfielders, there was little evidence that Mourinho and Guardiola were soon to endure one of the bitterest managerial rivalries in football. In fact, after Barcelona defeated Paris Saint-Germain in the 1997 Cup Winners' Cup final, the first player Mourinho hugged was Guardiola. The Catalan, though, was quick to downplay the significance of this in 2011: "We did talk about things when we both had doubts and we would exchange ideas, but I don't remember it as something which defined our relationship. He was Mr Robson's assistant and I was a player."

Samuel Okunowo believed there was nothing prophetic about Guardiola's early relationship with Mourinho: "When Mourinho and Guardiola were at the Nou Camp, everything between them was respectful... I'm not surprised that Guardiola went on to become the manager that he did. When we played together, he was just like a coach on the pitch and Mourinho recognised that. They 'played' together. Mourinho understood Guardiola's importance, as the club's captain. You have to respect your captain and huddle together to get their opinion and insight. There didn't seem any problems between them but when they became managers, of course, everything changed: Mourinho had his system, Guardiola had his."

If Mourinho's bond with Guardiola was shocking in hindsight, so, too, was his relationship with Barcelona's fans. There were two prime examples of this in 1996-97. When Barcelona played Athletic Bilbao at the San Mamés on 26 November, 1996, Mourinho managed to get under the skin of Bilbao's spiky coach, Luis Fernández. The Frenchman believed Mourinho was influencing refereeing decisions by constantly leaving the technical area and Fernández "warned the second coach, who I don't know, that the San Mamés dugouts are close together." Unsurprisingly, therefore, the pair clashed on the touchline when Fernández made a beeline for Robson.

Having memorably broken down in tears after Barça recovered from 0-3 down to defeat Atlético Madrid 5-4 in an astonishing second-half comeback four months later, the cult of *El Traductor* had been established. Unsurprisingly, therefore - with thousands of Culés cheering his name during

Chapter 3

Barcelona's open-air civic reception after the 3-2 victory in the Copa del Rey final against Real Betis on 28 June, 1997 - Mourinho declared in Catalan: "Today, tomorrow, always with Barcelona in my heart."

It was to prove the last time Mourinho was to share the stage with Robson.

Chapter 4: Going It Alone

Despite winning the European Cup Winners' Cup, the Supercopa de España, and the Copa del Rey in 1996–97, Sir Bobby Robson was moved upstairs by the restless Josep Lluís Núñez to the post of general manager. Robson lamented that, "If I was a coach in England challenging for three trophies, I'd be a bloody hero!" However, there was a genuine fear among the Barcelona hierarchy that Robson's outdated methods jarred with the *totaalvoetbal* principles - that Johan Cruyff had bred - of the likes of Pep Guardiola and Guillermo Amor. Heeding this, Núñez appointed Louis van Gaal - whose attractive football had won 11 trophies in just six years with Ajax - as the Englishman's replacement as head coach. Ironically, the initial approach had centered on van Gaal becoming Barcelona's head of youth development after his fine work in bringing through the likes of Edwin van der Sar, Michael Reiziger, Clarence Seedorf, Edgar Davids, and Patrick Kluivert with Ajax between 1991 and 1997.

In the hope of continuity, with Robson's recommendation, van Gaal retained Mourinho's services as the Dutchman had only studied Spanish for one week prior to his appointment. Interestingly, van Gaal initially planned to only give Mourinho a short-term contract to help with environmental assimilation, but Mourinho was to prove yet another Barcelona official wrong. Van Gaal was soon impressed with Mourinho's aptitude and application and, eventually, made Mourinho his official assistant alongside the Dutchman's long-term allies, Gerard van der Lem and Ronald Koeman. Certainly, the former gymnastics teacher, van Gaal, was as relatable and inspirational - in terms of ruthlessness, decisiveness and authority - to Mourinho as Robson had been.

Van Gaal let Mourinho take charge of Barcelona B and Barcelona's first-team for friendlies and shared insights on his mathematical interpretation of *Total Football*. The Dutchman, too, obsessively scribbled notes down in a notebook. In turn, Mourinho certainly learnt more and more about footballers' psychology upon witnessing the 1999 World Player of the Year, Rivaldo, and his vehement refusal to play out of position on the left wing for van Gaal after declaring that "trophies don't pay for the mortgage". In contrast to Robson appearing just ten minutes before training began, van Gaal's habit of arriving two hours early was also to strike a chord with Mourinho. So defined was van Gaal's daily schedules for training, too, Mourinho had few of the sprawling responsibilities he held under Robson. Instead, van Gaal ensured Mourinho's focus was only on training and tactics, meaning the Portuguese could arrive for training just 30 minutes before it began.

Samuel Okunowo played under van Gaal and Mourinho at Barcelona in 1998-99 and told me about Mourinho, the assistant: "Mourinho was a popular figure. I was an African guy and looked at him and thought, 'This man can help 'make me' and bring my game to the next level.' When I was there under van Gaal, Mourinho was good, very good. He was a man of policy. He was quick, he talked through drills, and he spoke the truth. In training, he asked a lot of you, he pushed you, and everything was drilled. But in the match, they didn't need to do that because everything had been prepared in training. In the first-half, they told you what to do; in the second, they didn't.

"He read the game very well; he knew what he was doing. Mourinho didn't like to show off or shout. To players that performed well, he liked to comment and praise them… I'm not surprised he went on to make it: he was able to show the players that - regardless of him not being a star as a player - he knew *this* and he knew *that*. Mourinho was very good in all aspects. If he went to watch a game, he was able to explain the opposition's strengths and weaknesses very well for us as players. He had the attributes that meant that he coped with the pressures of the Nou Camp.

"Van Gaal and Mourinho's only concern was that the team was playing well. They weren't obsessed about whether it was 1-0, 5-0 or 10-0; they just cared about winning. Win, win, win, win – they didn't want to lose. He fitted in perfectly with van Gaal's philosophy. He worked with Sir Bobby Robson for so long that it gave him the perfect preparation for that kind of policy. Van Gaal seemed to continue and elevate the work and philosophy that Robson had established… You see it every year: Mourinho has been able to tweak his style of football and, to be a coach, your philosophy has to progress every season. You cannot continue using the same policy you used ten years ago."

Clearly, the Dutchman was to have a massive influence on Mourinho's future methodology, with training sessions never lasting longer than 90 minutes for example. In fact, van Gaal would later remark: "José was an arrogant young man, who didn't respect authority. He was not submissive, used to contradict me when he thought I was in the wrong. I ended up listening to him more than the rest of the assistants. If I ever had to take a training session and didn't know what to do, I asked José."

Such was the seamless transition for Mourinho post-Robson, one member of Barcelona's playing squad even wondered if Mourinho had spent longer at the Ajax school of coaching than van Gaal had. The pair thrived at Barcelona: winning two La Liga titles, the Copa del Rey, and the UEFA Super Cup in van Gaal's first two seasons in charge. Van Gaal became the first Barça manager since Helenio Herrera, in 1958-59, to win the double in his first season and two titles in his first two seasons. Ironically, though, the Dutchman's first title was achieved with just 74 points – which was drastically lower than Robson's 90 points, when Barça finished as runners-up to Real Madrid in the previous season.

Still, following this success, the 36-year-old Mourinho now believed he was ready for his first foray into management and was headhunted by Braga in the summer of 1999 in case Manuel Cajuda departed as head coach. Benfica's Jupp Heynckes also contacted Mourinho to offer him yet another apprenticeship, as his assistant on a four-year deal. Both positions, remarkably, would only offer a fraction of the salary Mourinho was on at Barcelona.

Mourinho was frustrated that his break had not come yet, but such was his respect for van Gaal, the Dutchman convinced him to stay for, seemingly, the foreseeable future. Both targeted that one elusive major title during their time at Barcelona: the Champions League. In return, van Gaal awarded Mourinho even more autonomy and this resulted in Mourinho hoisting the first managerial trophy of his career after he led Barcelona to a 3-0 victory over CE Mataró in the Copa Catalunya final on 16 May, 2000. However, little did van Gaal know - despite Barça playing some of their best football, during his reign, that season - that it would be his final year at the Nou Camp after a trophyless 1999-2000.

So, after the Dutchman's dismissal and the uninspiring Serra Ferrer's appointment that summer, Mourinho was adamant that he would now go it alone. That did not mean that there were not emotional goodbyes when the Portuguese left, though, with Michael Reiziger remarking: "The players really missed him when he left. That's a big compliment to an assistant." Mourinho, too, declared: "I would only ever coach Real Madrid to destroy them: I will never stop being a *culé*."

In the eyes of Samuel Okunowo, though, the Nigerian did not forsee the rapid ascension that was imminent: "I didn't see anything that suggested Mourinho would become a star. When I saw what eventually happened at Porto, I thought, 'My God, this is a miracle!' It's still a miracle... he's a big man, he's a star. He's achieved, and changed, so much in football..."

* * *

While Mourinho realised he would have to be patient regarding his next move, he knew his homeland would eventually award him the opportunity. Mourinho recognised that Portuguese football was about to become one of the trailblazers in football management for managers who were not ex-players of clubs, or who had not had illustrious playing careers. This meant that one-time novices like Fernando Santos at Porto, Manuel Cajuda at Braga, Nelo Vingada at Marítimo and Luís Campos at Gil Vicente were all thriving in

Chapter 4

Portuguese football management. As a result, Mourinho rejected Sir Bobby Robson's offer of a potential long-term handover at Newcastle United once the Englishman had served a further two years at St James' Park and reached his planned retirement age of 69 in 2002.

Still, before Mourinho could even apply for managerial jobs, he had to finish the second part - some 12 years later - of his UEFA coaching course in Largs. This time, however, Mourinho's reputation preceded him. For example – in a remarkable contrast from 1988 – fellow students, Tosh McKinlay and Gary Bollan, remarked how outspoken and confident Mourinho was.

Now fully qualified, clearly, Mourinho was desperate to return to work despite the fact he had spent an enjoyable period with his family in their holiday home in Ferragudo, his father's birthplace in the Algarve. During this sabbatical, Mourinho had welcomed the chance to return to the terraces of the Estádio do Bonfim, Vitória de Setúbal's home, with his friends for the first time in nearly a decade. Also, Mourinho was wary of missing out on his children's upbringing. After all, Mourinho was already well aware of the devotion required to become a successful football manager. For example, the Tottenham legend, Bill Nicholson - who spent over three decades at White Hart Lane as both a player and manager between 1938 and 1974 - was in tears at the wedding of one of his daughters in the '60s, lamenting that he had not seen "her grow up".

However, following a very brief spell of near-purposeful unemployment – around the birth of his second child, José Mário Jr – Mourinho's opportunity came in September 2000, when Benfica offered him the opportunity to replace Heynckes on a six-month deal. This contract would be extended to two years if the presidential favourite, Joao Vale de Azevedo, won the December elections. Mourinho would become Benfica's youngest ever Portuguese coach, but it was a semi-ironic turn of events, with Mourinho having been offered the chance to assist Heynckes only months earlier. Mourinho may well have taken up Heynckes' offer but for van Gaal's fateful intervention before the Dutchman's eventual departure at the Nou Camp: "When I spoke with van Gaal about going back to Portugal to be an assistant at Benfica, he said: 'No, don't go. Tell Benfica if they want a first-team coach you will go; if they want an assistant you will stay.'"

Unsurprisingly, Mourinho had not been able to completely withdraw from football in his short hiatus and such was the importance of this 'break', he even devised the top-secret *Mourinho Bible*, which has proved a crucial thesis to his methods' evolvement and success across the continent as a football manager. The *Mourinho Bible* is a collection, and evolution, of Mourinho's notes from every single training session he has assisted and conducted since

1990. Mourinho has vowed to only show it to José Jr. if he ever wishes to see it when he is older. This thesis has laid the basis for what have become Mourinho's near-intangible, fate-driven ingredients for his undoubted success: "Quality, unity, passion, work methods: there is not just one or two reasons [for success]. When I go to a club, I wear the shirt; I feel the shirt like it's my first one or my last one. There are a lot of factors and they must work in unison."

* * *

Mourinho was a managerial rookie and to appease somewhat sceptical fans - because of his previous association with Sporting Lisbon and Porto, and an absence of managerial experience - Mourinho devised a future coaching hallmark: the 'Clarke role'. Mourinho held, and still holds, a crucial appreciation of the role of assistant from his time with Robson and van Gaal and has often used an ex-player as his right-hand man. Steve Clarke, the former Chelsea player, would eventually prove the most prominent Mourinho pupil but at Benfica, it was to be the ex-Benfica defender, Carlos Mozer. The former defender made 120 league appearances for Benfica in two spells, between 1987 and 1995, and won two Primeira Liga titles and a Taça de Portugal in the same period.

Mozer was a key appointment as Mourinho needed all the support he could get because Azevedo – who resembled Barcelona's then notorious president, Josep Lluís Núñez, for his lack of affection for football matters – afforded Mourinho a shoestring budget and wanted him to build a team around Academy players. Given these poor conditions, it was no surprise that Mourinho spent three days in a personal *ritui* (retreat) before his official unveiling in September, with near-endless video analysis of his squad and future opponents. This led to Mourinho promoting the likes of Diogo Luís, Geraldo, and Nuno Abreu from Benfica's B team; the trio were on just €215 per week.

Mourinho, though, would also leave his impact on established first-team players: being described by the late Robert Enke as "the best coach of my career"; and converting Fernando Meira from a central defender into a central midfielder. Mourinho brought a new level of intensity to Benfica, too, with mandatory shin pads, the reduction of training pitch sizes, and detailed scouting analysis of opponents. Remarkably, such was the state of Benfica's scouting analysis at the beginning of Mourinho's reign, one report Mourinho received had only nine outfield players.

Also, thanks to his experience at Barcelona, Mourinho was unfazed by star players like Pierre van Hooijdonk and Karel Poborský. Mourinho even played mind games with Poborský, who - resembling Rivaldo under van Gaal - was

Chapter 4

unhappy at being banished to the flanks. Sensing he could send a message to the dressing room, Mourinho let the Czech play in his preferred playmaker role in a Primeira Liga match and hauled him off after 30 minutes. Incensed by his audacity, poor fitness, and failure to track back, Mourinho condemned Poborský to the bench for the remainder of his reign.

It was a similar story for the flamboyant midfielder, Sabry. The Egyptian had not yet learnt Portuguese after just seven months in the country, but was a cult hero among *Benfiquistas* for his late winner in the 1-0 victory against Sporting Lisbon in the *Derby de Lisboa* on 6 May, 2000. The playmaker, through his agent, publicly complained to journalists about how Mourinho wanted to convert him from a free-roaming number 10 to a disciplined winger. Mourinho responded, in now trademark, all-seeing style. The Portuguese told Sabry how often he lost the ball, how rarely he recovered possession, and referred to the eight minutes and three boot changes the sulking playmaker needed before coming on as a substitute in a previous Primeira Liga match Mourinho had analysed. In contrast, Maniche encapsulated just what Mourinho could achieve in a short space of time, with the then 22-year-old initially struggling to adjust to Mourinho's methods at Benfica, but then going on to become club captain within just a few weeks.

Given this chaotic set-up and the fact that he only took over in September after pre-season, Mourinho performed admirably in his short spell. The highlight, undoubtedly, was defeating Sporting Lisbon 3–0 in the *Derby de Lisboa* on 3 December 2000. Clearly, a result like this was owed – heavily accentuated by Benfica's poor opposition scouting department, due to Azevedo's cutbacks – to Mourinho's meticulous analysis and motivational methods. Before this match, Mourinho brilliantly motivated the Benfica players by speculating that the Sporting players had been attending the Portuguese Tennis Masters two nights previously. Benfica's vice-president, José Manuel Capristano, paid tribute: "This man is born to be a coach. I have never met anyone like him before. He thinks 24 hours a day."

Still, regardless of Mourinho's mission to professionalise Benfica, Manuel Vilarinho, surprisingly, ended up winning the presidential election. When Mourinho requested a contract extension in good faith to recognise the landmark work he had done previously, Vilarinho refused. Instead, the nostalgic Vilarinho earmarked club hero, António 'Toni' José Conceição Oliveira – who led the club to their last European Cup final, in 1988 – as a replacement. After only nine games in charge, Mourinho resigned on 5 December 2000 - just two days after that momentous win over Sporting.

As well as his ultimatum for a new one-year contract, frosty relations between the new Benfica board and Mourinho were much to blame for the

Portuguese's departure. This had even led to Mourinho kicking the directors out of the players' hotel on an away trip in a sprawling two building hotel complex – that had originally housed a mixture of players and directors in each building – in Braga. Mourinho, too, had been upset in the run-up to the game against Sporting Lisbon after the board decided against the team staying in their usual hotel, the Meridien, and instead chose the less luxurious Hotel Altis. Also, the board had signed Rui Baião, Ricardo Esteves, Roger, and André without Mourinho's knowledge.

While undoubtedly disappointed by his departure, with Félix as a father – and having witnessed what happened to Robson and van Gaal – Mourinho was prepared for the cut-throat world of football management: "I was nine or 10 years old and my father was sacked on Christmas Day. He was a manager, the results had not been good, he lost a game on December 22 or 23. On Christmas Day, the telephone rang and he was sacked in the middle of our lunch."

It was far from the end.

Chapter 5: Shades of Herrera

Mourinho's next move would be crucial and in April 2001 – enthused by União de Leiria's president, João Bartolomeu's, belief in him after the sacking of Manuel José – he joined mid-table Leiria. Far from retreating to a steady safehaven, Mourinho was on half the wage he received at Benfica and his appointment caused uproar, with Manuel José declaring the following upon being notified: "If Mourinho thinks this is a jungle and that he is Tarzan, then he is greatly mistaken." Also, Tami, Matilde, and José Jr remained in Lisbon.

Without hindsight, it may have seemed a fairly knee-jerk decision by Mourinho to join Leiria amid tangible interest from Sporting Lisbon and their keen club official, Luís Duque. There was also an informal approach from Atlético Madrid to replace Claudio Ranieri. Although this was an appealing project - with the likes of José Molina, José Chamot, Rubén Baraja, Juan Carlos Valeron, José Marí, and Jimmy Floyd Hasselbaink at the club - Mourinho needed two years of top-level experience if he was to join Atlético. Also, the club was about to be relegated to the Segunda Division and had just entered administration. Regardless, Mourinho was not granted dispensation by the Liga Nacional de Fútbol Profesional (LFP).

Still, Mourinho saw a stable club in Leiria that could be moulded and following the chaos at Benfica, the importance of this cannot be understated. Buoyed, Mourinho immediately sought to leave his mark on Leiria. The traditional, but incredibly outdated, use of the surrounding forests for training was abolished; regular team meetings were used to strengthen team chemistry; and the similarly-aged Padre David Barreirinhas, who doubled-up as youth coach and religious counsellor, was recruited. Mourinho also requested, with much opposition, that the Leiria directors' tradition of a cosy friendly against the region's sports journalists at the club's training ground every Saturday morning be abolished.

Mourinho acquainted four crucial figures in his future success at Leiria. Firstly, there were the coaches, Baltemar Brito and Rui Faria. Brito had played alongside Mourinho and under Mourinho's father, Félix, at Rio Ave in 1981-82. Mourinho could not find an assistant in the ex-player mould at Leiria and, in fact, it was Mourinho's wife, Tami, who suggested Brito. Since then, Brito has always referred to Tami as his *madrinha* (godmother). Faria, meanwhile, had met Mourinho previously, in Barcelona - having graduated with a Sport Science degree in Porto - and was to act as Mourinho's methodologist. Leiria also housed Nuno Valente and Derlei, two pivotal figures in Mourinho's early success. Derlei, the Brazilian, epitomised Mourinho's shrewd month-long scouting trips of South America, with no work permit issues or foreign quotas in Portugal like there would be in other leagues. Nuno Valente, meanwhile, would soon become one of Mourinho's favourite, and most consistent, full-backs of all-time.

Mourinho also shook up the dressing room, with his prophetic opening declaration to the squad: "Don't doubt that sooner or later that I will go to a bigger club. And when I go, some of you are coming with me." Despite many of the Leiria region's football fans holding a long-standing preference and support for Sporting Lisbon – based 148km away – Mourinho's infectious confidence led to rising stadium attendances and heightened club enthusiasm at the Municipal da Marinha Grande. As a result, with barely months of the 2000-01 season remaining, Mourinho steered Leiria to their highest ever league finish, fifth.

While it may be tempting to suggest Leiria's fifth place finish in 2000-01 was a fluke, by January 2002, Mourinho had put Leiria in contention for the title. Not only was this overachievement owed to Mourinho's blossoming tactical nous, but also his passion for Leiria's cause. For example, when Leiria met Porto in a 2-1 defeat at the Estádio das Antas on 4 November, 2001, Mourinho clashed with Deco – Porto's talisman – over his play-acting.

Given his success, therefore, it was little surprise that Mourinho received offers from both Benfica and Porto. The semi-remorseful Manuel Vilarinho commented: "[Put me] back then [and] I would do exactly the opposite: I would extend his contract. Only later I realised that one's personality and pride cannot be put before the interest of the institution we serve." However, Vilarinho wanted to keep on Benfica's manager at the time and Mourinho's former tutor, Jesualdo Ferreira, as Mourinho's assistant. Vilarinho also prohibited Mourinho, as part of any deal, from bringing Faria and Brito with him and demanded that the goalkeeping coach, Samir Shaker, remain at the club. Given Mourinho's happier memories of Porto with Sir Bobby Robson – and without even addressing the disregard Mourinho held for the Benfica hierarchy – he chose to return to Porto's Estádio das Antas.

Mourinho had kept in touch with Porto's president, Pinto da Costa, from his time as Robson's assistant but Porto had fallen drastically since Robson had left. In Mourinho's own words, "It was one of the worst Porto teams for decades." This view was owed largely to Mourinho's belief that the decentralising of the club led to a lack of planning and stability. On the field, too, Octávio Machado, Mourinho's predecessor, had left the club in fifth place in the league, bottom of Group C in the Champions League second-round group stage, and out of the Portuguese Cup. Still, in his opening press conference, Mourinho declared that he was "sure that Porto would be champions at the end of [his] first full season." So desperate was club morale under Mourinho's predecessors, this statement led to the whole of the Porto press room giving Mourinho an immediate standing ovation.

The soon to be trademark self-belief was already evident but Mourinho was something of an unknown quantity to the Porto dressing room at the time, as César Peixoto, who played for Mourinho at Porto between 2002 and 2004, told me: "I knew little about Mourinho. In Benfica, it was over too quickly and he was unable to stay long enough to realise what he was capable of there. I knew he had done a good job at União de Leiria and that he was a young and ambitious coach. Through watching the playing style of Leiria, I realised that there was quality and that he was a coach with potential. Their game was exciting: a lot of attack, pressure, and no spaces for the opponent."

In the remaining months of the 2001–02 season, Mourinho led Porto to an admirable, and sweet (ahead of Benfica), third place finish after an impressive 11 wins, two draws, and two defeats in 15 league matches. One of those defeats, a 2-3 loss against Beira Mar at the Estádio das Antas, was to herald a landmark moment in Mourinho's management career, with the Portuguese to embark on a mammoth 151-match unbeaten-at-home run across four different leagues over the following nine years.

However, Porto's otherwise impressive form at the end of the season did not sway Mourinho's original transfer plans and the summer of 2002 saw drastic, but, ultimately, inspired transfer activity. Paulo Ferreira, Jorge Costa (recalled from loan at Charlton), Nuno Valente, Pedro Emanuel, Maniche, Derlei, and Edgaras Jankauskas were all brought in. Every member of the squad had to prove themselves to Mourinho, and Portugal's number one goalkeeper, Vítor Baía, initially fell out with Mourinho after Nuno took his prospective place following injury. Maniche, too - despite establishing a bond with Mourinho as his captain at Benfica - was often dropped by Mourinho if he felt the midfielder was losing his focus.

Although these names, Baía apart, were regionally known - rather than continentally or internationally - many of them would go on to inspire Portugal to the Euro 2004 final against Greece. Despite Mourinho's incessant quibbles with Luiz Felipe Scolari - who was appointed as Portugal's manager in 2003 - over the under-representation of Porto players, the Euro 2004 run owed much to Mourinho's man management and incredible coaxing of players' abilities. After all, 14 members of Portugal's 23-man squad were, at some point between 1993 and 2004, coached by Mourinho. Costinha was the perfect example: a 27-year-old who had never played in the Portuguese top-flight and lacked confidence, but who was convinced by Mourinho that he would be a starter for the Portuguese national team within just one month of being appointed as Porto's manager.

Chapter 5

It was not just Costinha who was driven to succeed and the Porto squad, overall, embodied the determination and strong-will that Mourinho exuded. Such was their eagerness to impress, they even arrived back early from a curfew in the vibrant city of Saint Étienne on the eve of a pre-season friendly in the summer of 2002. Peixoto believes this dedication was owed to the already mesmerising effect Mourinho was having on the new members of the squad: "Obviously, the first two months were about adaptation. Everything was new, very organised, and this was the biggest club in Portugal. I was surrounded by great players, so the pressure was huge…The games were always well prepared, but he gave special attention to pre-season. There were many new players in the squad at the time, so he wanted to outline the rules and pass on what he wanted for the team: the game ideas, training and methodology. We followed suit.

"Mourinho gave me a great opportunity. I had just arrived at the Primeira Liga with Belenenses from the Segunda Divisão but I'd had a very good season, with seven goals in the first year. My ability had, already, been well recognized after a good performance against Porto at the Antas in March. With the interest of FC Porto and the wave that was already being created by the arrival of José - supported by a solid project - I felt that the conditions were established to give a huge boost to my career."

Behind the scenes, Baltemar Brito, Rui Faria, Silvino Louro and André Villas-Boas also arrived. Mourinho's methodology, carefully harnessed with Faria, soon took hold; according to Peixoto: "The workouts were always about contact with the ball. They were very intense. Everything was very fast, explosive and very well organised. José Mourinho is very methodical and likes being in control."

This methodology was divided into two main outlets: ball-playing and aerobic exercises. Firstly, there were extensive ball-control sessions centred on Mourinho's core belief of 'resting' while in possession, that is, defensive-like possession for the sake of it rather than constant, penetrative-focused play for 90 minutes. Then, there were aerobic exercises and individual training regimes that maximised player fitness and combativeness in order to play Mourinho's high-tempo, *pressão alta* (pressing) game across the pitch.

* * *

As a running parallel to Mourinho's evolution as a coach, the Portuguese's self-belief soared, and there was a growth in the controversy that will inevitably serve as Mourinho's epitaph. The first real example of this was when Mourinho refused to shake hands with Boavista's then manager, Jaime

Pacheco, on 27 January 2003 after a fierce war of words surrounding Mourinho's claim that, "I don't shake hands with people I don't know."

Mourinho also incurred a one-match ban when he cynically blocked Lazio's Lucas Castromán from taking a quick throw in the first-leg of the 2003 UEFA Cup semi-final on 10 April. Remarkably, Porto were leading 4–1 going into this injury-time moment, but Mourinho is a man of principle and felt that his marauding full-backs would be outnumbered by a quick throw. With his darkened crew cut and athletic build, this tactical foul from the dug-out was the first real example of Mourinho's status as a 12th man in that Porto team. Incredibly, though, using a micro device that Villas-Boas wielded beside him in the stand, the banned Mourinho still conveyed a whopping 30 messages – such as "tell the players where I am", "I want them to look at me before the game" and "pressure on linesman, everybody" – in the return leg against Lazio at the Stadio Olimpico two weeks later.

Certainly, there are remarkable parallels between these examples of Mourinho's contentious methods and those of Helenio Herrera, one of the most controversial managers of all-time. The Argentine pioneered the use of psychological motivational skills in football and popularised the use of the defensive *catenaccio* (The Chain/Door bolt) tactic in the 1960s. A ground-breaking trailblazer in football management, Herrera won seven league titles and two European Cups in a glittering 37-year managerial career. *Il Mago*, the magician, did not tolerate a lack of discipline, tactically or personally, and even dropped his fellow countryman, the great Antonio Angelillo, at Inter in 1960. Herrera resented the fact that Angelillo - who netted 68 goals in 113 games for Inter - was in a relationship with the popular Italian singer, Ilya Lopez.

Perhaps, Mourinho even took Herrera's antics one step further with open-door practices after defeats and, to this day, Mourinho claims to have pre-planned the silver goal finish against Celtic in the 2003 UEFA Cup final in Seville. However, Mourinho did not share all of Herrera's eccentricities. After all, the Argentine believed in the idea of the *ritui* (retreat) and 'sugar' supplements in the days running up to matches for *all* of his players and staff.

Also, Herrera used cult-like huddles where he threw footballs and screamed at his players before embracing them as they left the dressing room; and shared bizarre superstitions with his star forward, Luis Suárez Miramontes, such as getting the said striker to dip his finger into spilt 'anointed' wine and bless himself the evening before a key match to instigate a goalscoring display. Mourinho, by comparison, likes his players to spend their first day of away trips immersed in the foreign city's culture before beginning his intensive PowerPoint and whiteboard presentations.

Chapter 5

So, while Mourinho had not yet sunk to his most controversial state, or anything yet resembling Herrera's abrasiveness, the Portuguese certainly enjoyed Porto's bitter rivalry with Benfica. In fact, Mourinho cranked it up upon his winning return to the Estádio da Luz – a match which led to an unassailable 13-point lead and which gave the team even more belief in their treble dream. On 4 March 2003, Mourinho declared: "I made the point of walking on alone, before the team. I had never been a first-class player who could feel, for example, what [Luís] Figo had felt upon returning to Barcelona. Upon hearing the whistles and jeers, I felt like the most important person in the world."

The seeds had been sown.

With Porto's renewed success, fan support was revived - amid the eventual opening of the state-of-the-art, 52,339 capacity Estádio do Dragão on 16 November, 2003 - and Mourinho was keen to tap into this. The Portuguese even posted in-depth training details and fitness programmes for Porto's fans on the club's website, with a 20km jog being referred to as "an extended aerobic exercise", for example. What followed was Porto's president, Pinto da Costa, referring to Mourinho's Porto as the "best in 50 years" and Porto completing a remarkable treble. Firstly, there was the league title with 86 points (just two defeats), a then record in the three-point era in Portugal and a satisfying 11 points ahead of second-placed Benfica. Then, there was an emotional 1–0 Portuguese Cup victory against Mourinho's previous club, União de Leiria.

The UEFA Cup was to prove the most impressive achievement, with the highlight being Porto defeating Panathinaikos 0-2 in the quarter-final second-leg after losing the first-leg 0-1 at the Estádio das Antas on 13 March, 2003. Following the 4-1 aggregate defeat of Lazio in the semi-final, the treble was completed after an epic 3–2 UEFA Cup silver goal final victory over Celtic in Seville. Porto had become the first ever Portuguese team win the UEFA Cup. Already, Mourinho had established himself as one of the most successful Portuguese managers of all-time, and the first in 16 years to win a major European trophy.

However, this remarkable victory was marred slightly by Mourinho complaining about Celtic's aggressive style and defending his team's diving. Privately, though, Mourinho relished the war-like conditions of Porto's hotel being flooded with zealous Celtic fans. César Peixoto's testimony to me about Seville reflects this: "Luckily we had two wonderful years. We won everything, so there are many good memories. But what really marked me was the UEFA Cup and how it was obtained. For many years, a Portuguese team had not won an international trophy and the game itself was very emotional. The atmosphere was fantastic and the Scots made a big party. We were focused at the hotel and saw on the television that people were partying in the street and that there was a lot of excitement around us. We took a stroll through the city park and felt the heat and excitement of the game. It was, undoubtedly, a special environment.

"Mourinho is always methodical in the preparation of the games, but that was more to do with detail than motivation. In motivational terms, he did not have to say anything because it was a final that all the players were ready to play. But, as we always did, we knew by detail the whole team of Celtic and we went into the game with the exact notion of how Celtic played and their strengths and weaknesses."

2002–03 had been an unqualified success but, in Mourinho's eyes, "It was unforgettable… not unrepeatable". While the idea of winning the Champions League was certainly not at the forefront of his thoughts - amid the 'sharks' who could spend £40 million on one player - Mourinho clearly saw the treble success as merely the foundations for further silverware with Porto.

Still, with his treble success inevitably attracting interest, Mourinho was offered a much higher salary and bigger budget to join Paris Saint-Germain. Mourinho, however, was soon to advocate the nomadic Béla Guttmann's three-year rule, whereby coaches should never leave before their three years are up – as it is near-impossible to complete all objectives in this time; in turn, they should never stay beyond this period as players and staff get complacent.

Guttmann had 25 spells - returning to separate clubs he had previously managed on four different occasions - in a 40-year spell in management between 1933 and 1973. Spreading his message across 12 nations - in Europe and South America - Guttmann was the forerunner of the modern cult football manager: one who always wore a suit, provided a memorable quote, and who sought to be the central voice of the club. The Hungarian won 11 trophies in this period, with the highlight being his back-to-back European Cups with Benfica in 1961 and 1962. Far from coincidentally, the Estádio da Luz was where Guttmann had his longest individual spell, a mere three years. To put his achievements there into context, Benfica failed to win the five European Cup finals they contested, amid the 'Guttmann curse', between 1963 and 1990.

Thus, like Guttmann, in the words of the anthropologist Desmond Morris and his acclaimed work, *The Soccer Tribe*, Mourinho is a 'witch doctor'. This is a man whose charisma and magic remedy the failings and bad habits of the *other* [his predecessors] in the short-term with his unique form of medicine [coaching], but who cannot guarantee the disease will not return in the long-term post-treatment [after departure]. This has been accentuated by Mourinho's general preference for peak-aged players, leading to something of a scorched earth policy when he leaves as these players' abilities have been exhausted.

* * *

Without changing his treble-winning squad dramatically – with José Bosingwa, Pedro Mendes, Carlos Alberto, Benni McCarthy and, eventually in January, Maciel and Sérgio Conceição arriving and only Hélder Postiga departing – Mourinho sought to keep his players on their toes. The

Portuguese aimed to achieve this, tactically, with his wish for them to effortlessly shift from 4-4-2 to what was to become 'Mourinho's' 4-3-3. Having already laid the foundations of his high-tempo, *pressão alta* game throughout the pitch, this was to prove a potent combination in tandem with the 4-3-3.

With the permanent signings of Carlos Alberto and McCarthy in particular, Mourinho felt Porto, with a bit of luck, could be well-equipped – even with Derlei's and César Peixoto's injuries – for a decent assault on the Champions League. Still, Peixoto's anterior cruciate ligament injury had been a particular blow, with the midfielder thriving in Mourinho's shift to a 4-3-3 and Mourinho had never seen one of his own players suffer such a serious injury up to this point. Mourinho remarked: "It is the first time that an injury so severe has happened to a player of mine since I'm coach and it is a very strange feeling. We cannot rely on the player for a long time and because it's César, the sadness is too big. We thought we'd found the player we wanted for the left flank. When he injured himself, I immediately thought that in terms of the team, we'd have to return to the 4-4-2 formation, as without César we couldn't play with three forwards. Together, we have to overcome this situation, but it's a shame what happened. It's a shame also for Portuguese football because, for sure, [Luiz Felipe] Scolari was already eyeing him."

In contrast to future reports that Mourinho – like the legendary Bill Shankly at Liverpool – would freeze his injured players out, Mourinho made sure to maintain Peixoto's focus and morale: "As a man, he was always positive and always treated me well. He was present at the clinic for the operation and gave me support before, during and after surgery. It made me feel great and I am grateful for that. I remember that two days before the operation, José told me he did not have high expectations of me but now he was concerned because he felt that I was becoming a major player. On confirmation of diagnosis, he called me and gave me strength."

* * *

The turning point in the Champions League dream proved to be the 2-3 away victory over Marseille on 22 October, 2003, with Porto having claimed just one point in their opening two matches against Real Madrid and Partizan Belgrade in Group F before this. It was a telling match for Mourinho's future plans, too. Before the game, Mourinho had been contacted by Tottenham representatives who wished to interview him about replacing Glenn Hoddle. Mourinho politely declined. That night, also, Mourinho met Marseille's towering forward, Didier Drogba, in the tunnel for the first time and so mesmerised was the Portuguese by Drogba's physique and goalscoring performance, Mourinho quipped: "Do you have a brother or cousin in the Ivory Coast, because I don't have the money to bring you to Porto!"

Porto went on to record a further seven points in their final three group matches to finish second behind Real Madrid on 11 points. Interestingly, Mourinho had sought either Monaco ("weakest" and "lack of home atmosphere") or Manchester United ("great European stature") as the perfect scalp to send Europe a message. It was clear that Mourinho saw the second-round as a pivotal stage in judging his squad's merits for a serious challenge for the trophy and Manchester United was the perfect test. In contrast, the Group E winners, United, knew that they could have had a somewhat easier draw, with Celta Vigo, Sparta Prague, and Lokomotiv Moscow being among the seven options.

Given the volatility of both managers, it was perhaps little surprise that the first-leg at the Estádio do Dragão on 25 February 2004 ended in controversy. After all, Sir Alex Ferguson refused to shake Mourinho's hand following a frustrated Roy Keane's red card in the 87th minute. The Irishman left his dangling foot in on Vítor Baía and Ferguson was soon to echo Martin O'Neill – who managed Celtic against Porto in the 2003 UEFA Cup final – with his criticism of the goalkeeper for "lying out on the turf for three or four days".

Remarkably, this hostility occurred even before Mourinho's post-match taunts of assembling Porto's squad with just 10% of Ferguson's budget. In hindsight of the tie's eventual result, it is telling that Ferguson would rarely taunt Mourinho when the duo were to go on to face each other in the future. Still, hopes were high for United, with Quinton Fortune having scored a crucial away goal in a 2–1 first-leg defeat for United at the Estádio do Dragào.

In the second-leg, at Old Trafford on 9 March, Paul Scholes put a dominant United ahead just after the half-hour mark. United, though, did not add to their lead and Porto were awarded a 20-yard free-kick deep into stoppage time. All European champions, let alone outsiders like Porto, need a degree of fortune along the way and that moment of luck, or *azar* (fate), came with 89.21 minutes on the clock. With McCarthy striking the ball centrally, but at a relentless pace, Tim Howard could only punch. It was an unorthodox reaction, as if fate-like, particularly when he knocked it straight into the path of Costinha. What followed was Mourinho announcing himself on the world stage: leaping from Old Trafford's famous red-brick dugout and sprinting, arms aloft in a helicopter fashion, towards his ecstatic players as the ball fired into the goal.

From a distance, even with the cashmere coat, Mourinho's naturally coloured crew cut and his mid-air punch seemed to affirm his 12th-man status and, as he hugged his players, it was clear that he had achieved a delicate balance between player popularity and a never-say-die mentality. After all, Porto never gave up, alongside their good fortune of Scholes having a goal disallowed just before half-time. Mourinho's antics, too, had established a new phenomenon for major European nights: managers, ahead of their players, becoming the central attractions.

After putting the first-leg bickering behind them, Gary Neville - who filled in for Keane as United's stand-in captain that night - and Ferguson knocked on the away dressing room door following the match. Both congratulated Mourinho and the whole of the ecstatic Porto squad. It was then, in Mourinho's eyes, that he knew that something special could be in the offing.

* * *

Brian Clough - the man alongside Helenio Herrera who so clearly influenced Mourinho without ever coming into direct contact with him - was soon impressed and, remarkably for an anglophile like Clough, that was before Mourinho even managed in England: "I like the look of Mourinho, there's a bit of the young Clough about him. For a start, he's good-looking and, like me, he doesn't believe in the star system. He's consumed with team spirit and discipline. The players have to fit in with his vision and pattern of play, which is right. Don't confuse footballers - keep it simple."

While Clough and Mourinho shared the same audacity – with Mourinho's eventual tapping up of Ashley Cole in 2005 echoing Clough prematurely parading Ian Storey-Moore at Derby County's Baseball Ground in 1972 – there was a clear contrast between Clough's respect for discipline and referees and Mourinho's incessant criticism of officials. Sir Bobby Robson, too, believed the duo had a crucial difference in personality: "Clough was arrogant, no doubt about that, not like José Mourinho, who's simply self-confident."

* * *

Porto defeated Lyon 4–2 on aggregate in the quarter-final, before a semi-final against Deportivo de La Coruña. Feeding off their unstoppable momentum, *Os Dragões* won 1–0 on aggregate, with Deco inspirational and Costinha brilliantly shackling the classy heartbeat of Deportivo, Juan Carlos Valeron. Mourinho's brave decision to drop McCarthy for the returning Derlei in the second-leg proved inspirational, with the Brazilian netting the only goal of the two games. Given the fact that Deportivo dominated both matches, their manager, Javier Irureta, felt that "fate was against us". Hyperbole, certainly, but Mourinho's Porto had a pre-determined and well-drilled quality in stifling teams, working the whistle, and counter-attacking with real menace.

Chapter 6

Having already won the league with an eight-point advantage over Benfica, and an unbeaten home record to boot, Porto were slight favourites for the Champions League final against a talented Monaco outfit featuring the likes of Jérôme Rothen, Ludovic Giuly, Dado Pršo and Fernando Morientes. Despite these attacking talents, Monaco had proved vulnerable at the back: conceding a whopping 16 goals on their run to the final, and Porto easily exploited this. Admittedly, Porto were helped by the mercurial Giuly's injury mid-way through the first-half at the Arena AufSchalke in Gelsenkirchen - with the Frenchman an influential captain - but Monaco were soon gripped by complacency following a decent start.

Monaco's key tempo dictator, Rothen, carelessly conceded possession in the middle of the park on multiple occasions and when Paulo Ferreira sent in an awkward low cross from the byline – owing to one of these concessions – Alberto hit a hooked finish past Flavio Roma just before half-time. Monaco were shell-shocked: Mourinho smelt blood and made soon-to-be-trademark use of his bench. The move on the hour mark seemed risky as Mourinho substituted the goalscorer, Alberto, for the 32-year old Dmitri Alenichev; it proved inspirational.

With Monaco going prematurely gung-ho, Alenichev set up Deco on 71 minutes and just four minutes later, Derlei crossed for Alenichev to strike a brilliant volley. Alenichev's goal saw the only emotional response from a near-tearful Mourinho during the final, with an ecstatic punch and his tongue almost involuntarily hanging out. Porto's captain, Jorge Costa - who was among the Porto squad when Mourinho assisted Sir Bobby Robson between 1994 and 1996 - made a beeline for an emotional embrace with Mourinho: "When the third goal went in, I went and hugged Mourinho, not a team-mate. It felt right."

For the first time in 16 years, Porto had won the European Cup. However, while the squad was, naturally, euphoric at the final whistle, Mourinho was remarkably composed alongside Tami, Matilde, and José Jr. The Portuguese gave each member of his staff and playing squad a nonchalant, but telling, handshake and took his medal off once the trophy had been lifted.

"One of the most important things I learnt from Bobby Robson is that when you win, you shouldn't assume you are *the* team and when you lose, you shouldn't think you are rubbish."

[On van Gaal] "We had a really special rapport.
He showed faith, gave me confidence and responsibility."

[The UEFA Cup with Porto] "It was unforgettable, not unrepeatable."

[On Champions League success with Porto] "It's time for people to stop speaking about my past and start speaking about my recent past, because I did what almost nobody has done."

Chapter 7: Revolution

Chelsea Football Club, where the terraces were once a breeding ground for the National Front, had now become a trailblazing, free-spending superpower under a Russian Jew, Roman Abramovich. The Russian and Peter Kenyon, Chelsea's then chief executive, clearly saw Mourinho as the man to lead a new, dynamic Chelsea project. Impressing this impetuous Chelsea hierarchy, Mourinho analysed the management styles at Microsoft and Apple; read Colin Powell's *It Worked For Me: In Life and Leadership*, and Phil Jackson's *More Than a Game* and *Mindgames*; and studied John Wooden's *Pyramid of Success*.

So, while the media had built-up the 2004 Champions League final as a winner-takes-all duel between Didier Deschamps and Mourinho for the Chelsea job – soon to be vacated when Claudio Ranieri was inevitably sacked – Mourinho had already convinced Abramovich, Kenyon, and the influential director, Eugene Tenenbaum, of his merits. Such was the hierarchy's audacity and keen interest in Mourinho, this initial meeting had occurred the day before Chelsea's Champions League semi-final first-leg against Monaco at the Stade Louis II on 20 April.

The result? Instantly charmed, Kenyon did not even consult Sir Bobby Robson about whether Mourinho would be a suitable fit. Interestingly, though, in advance of what would happen nearly three and a half years later, Tenenbaum and Kenyon – behind closed doors – feared that there was a potential personality clash in the offing between Mourinho and Abramovich. The Russian, after all, had fallen in love with fantasy football after seeing Milan's gleaming trophy cabinet during a private tour of the San Siro with Silvio Berlusconi, and witnessing Manchester United's 4-3 epic victory over Real Madrid in 2003.

Mourinho, though, convinced Kenyon and Tenenbaum that their mutual will to win and similar self-made successes would be enough to ensure that his partnership with Abramovich would be a successful one. Arguably, of the near-endless list of managers in the Abramovich era, it is only Mourinho who has come the closest to calling Abramovich a friend as much as a boss. Reflecting this, the duo would fly on Abramovich's private jet to attend England's friendly against Spain on 18 November, 2004.

Regardless, having previously flirted with Sven-Göran Eriksson during the same season, it was clear that Kenyon really did not rate Ranieri – even before *the Tinkerman's* debacle in Monaco. The episode cemented the then 52-year-old Ranieri's dithery epitaph, as Chelsea had been 1-1 'up' on away goals and in firm control against ten-man Monaco by half-time at the Stade Louis II. Perhaps Ranieri was feeling the pressure to deliver a season-defining, and potentially prospect-boosting, away victory, but he made unnecessary, imbalanced and impulsive changes in bringing on Juan Sebastián Verón, Jimmy Floyd Hasselbaink, and Robert Huth in the second-half. Chelsea went on to lose the game 3-1.

With Ranieri's white hair, reading glasses, and outdated methods, it seemed that there was a generation gap between the pair – despite a mere 11-year age difference. Mourinho, who was, even then, already one of the game's top masters at the art of substitution and holding leads – and embodied the brashness and modern values that Kenyon and Abramovich so badly sought after the dithery Ranieri – therefore seemed the perfect fit to restore Chelsea's famed King's Road swagger. The Portuguese even had a dog named Gullit, called after the legendary Dutchman, Ruud, who was Chelsea's player-manager between 1996 and 1998.

Still, initially, an agreement with Chelsea was not so concrete – with Internazionale and Liverpool also interested – and Mourinho, a childhood supporter of Liverpool, originally publicised his interest in taking over from Gérard Houllier, declaring on 23 April: "Liverpool are a team that interests everyone and Chelsea does not interest me so much because it is a new project with lots of money invested in it. I think it is a project which, if the club fail to win everything, then [Roman] Abramovich could retire and take the money out of the club. It's an uncertain project. It is interesting for a coach to have the money to hire quality players but you never know if a project like this will bring success."

However, this was Mourinho using Liverpool interest as a public bargaining position and the Portuguese saw the Chelsea job as a once in a lifetime opportunity, given the rarity of oligarchical investment in English football at the time. It was a quantum leap in Mourinho's career and reflecting this, Mourinho dispensed with his agent of three years, the regionally-known Brazilian José Baidek, for football's first ever super-agent, Jorge Mendes. With Mendes' trademark tough negotiating, Mourinho was awarded a lucrative three-year contract on a whopping £4.2 million per year. To put this ascension into perspective, only four years earlier, Mourinho had finished the second part of his UEFA coaching course.

While it was a massive wage rise, there was no doubting what a difficult and emotional decision it was for Mourinho. After all, he did not partake in Porto's homecoming celebrations when they paraded the Champions League trophy and many of Porto's fans would never forgive him for the move. Even though Porto had won every major club honour under Mourinho's leadership, the Portuguese was sent death threats and was even spat on when Chelsea fatefully played Porto in a 2-1 defeat in Group H of the Champions League months later.

This ill-feeling was not present among the squad when the teams met, though, as César Peixoto – who set-up Benni McCarthy for the winning goal in injury-time that night – told me: "It is always emotional to look back on that time. We spent many great years together: we won everything. We just greeted each other. He helped me and my colleagues helped him. There was plenty of empathy among everyone within the team."

Regardless of the difficult divorce, Mourinho had impressed the Chelsea hierarchy with a PowerPoint presentation that convinced them that he would have the command, drive, and image to represent what Kenyon hoped would soon become the "biggest club in the world". In the presentation, Mourinho talked about the need to upgrade Chelsea's dilapidated Harlington facilities and improve the club's Academy exploits. This would lead to Mourinho, personally, selecting Brendan Rodgers as the head of youth development in September 2004 and it was no coincidence that planning permission for the building of a state-of-the-art training facility at Cobham was granted just months after his arrival.

Rodgers' cousin, Nigel Worthington, believes Mourinho was crucial to Rodgers' eventual elevation to the frontline of football management: "Mourinho's influence on Brendan has been immense. Brendan would be the first one to say this himself. He worked very closely with Mourinho, gaining much knowledge along the way, which helped Brendan to be where he is now. Brendan, Steve Clarke and [André] Villas-Boas all worked under him and became top-class managers. It would be very difficult not to learn from someone of Mourinho's ability."

On the playing side, Mourinho also had concrete plans to, eventually, cull Chelsea's 27-man squad – pointing to his inspired transfer dealings with Porto in the summer of 2002 – to a two-per-outfield position, 23-man alternative. Such was the state of Chelsea's squad at the time, out-of-favour high earners like Winston Bogarde, Emmanuel Petit, and Marco Ambrosio were still under contract. Mourinho, instead, planned to build the team around five key figures: Carlo Cudicini, John Terry, Frank Lampard, Deco/Steven Gerrard, and Hernán Crespo. Captain-wise, Mourinho plumped for Terry over Lampard following an introductory meeting with Terry, Lampard, Wayne Bridge, and Joe Cole at England's team hotel before a friendly against Japan at Eastlands on 1 June 2004.

Mourinho also wanted to break-up the cliques in the Chelsea squad - partly due to a fear that the influx of Portuguese players that he was soon to recruit could be alienated - and demanded that only English was spoken. Before Mourinho began his revolution, though, he evaluated the squad with an interview with each player and did not hold back, particularly in one off-the-record case: "I wanted to show them that I can be a sweetheart but at the same, can be very nasty: 'Hey, last two seasons, eleven matches – why? You play nothing, you don't work, you don't sleep, you are always injured. You say the manager was s***, racist and did not like you?'"

Thus, Mourinho set up a strict code of conduct, whereby a booklet was posted to each member of the squad upon his arrival and featured the recurring mantra of: "Each practice, each game and each minute of your social life must centre on the aim of being champions." The booklet also contained a curious equation – "Motivation + Ambition + Team + Spirit = SUCCESS" – and this phrase: "First-teamer will not be a correct word. I need all of you. You need each other. We are a TEAM." Mourinho had used the same booklet at Porto in 2003-04 and among the outlined advice was keeping mobile phones on silent on the team bus, no hotel room service, and the players being role models at all times.

Steven Watt - who started Mourinho's first pre-season match, against Oxford United on 18 July - told me about that momentous pre-season: "I've still got the booklet! It was a detailed layout of the pre-season schedule. I remember thinking how organised he was, as everything had been covered - right down to the finest of details. He stressed that we should never lose a game at home. It was well organised from start to finish, high standards were always expected. At training, you were expected to work to your maximum ability the whole time you were on the training pitch. Everything we worked on was game related and had a point. It all reflected the manager's philosophy. Every session was enjoyable and educational because of the high standards that they set.

"I was excited to see a change but, as a young player, I was unsure where my future would lie with the money being invested into the club. Thankfully, Mourinho had a great way of making you feel a part of the first-team. Even as a young player, he made you feel as if you belonged there."

Mourinho knew that some of his squad would struggle to adjust to this approach, but he aimed to give all members of Claudio Ranieri's squad a chance before wholly dipping into the transfer market. Method-wise, though, Mourinho was to dramatically change Chelsea's approach – ditching Ranieri's cardiology-focused double-training sessions for more popular, ball-centred training and even showering alongside his players. Clearly, Mourinho had little time for Ranieri's foundations, evident in the Portuguese's criticism of Ranieri's use of Ridley Scott's *Gladiator* as a motivational tool before a 2003-04 Champions League match: "If I did that they'd just laugh at me and think I was sick."

Craig Rocastle was part of Chelsea's first-team squad under both Ranieri and Mourinho, between 2003 and 2005, and the midfielder told me about two distinct individuals: "I could not ask for more from Ranieri - he gave me a chance and put me on a platform due to my performances with the reserves. Yet, the difference between Ranieri and Mourinho was basic man management. Ranieri was more closed circuit and only addressed people he needed; Mourinho would speak to all players and made you feel welcome on a daily basis. It is what all players love and need.

"The booklet even had his mobile number. All I was thinking under him was, 'I'm finally here'. I could not wait to start training that same afternoon. This is why he is so successful. Typical training sessions involved game-like situations. Nothing was fake; no player went through the motions. All sessions were intense, technical, and tactical. Put it this way, not one player in the entire club did not understand their tactical role or position. He created a style, a system, and wanted all players and coaches to follow his plan… Mourinho would always encourage players in training, especially young players, and I'll never forget when an afternoon session did not go to well for me. He came up to me and put his arm around my shoulder. He told me my history before Chelsea and whilst at Chelsea and said, 'People only remember the good things, so keep doing the good things. Never lose focus.' He is the best manager I've been under."

Mourinho also brought in his own backroom staff, with Abramovich forking out £1.75 million in compensation to buy four members of Porto's staff - Rui Faria, Baltemar Brito, Silvino Louro, and André Villas-Boas - out of their contracts.

Faria was brought in as a methodologist, rather than simple fitness coach. Such was Faria's advancement, he compiled individual training programs and varied player diets that were near-unprecedented - even by Arsène Wenger's standards - in England at the time. Ricardo Carvalho and the Portuguese contingent favoured crab meat; Arjen Robben and Eidur Gudjohnsen liked tuna; and Terry and Lampard stuck to simple, healthy staples.

The training ground became a sacred temple for Mourinho and Faria as Lawrie Sanchez, manager of Northern Ireland at the time, told me: "I met José the week after we beat England in 2005. Our Under-19s were playing in Harlington at Chelsea's training ground, as it happens. I went down to watch them and one of the press officers at the time was an ex-Wimbledon press officer. He came up to me at the end of the game and said, 'Can I get your picture with José?' We lined up, taking our picture, and, unfortunately, the flash wouldn't go off. So, the cameraman had to change the batteries. We had a quick chat, but the good humour evaporated the longer the photographer took to take it. He was very much, 'This is my domain'...A lot of people were congratulating me on that win against England a week earlier; some of the Chelsea boys were in the England squad and even they said well done. He didn't seem to like outsiders coming in and taking credit. Mourinho was very much, 'Time to go now, this is my place, I'm the king here.'"

Pre-match warm-ups, too, took on massive importance, with immense concentration needed to keep up with Faria's 'peep whistle', sprinting and jogging exercises. Even though Mourinho announced his team some five days before kick-off for the majority of matches, if a member of staff felt that a starting player was too relaxed or lethargic in the warm-up, a Roman-style thumbs down towards Mourinho from Faria could result in said player being dropped. The Chelsea staff would also choose the player to give the final rallying call in the dressing room before the start of a match, with Mourinho, generally, preferring not to have the final word before the players crossed the white line.

Chelsea legend Steve Clarke was recruited as Mourinho's first assistant, to act as a tactical consultant, and the gesticulative Baltemar Brito was appointed as his second assistant, who would be the players' confidant despite, ironically, speaking very little English. Silvino Louro - the Benfica great, who won 23 caps for Portugal - was brought in as the sole goalkeeping coach. Silvino trained the goalkeepers in isolation and would act as their key morale booster due to their absence from Mourinho's outfield-focused training activities. André Villas-Boas, recruited as Mourinho's 'eyes and ears', compiled scouting dossiers and was, clearly, one of Mourinho's most ardent disciples. After all, Villas-Boas would often go days without sleep and Mourinho knew only too well how valuable his five-page dossiers were due to the difficulty of maintaining the squad's attention span during a tactics discussion in a dark room for 45 minutes.

The Chelsea squad embraced Mourinho's methods, and it would be this set-up and discipline, just as much as Mourinho's eventual success, that would haunt every one of Mourinho's successors. After all, the Portuguese brilliantly struck the delicate balance between player-favoured ball-playing sessions and honing the immense fitness needed to play Mourinho's *pressão alta* tactic throughout the pitch.

The foundations were now in place: enter *the Special One*.

Chapter 8: Self-Anointed

Ahead of his Chelsea unveiling on 2 June 2004, just one week after Porto's Champions League triumph, Mourinho was restless. The Portuguese knew that he was already under immense pressure to succeed and it was clear that he had picked up on the English media's mixed reaction to his appointment. This, initial, lukewarm reaction to Mourinho's arrival was owed to numerous factors: the despicable manner of the popular Claudio Ranieri's dismissal, Mourinho's lack of experience outside Portugal, the Portuguese's league-record £4.2 million wage, Mourinho's controversial run-ins with Martin O'Neill and Sir Alex Ferguson in the past, and an 'easier' 2004 Champions League tournament which lacked the football aristocracy in the latter stages.

Peter Kenyon picked up on this and immediately backed Mourinho, who even had a name card in front of him on the desk, at that infamous first press conference: "You'll all look at the Chelsea trophy room in ten years' time and think what a good acquisition José Mourinho was." However, Mourinho, himself, needed to address his insecurities in a new environment by reminding the media just who this 41-year-old upstart was, after being asked if he felt he was ready to manage in England: "If I wanted to have an easy job, working with the big protection of what I have already done before, I would have stayed at Porto – beautiful blue chair, the UEFA Champions League trophy, God and after God, me... please don't call me arrogant, but I'm European champion and I think I'm a special one." In that one pre-planned moment, Mourinho - who was not wearing a tie in a new precedent for English football unveilings at the time - had set the tone for not only his time in England, but, also, his career: revolutionising press conferences into box office events.

* * *

Mourinho had penetrated a new sphere for football managers and Lauren Cochrane, fashion writer with *the Guardian*, told me about the power of Mourinho's aesthetic qualities: "I think it's a few things that make him so attractive to females. Mourinho has a classic, monochrome, neat and minimal style. He's good-looking and has a personality that extends beyond the *Match of the Day* routine. But, also, I think his clothes are just different enough so they're not scary for straight men, but, equally, fashion observers will notice them, too. The cut of his clothes will always be appreciated in this arena.

"Maybe his slickness has helped his appeal with his players – even though I don't think Chelsea have had particularly style conscious players in recent years. But, I definitely think his personality has had an impact and that's probably more to do with him being a winner, a 'Special One', and an alpha male. All three are going to go down well in the training ground."

Chapter 8

Mourinho's audacity was also evident in a less-heralded, but equally intriguing, psychological moment when the new Chelsea manager signed his showpiece contract after his unveiling. With the on-looking media, Bruce Buck, Chelsea's chairman, and Kenyon, Chelsea's then chief executive, were eager to give the world the perfect revolution-instigating image: Mourinho signing on the dotted line. Just before this moment, Buck took a pen out of his pocket for Mourinho to sign but Kenyon, somewhat tongue in cheek, commented that Mourinho "needs a decent one [pen]". Just as Kenyon was about to hand Mourinho *his* fountain pen, the Portuguese retrieved his very own pen from the pocket of his Armani blazer and proceeded to sign. It was the clearest signal of how Mourinho was going to manage the delicate dynamics and set-up of Chelsea Football Club: he was going to do it his way and with his sword.

Still, there was no doubting the fact that there was an element of insecurity to Mourinho's brashness, given that this was the first time he was managing abroad. It was an isolated initial period in the family's lavish new home in Eaton Square, Belgravia - with Mourinho only frequenting a pub once to buy a packet of cigarettes for Tami. In truth, Mourinho much preferred to stay in and read a José Saramago book rather than visit the West End. Mario Stanić, who went on to confirm his retirement with the Portuguese on the first day of pre-season, picked up on Mourinho's nerves and made a point of re-assuring Mourinho: "A lot of people have arrived in England and they just adapt to the English reality of football. But I know that your methods and your philosophy and your way of thinking are very special. Don't ever change, even if it takes time."

Buoyed, Mourinho soon got to work on his transfer targets ahead of the beginning of pre-season on 5 July. Incidentally, Mourinho requested his squad spend their first day of pre-season at Stamford Bridge, as opposed to Harlington, in an attempt to drive home the importance of turning Stamford Bridge into a fortress. Ranieri's respectable record of 47 home league wins - just 12 defeats - from 74 league games was soon to be put into perspective.

With the Petr Čech and Arjen Robben deals already sanctioned by Ranieri before Mourinho arrived, Paulo Ferreira, Ricardo Carvalho, Nuno Morais, Tiago, Didier Drogba and Mateja Kežman were also signed. Mourinho was wary of the dangers of bringing in too many Portuguese players - having witnessed Louis van Gaal sign nine of his Dutch compatriots at Barcelona between 1998 and 2000 - and even claimed he would not sign any of his former players during his unveiling press conference. Such was the poisonous atmosphere that van Gaal's Dutch bias created at Barcelona, even Patrick

Kluivert admitted: "Having so many Dutch players is dangerous. It is going to be too easy to blame us if things go wrong." Even though Mourinho went back on his word, he knew that he could not afford to isolate the English bloc within the squad. So, when Ferreira was signed from Porto, Mourinho immediately phoned the English right-back, Glen Johnson, to reassure him about his future.

While, tellingly, £43 million of the £72 million that Mourinho spent in that first window was on players from his homeland, Drogba's signing, at a whopping £24 million from Marseille, concealed this and was the deal to grab the headlines. The Ivorian's expensive arrival came as something of a surprise given the fact that he had played just one season at Marseille, but Hernán Crespo had let Mourinho down. Crespo arrived two days late for pre-season, following an extended holiday in Argentina, and was adamant that he would follow Juan Sebastián Verón in leaving Chelsea on a loan move to his European home, Italy.

Crespo turned up on Wednesday at lunchtime for his one-on-one meeting with Mourinho – which every other member of the squad had held, predominantly in English, two days previously. Mourinho addressed the Argentine in Spanish due to Crespo's poor command of English: "You have always to be there. If the plane is full from Argentina, come by bus. You can call. There's always a solution." Clearly, Mourinho had to act to send a message to the dressing room. After all, such was Crespo's unprofessionalism, the Argentine's payslip (£94,000 weekly wage) was leaked to the press after Crespo had left it lying around the Harlington training ground.

Even Mourinho's predecessor, the affable Ranieri, would not have stood for this, as he outlined in *Proud Man Walking*: "There can be no place for nancy boys in my group. A player cannot use every slightest set-back as an excuse for malingering." Such was Mourinho's disgust, and the hierarchy's backing of him, Chelsea paid two thirds of Crespo's wages to fund the Argentine's loan move to Milan. The episode epitomised the fact that Mourinho's original plans were now completely flipped: Deco plumped for Barcelona; Steven Gerrard performed an eleventh hour u-turn about leaving Liverpool; and Cudicini - Chelsea's Player of the Year in 2002-03 - did not wholly impress Silvino Louro in pre-season.

Still, Crespo was far from the only rebel in the camp and Adrian Mutu was another *enfant terrible* Mourinho had to deal with. Perhaps, their eventual parting - following Mutu's positive drugs test for cocaine and a controversial claim that Mourinho had prevented him from playing for Romania against the Czech Republic in October, 2004 - should have been of little surprise. After all, Mourinho's prophetic opening words to the Romanian on 5 July were telling: "You are already a rich boy, you won a lot of money, you are still in a big contract. So no problem with your future about money, no problem about prestige in your home country. When you go back to Romania, you will be one of the kings. But five years after you leave football, nobody remembers you. Only if you do big things. This is what makes history."

In contrast to Mutu and Crespo, Drogba would soon become one of Mourinho's leading disciples. Having closely monitored the Ivorian's progress at Marseille in 2003-04, Mourinho was the key to Drogba's signature: "Some people said to me: 'Is it real that Chelsea wants to buy you?' I said: 'I don't know.' Then, when my agent came and said to me: 'Chelsea have made a proposition for you' and I say: 'Fantastic, but I don't want to go.' Two days after, I met José Mourinho and, *clicks fingers*, it was in the pocket."

Drogba's eventual evolution into *the* most feared hold-up player of his generation was, perhaps, unsurprising. Sure, the Ivorian would enjoy his most groundbreaking years under Carlo Ancelotti and Roberto Di Matteo, but it was Mourinho who took the initial gamble. After all, Drogba had only played two and a half seasons of top-level football in France before his move to Chelsea and Mourinho's loyalty towards him – while the English media hounded Drogba over his play-acting and initial poor finishing from 2004–06 – shaped Drogba's soon to be trademark self-belief.

Like Mourinho, too, Drogba was to leave an irrevocable mark on Chelsea's history.

Chapter 9: When Mario met José

To some, the name Mario Rosenstock may appear to be the latest German international signing on José Mourinho's wishlist but, in actual fact, Rosenstock is an acclaimed satirist and impressionist from Dublin.

Such is Rosenstock's popularity, since 1999, he has held a near-daily mimic sketch slot, Gift Grub, on Ian Dempsey's Breakfast Show on Today FM - one of Ireland's national radio stations. Rosenstock also starred in Arthur Matthews' immensely popular musical comedy, *I Keano* - which brought the 2002 Saipan fiasco involving Mick McCarthy and Roy Keane to the stage - and achieved an Irish Christmas number one with *I Think I Better Leave Right Now*, a parody of Keane's fall-out with Sir Alex Ferguson in 2005.

Up until 2005, Rosenstock had made his name nationally for his lampooning of Irish figures, ranging from Roy Keane to Bertie Ahern, Ireland's former Taoiseach. José Mourinho, as one of the first foreign names Rosenstock impersonated, was to send Rosenstock's career into orbit as the Irishman told me: "We've always loved football and doing football stuff on Gift Grub and when Mourinho came on the scene, it very quickly appeared that this guy was a bit special in terms of his charisma and character. He turned the league upside down a little bit in his first year and, actually, when someone like that comes on the scene you don't think of doing them.

"It's very bizarre, it never actually occurs to you. You're taken in by who they are and you watch them like everyone else does. No one had depicted him up until that point. The beauty of football and the Premier League is that it tends to provide you with the ammunition itself and to try and pre-empt it and to try and write stuff yourself is foolish. At times, the Premier League is farcical pantomime that you can never guess - so to even pre-empt what he might do is wrong.

"I always mess around with voices in the office and it just turned out that a sort of pitch in my voice really matched his. It was a raspy pitch in my voice and I had no problem doing a Portuguese accent, which had a little bit of a Slavic, Eastern European vibe to it as well - which is strange, because they're not from the same part of the world. Then, it was a question of what kind of character we'd give him. We decided to give him a Latin lounge singer, mega confident, almost like Julio Iglesias. There's a supreme confidence in his voice: he makes categorical statements that cannot be refuted."

Rosenstock's impersonation of Mourinho was to first crystallise in his ingenious song, *José and his Amazing Technicolour Overcoat* – which was set to the tune of Andrew Lloyd Webber's *Any Dream Will Do* from the musical, *Joseph and the Amazing Technicolour Dreamcoat*. Rosenstock, as Mourinho, riles his underperforming players at half-time through the power of song. Featuring lyrics such as "they are all hating, but I like rotating" and "a corner kick is just enough, a little flick from Damien Duff", it proved inspired comedic song-writing. One man, in particular, took note: "I was in a wedding in the Radisson Hotel in Stillorgan in Dublin. The next day, I was downstairs hung-over - as loads of us were - and was watching Sky Sports' Gillette Soccer Saturday. José came on screen. I'm sitting downstairs in the lounge of the hotel and he looks up to the screen and says, 'So if he's out there, I want him to come over to me and I want him to sing the song for me.' I nearly spilt the pint all over myself! Have I completely gone nuts? Alcoholic psychosis, here – José Mourinho's just looked out from the television and is talking to me!"

Within hours, a formal invitation from Chelsea's then director of communications, Simon Greenberg, arrived in Rosenstock's inbox and he and his wife were whisked to the Marriott Hotel in Liverpool on the eve of Chelsea's next game, against Everton on 12 February 2005. It was the first time that Mourinho had brought someone from outside the squad's circle into the team's hotel before an away game and Rosenstock requested no fee for the privilege. Such was the tight security, Rosenstock's wife, Blathnaid, was not even allowed in. Also, Rosenstock did not get to meet the squad or Chelsea's staff beforehand and the only detail he was told was that there was to be just 30 people in attendance: "I'd arranged that the director of communications give a couple of questions - which I wrote on a tiny piece of paper - to the players in the room. So, I just came into the room with my overcoat and my scarf as José and walked through the players, past him [Mourinho] up to a little desk which said *the Special One* on it. I began the press conference and all the players started asking me questions.

"I was giving them the answers as himself, as José, and then I sang *the Technicolour Overcoat*. The thing was, the gig didn't go as well as I had hoped; in fact, it was a bit flat. First of all, there were only about 30 people in the hotel room and, second of all, half of them didn't know what I was talking about because they didn't speak English! [Didier] Drogba and [Claude] Makélelé hadn't a clue what I was talking about, but I looked down the back and saw [Frank] Lampard and [John] Terry pissing themselves and they were videoing it on their mobile phones.

"You walk into a room and two thousand people come to see you and they pay for a ticket. They're really hoping I'll be great so when I walk on stage, they give you a big welcome. That means people really warm to you. But these people hadn't a clue who I was and they didn't have a clue what I was going to do. For all they knew, I could've been a maniac…Really, the gig was a bit fraught and full of tension. Whereas, a gig you do in front of lots of people, it's much easier. The fewer people you perform to, the harder it is."

While much of Chelsea's foreign contingent seemed unimpressed - even when Rosenstock, as Mourinho, made a prank phone call to the injured Damien Duff to demand he played against Everton - one Portuguese was particularly delighted by Rosenstock's performance: "José sent them to bed – it was only 9.30pm! Then it was just me, him, and his Portuguese staff. We sat around, had a bottle of wine, and talked. He had listened to other sketches in the meantime on the radio. He loved my take on Mick McCarthy, so he put his hands over his eyes and said, 'Do your Mick McCarthy! Do your Mick McCarthy!' So I proceeded to do it… 'It's Mick McCarthy! He's beside me! It's Mick McCarthy!' At the time, as well, I joked, 'Would you come and manage Ireland?' He just looked at me and said, 'Roy Keane should be your next manager - he's invincible.'"

While this relaxed side of Mourinho - especially on the eve of what was sure to be an incredibly close match against Everton - may seem surprising, Rosenstock believes the request for his performance was not just for comedic effect: "Mourinho's a very, very clever guy in his own right. One of Mourinho's geniuses is that he manages to make players die for him and respect him. One of the ways he does that is by showing the players that he is cool. He really is the business. What I think he was doing was, 'Look at all you guys – you're all on £150,000 per week, you all have Bentleys and Ferraris, you all are very, very rich and arrogant and you think the world is yours.'

"It must be difficult for players, sometimes, to have respect for authority. What better way to show the players you're the man than going, 'Guys, I'm so famous that there's even guys in other countries doing impressions of me and doing songs about me. You might be on £150,000 per week, but you're not quite in my league yet. I'm the boss here.' He probably took a risk, because they didn't ask me about any script or anything so, maybe, I would've come in and humiliated him in some way. Maybe, it could have gone really wrong but, then, I think he felt confident enough that he could handle any situation."

Mourinho remains one of Rosenstock's favourite muses to this day and the Irishman went on to achieve further acclaim with another Mourinho song, *Sign Another Player or Two* (set to Aretha Franklin's *I Say A Little Prayer*), in 2007. Rosenstock even has his own Mourinho puppet series called Special 1 TV - which has appeared on Setanta Sports and BBC3 - and has starred in the *Mario Rosenstock Show* on RTÉ2 since 2012.

Chapter 9

Still, that famous day in February, 2005 would not prove the last time that Rosenstock was to receive an email from Chelsea's director of communications.

Chapter 10: Shifting Perceptions

Whether it was Glenn Hoddle, Ruud Gullit, Gianluca Vialli or Claudio Ranieri, Chelsea – as a team who thrived in cup competitions with an attacking philosophy – were, for many neutrals, a wholly likable club under proactive managers between 1994 and 2004. This was to change radically under Mourinho as tactically – with wingers Arjen Robben and Damien Duff, as almost fate would have it, being injured during pre-season – the Portuguese initially set up a narrow 4-4-2 diamond with Claude Makélélé, Alexey Smertin, Tiago and Frank Lampard. The flaws of the diamond were to crystallise, infamously, in Mourinho's failure to break down Tottenham's "parking of the bus" tactic in a 0-0 draw on 19 September 2004. Thus, it was not until the implementation of a 4-3-3 that Chelsea really took their mantle as the rich, 'boringly-consistent' club that everyone wanted to beat.

* * *

Several signature Mourinho moments stood out in Chelsea's momentous campaign in 2004-05 and were to set the tone for his reign. Firstly, after Joe Cole netted the only goal in the 1–0 victory over Liverpool on 16 October, Mourinho lamented: "I think he has two faces: one beautiful and one that I don't like. He must keep one of them and change the other one." Mourinho planned to mould Cole - who, privately, he admired much more than, say, the similarly raw Sabry at Benfica - into an all-round player. Mourinho wanted the Englishman to use his endless energy for crucial defensive purposes, in tracking back, and to adapt his game to play on either flank.

So, while Duff and Robben took most of the headlines in 2004-05, Mourinho had a preference for rotating his wingers and wanted each of them to play their part: "Why drive Aston Martin all the time, when I have Ferrari and Porsche as well? That would just be stupid." Still, admittedly, Cole remained fairly confined to cameo appearances until Robben's metatarsal injury in February 2005. Displaying newfound energy, determination and hunger, Cole's improved attitude was evident in a brilliant goal against Norwich on 5 March 2005, when he surged past two heavy challenges to hit a fantastic 20-yard strike past Robert Green.

It was again witnessed against Bayern Munich in the Champions League quarter-final on 12 April 2005 at the Olympiastadion, when Chelsea were drawing 1–1 and leading 5–3 on aggregate. In the 80th minute, it seemed Cole, wisely, would run down the clock by keeping a loose pass in the corner. However, instead, the Englishman showed remarkable energy to sprint to the edge of the box and pick out Didier Drogba for what proved to be a crucial goal in a 6–5 aggregate victory. Cole, as a reformed, orthodox winger, finished the season with an impressive nine goals and a new-found attitude. Perhaps,

Chapter 10

out of all the Chelsea squad who played under Mourinho, it would be Cole's consistency - admittedly, partly owed to a cruciate knee ligament suffered in 2008–09 - that would suffer the most post-2007.

* * *

The next moment, on 30 October, was when Chelsea went top of the league – on goal difference – ahead of Arsenal after beating West Brom 1–4 at the Hawthorns. Eidur Gudjohnsen, who had been at the club since 2000, summed up what a key date that was: "We played West Brom away and the boys on the pitch, sort of, realised that Arsenal were losing because our fans were chanting, 'We're top of the league.' It was the first time in a long, long time that we were top of the league and from that moment on, we did not want to let it go."

Chelsea kept their lead in the league and two months later, met Arsenal at Highbury on 12 December 2004. Incidentally, unlike some continental managers working in England, Mourinho relishes working over the Christmas period and would even go on to watch Premier League games on holiday in New York and Brazil during the Spanish winter breaks in 2011 and 2012. In this instance, though, Chelsea had gone into half-time 2-1 down after Thierry Henry scored a semi-controversial, but ingenious, quick free-kick before the half-hour mark. Mourinho was livid, criticising his team for playing so well without scoring. This led to Mourinho's first major outburst in the dressing room at Chelsea: volleying what he thought was an empty plastic cup, which actually had Lucozade in it, and a tub of Vaseline which hit Steve Clarke in the chest and went all over Carlo Cudicini's pre-match suit.

So riled was the Chelsea dressing room, tellingly, they fought back to draw the match 2–2 and the hoodoo that had gripped Chelsea against Arsenal in the Premier League for nine years was soon to be over.

This was a rare Mourinho outburst and, in fact, he shared immense empathy with his squad and even gave one off the record member a leave of absence to care for his sick son. Steven Watt told me about this side of Mourinho: "He was like a father figure: he knew when you needed an arm around you and he knew when you needed a kick into gear to make an improvement. I respected him and did not want to disappoint him… One of my best memories is when he told me I was going to be making my first-team debut against Scunthorpe in the FA Cup in 2005. There was no meeting and nothing official about it. He just casually strolled up to me in the canteen while I was queuing for my lunch and said, 'Steve, do you want to play for me this weekend?' I said, 'Yes, boss!' Then he just smiled and said 'Okay,' and walked out of the canteen.

"I had been suffering with a proper flu bug up to then and couldn't even get out of bed. I even had to spend Christmas Day in bed, but up until the illness struck I had been doing really well in training and was involved with a lot of the first-team sessions. I was feeling confident, but the Scunthorpe game came out of the blue as I thought I might get a chance towards the end of the season… Mourinho took this game very seriously and [André] Villas-Boas' pre-match dossier was incredibly detailed. No stone was left unturned. During the pre-match meeting the day before the game, they went through Scunthorpe's entire starting XI from their previous game. Everything was analysed: the heights and weights of each player, their strengths and weaknesses, video clips of how they play, their set-piece routines, and how we could exploit their weaknesses. It was treated with the same respect as if it were a Champions League match."

* * *

Jiří Jarošík joined Chelsea from CSKA Moscow for £3 million in January 2005 and the Czech told me about adjusting to life at Stamford Bridge: "The first time I met José was during the Champions League in 2002, when Sparta Prague played Porto at the Letná. I had a very good game and scored, and he told me that he wanted to sign me in the summer. I ended up eventually moving to CSKA Moscow and we met again in the Champions League in 2004, when he was at Chelsea. He was looking for a bigger squad and they had some injuries. That's why he asked Petr Čech about me because Petr was with me at Sparta and the national team, and he wanted to know a little bit more about me.

"For me, it was a big step because there was a big difference between the squads and methods of CSKA and Chelsea. For example, training sessions were not that long at Chelsea: they were very quick and he was always looking for the utmost quality and effort. At this time, José had a very good squad at Chelsea. A lot of games, we were winning 1-0; we had a very good defence but in the middle, we were not always that strong in depth… If we lost one game or two games – or didn't play well – he prepared 10 minutes of footage before the next game of our mistakes. It was actually very funny footage, with gaffes from other sports included too. It was funny for everybody and everyone went onto the pitch smiling."

* * *

On 2 February 2005, Chelsea played Blackburn in a bruising encounter, which saw Petr Čech save a penalty and set a record at the time of not conceding a goal in 1,025 minutes. In frosty conditions – with Robben particularly targeted by Blackburn's players and Mourinho refusing to shake Mark Hughes' hand – Mourinho ordered that every Chelsea player take off their shirt and salute their travelling support after a brilliant, Champions-like 0–1 victory.

Čech's record of not conceding a goal was to end in a 1-3 win at Norwich on March 5, 2005. Nigel Worthington was Norwich's manager at the time and he told me how memorable that evening's events were: "Our technical plan pre-match was to be as positive as we could, bearing in mind the quality that the Chelsea team possessed. The word 'weakness', that was something that I could not find in the Chelsea team at that time. This situation with Čech not conceding in ten consecutive games again showed quality that this Chelsea team had acquired under Mourinho... While Arsenal were on their record-breaking run of 47 league games unbeaten, we hosted Arsenal for the 42nd game and became one of the stats. At least here, despite being a smaller club, we left our mark.

"Pre-match, I referred to José as a breath of fresh air for English football and I stand by that comment. He put some humour into press conferences; I think it's very important not to be serious all the time... We shared a memorable glass of wine post-match on both occasions that season and for all that he had achieved in the game, he was a very humble and pleasant individual."

* * *

Another moment that stood out in Mourinho's debut season was his Sir Bobby Robson-like triple substitution at half-time against Newcastle in the fifth round of the FA Cup on 20 February. Robson used to advocate the idea of bringing "three fresh pairs of legs on" when his team were seeking an equaliser, believing their energy could bring renewed vigour, psychologically, to their flagging team-mates.

Thus, Mourinho bravely brought on Duff, Lampard and Gudjohnsen after resting most of his first XI in preparation for the first-leg of the second-round Champions League match against Barcelona on 23 February. It ultimately backfired: William Gallas and Duff suffered knocks and Carlo Cudicini was sent-off, leading to Glen Johnson wearing the goalkeeping jersey for the final minutes. Still, multiple substitutions would go on to become a hallmark of Mourinho's time with Chelsea if he was unhappy with a poor, torpid showing. This infamously occurred after just 26 minutes in the eventual 1–0 defeat to Fulham at Craven Cottage on 19 March 2006, with Shaun Wright-Phillips and Joe Cole being replaced by Duff and Drogba.

Still, days after this FA Cup exit to Newcastle, it would be the second-round tie against Barcelona that epitomised the ultimate paradox of Mourinho; the tactical brilliance and the ingenious mind-games, but also the cynical foul play, fabricated allegations and intimidation of the referee, Anders Frisk. First, the mind games...

Chapter 11: Machiavellian Deceit

"The end justifies the means" – the infamous mantra of Niccolò Machiavelli's *The Prince*. This scheming masterpiece acted as an unethical guide to seizing and maintaining power for those who have not inherited it. Centred on the difference between good cruelty and bad cruelty, *The Prince* outlines how good cruelty – a one-off action one gets away with – is justifiable if it leads to victory.

* * *

Damien Duff's knock against Newcastle meant that he was a massive doubt for the Barcelona game. Perhaps – though, somewhat ironically – Mourinho sensed a potential advantage with Duff's fitness ahead of the Portuguese's first ever return to the daunting Nou Camp, on 23 February. Thus, the day before the first-leg, Mourinho took the liberty of naming both teams in the pre-match press conference:

"Do you want to know the team? I can say my team and the Barça team, and the referee. Referee: Frisk. Barcelona: Valdés, Belletti, Puyol, Márquez, Giovanni; Albertini, Deco, Xavi; Eto'o, Giuly, Ronaldinho. Chelsea: Petr Čech, Paulo, Ricardo, John Terry, Gallas at left-back; Tiago, Makélélé, Frank Lampard, Joe Cole; *telling pause and bite of tongue* Drogba and Gudjohnsen. It's a good finish."

In eventually picking Duff instead of Eidur Gudjohnsen - who would go on to play a key role in a tight midfield trident with Frank Lampard and Claude Makélélé in the second-leg six days later - Chelsea's formation shifted from 4-4-2 to 4-3-3. It was the perfect tactic to counter-attack the flair-filled Barcelona and Frank Rijkaard was paralysed in being unable to change his plans - with this exact XI having started in the 2-0 victory over Real Mallorca two days previously - on the eve of the tie.

However, Damià Abella, the then 23-year-old right-back, was on the Barcelona bench for both legs and he told me that Mourinho's antics did not have a profound impact on the Barcelona camp ahead of that first-leg: "I think José Mourinho is a great coach who has had a big impact on football, making teams strong defensively and decisive in front of goal. However, his way of liaising with the press has occasionally hurt him and, personally, I think in the long run this attitude does not benefit anyone. Mourinho is a provocative coach and sometimes he has benefited from his actions off the field but on many other occasions, he has lost.

"For him, the match starts long before the day on which it is played. He tries to use 'weapons' that have benefited him on occasions, but ethically they seem ambiguous and wrong... [Frank] Rijkaard was focused on the players, but only the ones he trained – not Chelsea's. In the long run, I don't think the fact that Mourinho said he would play one [Eidur Gudjohnsen] and then played another [Damien Duff] benefited them greatly or shook our camp up."

Still, in some ways, there proved to be parallels with Chelsea's last visit to the Nou Camp, a 5–1 defeat under Gianluca Vialli on 18 April 2000. It was a balmy night, Chelsea were again kitted out in virgin white in their most daunting European away test up to that point, and there was to prove a game-changing red card in an echo of Celestine Babayaro's dismissal mid-way through extra-time in 2000. There was one crucial difference, though: Mourinho, alongside Louis van Gaal, was on the Barcelona bench that night.

Nearly five years on from the last time he sat in the Nou Camp dugout, Mourinho looked unfazed: outrageously slapping Carles Puyol on the cheek, before sitting slouched alongside a noticeably fidgety André Villas-Boas. Mourinho, after all, knew that he had armed himself with a trump card in recognising 30-year-old left-back Giovanni van Bronckhorst's flagging tackling ability in dealing with nippy wingers. Tellingly, therefore, Duff's brilliant influence was to be made clear with Juliano Belletti turning in the Irishman's cross, after Duff narrowly beat the offside trap, to put Chelsea 1–0 up just after the half-hour mark. It was the kind of tactical genius that Didier Drogba was to praise Mourinho for: "On the bench, I've heard him describe what would happen in an almost surgical way. Sometimes this was almost disquieting, as if he could see the future."

The goal was, arguably, Mourinho's defining Chelsea moment up to that point and was the perfect evidence of the belief he had in an 80% fit Duff. Then, though, came the nadir of Mourinho's career.

When surrounded by the red and blue of the *blaugrana*, it is safe to say that Barcelona are nothing short of catalysts for Mourinho controversy. Reflecting this, after the first leg, Mourinho declined UEFA's mandatory post-match press conference and the Portuguese claimed Steve Clarke and Chelsea's security officer, Les Miles, saw Rijkaard enter the referee Anders Frisk's dressing room at half-time over the decision to allow Chelsea's goal – which the Dutchman believed Duff was offside for.

Rijkaard, himself, did not deny this - but was keen to stress it was nothing illegal: "I was there, I talked with the referee and the reaction of the Chelsea side kind of exaggerated it all. I talked to the referee really politely, nothing in particular; they were upset about that. They started the thing for me; nothing happened and if something did happen it is because of them. They were upset, maybe because of me talking to the referee. I don't understand it; I am curious in what will be their complaint. They definitely didn't hear me speak. I said [to Frisk] 'Hello, pleased to see you,' something about the game, not in an aggressive way; I just said hello and nothing more."

UEFA's report of the night's events, meanwhile, read as follows: "The latter [Frisk] reported that he could not understand what the Barcelona coach was saying. It appears that in the tunnel a member of the Chelsea technical staff, the goalkeeping coach Silvino, tried to pull the Barcelona assistant coach, Henk ten Cate, away from the referee, causing a further gathering of representatives from both sides. At the top of the stairs, Anders Frisk and his assistants went through the left glass door and turned left for gaining [sic] their dressing rooms that were locked. Frank Rijkaard and his staff went through the right glass door and it appears that Frank Rijkaard tried to address some words to Anders Frisk at the end of the reception area. However, the referee told him to gain [sic] his dressing room, and Frank Rijkaard did so immediately…"

Still, Mourinho then manipulated this incident – particularly when Drogba, harshly, received a second yellow card before the hour mark after an innocuous challenge with Victor Valdés – in his post-match interview with *Dez Record*: "When I saw Rijkaard entering the referee's dressing room I couldn't believe it. When Didier Drogba was sent off, I wasn't surprised." So, then, was it Mourinho - as opposed to Clarke or Miles - who witnessed Rijkaard liase with Frisk? Regardless, Barcelona went on to win the match 2–1, through second-half goals from Maxi López and Samuel Eto'o after Drogba's sending off.

It seemed that Chelsea's complaints centered on Rijkaard's conduct, as opposed to Frisk's 'complicity'. However, what followed for Frisk was nothing short of vilification and he received numerous death threats in the aftermath of the match. Mourinho was accused of being the "enemy of football" by UEFA referees' committee chairman, Volker Roth, and "using lies as a pre-match tactic" by William Gaillard, UEFA's director of communications. Frisk was so shaken that he retired from refereeing indefinitely. To put this into context, it is important to stress that the flamboyant Frisk was the same age as Mourinho at the time, just 42, and was planning a dream swansong: refereeing in the 2006 World Cup in what would have been his 20th year of refereeing.

Mourinho, though, was unmoved and even felt entitled to quip about Frisk's decision when asked by Portuguese television to comment on João Ferreira's refereeing during nine-man Porto's 2-0 defeat to Sporting Lisbon on 21 March: "I have to be very careful when talking about referees because Mr João Ferreira may also quit refereeing." Also, this was far from an isolated incident of referee intimidation by Mourinho and just one month previously, the Portuguese claimed referee Neale Barry had been influenced by Sir Alex Ferguson in the first-leg of Chelsea's League Cup semi-final against Manchester United.

Even a hardened figure like Rijkaard was left shaken by the events and Mourinho's abrasive tactics did not stop there: "My history as a manager cannot be compared with Frank Rijkaard's history. He has zero trophies and I have a lot of them." Yet, interestingly on the Barcelona side, it was Mourinho's style of football - rather than his conduct - that irked Johan Cruyff, who was an unofficial adviser to Barcelona's then president Joan Laporta. Cruyff claimed that Mourinho had "done everything to make me loathe football," after his compact football, use of a sole, physical centre forward and, particularly, his substituting of Joe Cole with Glen Johnson after Drogba was sent-off early in the second-half. Cruyff believed that managers like Mourinho – with their siege mentalities from 'smaller' football nations – were skewing the gentlemanly (we attack, you attack) tactical traditions of football.

Regardless, with Anders Frisk now in retirement, the imperious Pierluigi Collina took charge of the second-leg, which was one of the most vitriol-anticipated matches in Champions League history – all thanks to Mourinho. Thus, it was perhaps no surprise that Chelsea's winning goal – their fourth of the night, scored by John Terry – was marred by Ricardo Carvalho illegally jostling with Victor Valdés. What followed echoed the fracas that gripped the first-leg: Mourinho and his backroom staff clashed with Rijkaard, Samuel Eto'o and Ronaldinho in the tunnel.

Eto'o claimed that a Chelsea steward made a racist slur and declared: "Mourinho is shameless. If this team wins the Champions League, it would make you want to retire. With so much money and so many players, what they do is not football." Even the, seemingly, meek Villas-Boas spat his chewing gum at Barcelona's assistant manager, Henk ten Cate.

Such was the whirlwind of fury at full-time, Damià Abella missed out on what happened: "Many times, we tend to look for excuses in defeat and, also, in football, everything is magnified. I do not think Mourinho is the enemy of football in any case. But it was a shame because that goal should not have gotten on the scoreboard in my point of view, but errors are constant in football from both players and referees… I remember there was a lot of tension at the final whistle, as we realised we were now out of the competition. We thought it was unfair, because of the referee's mistake for the final goal. Then, there were some unfortunate comments and actions after the whistle. I did not see exactly what happened, but I do remember Eto'o and Rijkaard's reactions being forceful…"

While Chelsea were to incorporate Mourinho, Miles and Clarke's observations in their official complaint about Rijkaard's interaction with Frisk to UEFA, the club did not appeal Mourinho's eventual two-match ban awarded after the second-leg. With Chelsea having ridden out the controversy of Mourinho and Peter Kenyon illegally tapping up Ashley Cole in January, 2005 - leading to a £300,000 fine for the club - and the Portuguese's subsequent condemnation of Arsène Wenger as a "voyeur", it was to prove the first real crack in the relationship between Mourinho and the Chelsea hierarchy.

* * *

It is important to distinguish Mourinho the football manager and Mourinho the man. After all, not even a supposed megalomaniac like Mourinho would have condoned Portuguese television cutting short their coverage of Pope John Paul II's final moments to discuss rumours of Mourinho's departure from Chelsea after the Barcelona fall-out. Instead, the noble side of Mourinho was evident in March, 2005, when he voluntarily flew at no charge – following an ambitious and surprising invitation by Shimon Peres, Israel's then deputy Prime Minister – to the Peres Centre in Israel to encourage the setting up of a mixed Israeli and Palestine youth team.

The centre was founded in 1996 by Peres and had a total of 14,000 members by the time of Mourinho's visit. Upon witnessing 200 primary school children - Jewish and Arab - playing in the same blue shirt, a humbled Mourinho commented: "I'm supposed to be a VIP, but I don't feel like one. Football is nothing compared to those who work for a better world."

Also, regarding his conduct with referees, Mourinho's attitude towards them changed, accordingly, once he exited their sphere. For example, two-and-a-half years later, when Mourinho had left Chelsea, the Portuguese got in touch with Mark Halsey. The 38-year-old Premier League referee was diagnosed with throat cancer in August, 2009. Horrifically, Halsey's wife, Michelle, had only recovered from a lymphoma, herself, just one year previously.

Over two years after Halsey failed to award Chelsea a penalty - when Antoine Sibierski appeared to foul John Terry in a 0-0 draw with Newcastle on 22 April 2007 - Mourinho emailed Halsey his phone number. This draw had been a particular blow to Mourinho's hopes of a third-straight Premier League title, as Chelsea would have gone within just one point of leaders Manchester United with only four games to play. Mourinho, though, was not one to bear a grudge and as well as paying for a holiday for the Halseys at the five-star Lake Resort at Vilamoura in his native Portugal, Mourinho invited Halsey to a series of matches between 2009 and 2011. The duo built up a close relationship and Mourinho claims Halsley is the only referee he can call a friend. Halsey, meanwhile, referred to Mourinho as a "wonderful, wonderful person".

* * *

Even with Mourinho's two-match European ban, the Portuguese's presence remained for the quarter-final matches against Bayern Munich. Whether it was Rui Faria allegedly wearing an earpiece under a woolly hat or Silvino Louro making frequent trips down the Stamford Bridge corridor and returning with instructions – supposedly delivered from Mourinho out of a laundry basket – Mourinho's spirit dominated proceedings. So paranoid was German TV, pre-match cameras were fixed on seeing whether Mourinho sneaked into the VIP area of the Olympiastadion. Coupled with Mourinho's debut television advert, with American Express, there was no escaping *the Special One*. In the end, though, Mourinho stayed put in his hotel in Munich and Chelsea went on to progress on away goals to meet Liverpool in the semi-finals.

It was Luis García's 'ghost goal' decider in that semi-final which proved a body blow, in Liverpool's 1-0 aggregate victory, and which left Mourinho incensed post-match: "I felt the power of Anfield, it was magnificent. I felt it didn't interfere with my players but maybe it interfered with other people and maybe it interfered with the result. I went through many experiences in football in difficult atmospheres. I never found cannibals in the stands, only noisy people. I saw a stadium where the crowd scored the goal. You should ask the linesman why he gave a goal. Because, to give a goal, the ball must be 100% in and he must be 100% sure that the ball is in."

Still, Chelsea's first league title for 50 years and their first League Cup for seven years were welcome consolations. Incidentally, the 3–2 League Cup final win over Liverpool in February marked the beginning of Chelsea's siege mentality, following Mourinho ridiculing Wenger and Sir Alex Ferguson's predictions of an inevitable Chelsea blip in the final's pre-match press conference. Amid the booing of Liverpool's fans, Mourinho putting his finger towards his lips was aimed just as much at the media and his managerial rivals, and that League Cup victory was key. It was Chelsea's first trophy for five years and whetted the appetites of the squad. After all, Mourinho took this often-derided competition incredibly seriously, with near-full-strength XIs picked whenever possible. It was, therefore, little surprise that there were over-zealous celebrations after the final in Cardiff.

Jiří Jarošík, who started in central midfield alongside Claude Makélélé and Frank Lampard that day, summed up the occasion for me: "The League Cup final was a very special game for everyone. We wanted to win it badly, and

Liverpool was very strong at this time as well. We didn't play at Wembley, but the Millennium was full. The roof was shut. Half was red and half was blue: it was a special atmosphere. I was so happy to win it."

Elsewhere, the pivotal title moment came on 30 April 2005 against Bolton Wanderers, with Mourinho uncharacteristically decked out in a tracksuit – perhaps reflecting his confidence in a champagne-soaked result. As well as predicting, in November 2004, that Chelsea would have wrapped up the title at the Reebok, Mourinho spoke in the pre-match team meeting of: "You cannot lose the game. I am not putting pressure on you with 'we have to win' – I don't like that kind of pressure – but we cannot lose. We cannot lose."

At the Reebok Stadium, the Portuguese's words in the dressing room beforehand, though, were somewhat clichéd and did not inspire his team: "We've played in rain, sun and snow, in heat and cold, in north and in south, at home and away. We've played 3,060 minutes. With these next 90 minutes, we can become champions. Go out there, play as a team, win the game! I want this dressing room to be celebrating when the game is over!"

Therefore, uncharacteristically, under Mourinho, Chelsea were insipid and filled with stage fright in front of the on-looking Roman Abramovich and headed into the break scoreless against Bolton. Echoing his dramatic actions at half-time against Arsenal four months previously, Mourinho gave yet another profound team-talk. The Portuguese declared that his team had performed so badly that it would be as well for him, Baltemar Brito, and Clarke to go out there and play.

Following two goals from Lampard in the second-half, a rejuvenated Chelsea claimed a deserved first Premier League title with a record 95 points and just 15 goals conceded. Echoing Mourinho's embrace with Jorge Costa after the third goal in Porto's Champions League win in 2004, Mourinho made a beeline for Lampard, remarking: "What you saw was more than a hug – it was trust." Afterwards, Mourinho immediately rang Tami, his wife, at the final whistle while the team's celebrations were underway.

It was Jarošík's eighth league title of his career, at just 27 years of age, but this one was particularly special: "Chelsea had waited 50 years for the title and everyone was working incredibly hard behind the scenes. During the season we played well, but we were very focused on giving this game 110%. They had a very good, strong team. We badly wanted to win the title and it was a very special test, because we played away and Bolton played very well. We wanted to do our best to win and, finally, we did it and it was amazing. We had the trophy; it was a magical time."

Chapter 11

Incredibly, Chelsea suffered just one defeat that season, a 1-0 loss away to Manchester City on 16 October, 2004. So impressed was Mourinho, the Portuguese decided not to give a press conference after the game - preferring, for once, that his players be the centre of attention instead. After cleaning up, the coaching staff and players had dinner together at their hotel in Manchester city centre and watched the madness on Fulham Broadway – some 336km away - unfold on television.

Given that the Champions League semi-final against Liverpool was just days after the Bolton game, the real celebration was to come in Chelsea's final home game of the season, against Charlton a week later, when Chelsea lifted their first league title for 50 years. Reflecting the enormity of the occasion, 13 members of the class of 1955 were present. Also, instead of his usual prose, Mourinho listed 101 names that had contributed to Chelsea's 2004-05 success in in his programme notes. Among those was Craig Rocastle, who departed mid-season for Sheffield Wednesday, and he told me how that made him feel: "That is the type of man he is - he is loyal and respects all his players. He rewards the players and people for their work. He made Chelsea a happier place of work when he took over. The club was more unified and obviously we won trophies immediately. I'd have loved to be on the podium, but knowing he mentioned me in the programme almost meant more… When I accepted the offer from Sheffield **Wednesday,** he said, 'I respect you that you're leaving and I wish you the best. If you need anything you have my number. Go and be a player!' He is just a class act. I could talk all day about *the Special One.*"

Defender Steven Watt had not made enough Premier League appearances to merit a medal, but he told me how momentous that final week of that season was for him: "It was pleasing to be mentioned by Mourinho in the programme, although I was disappointed not to be on the podium. However, I didn't miss out on being involved in the celebrations. I was on the pitch when the trophy was presented and, from then on, it was just a non-stop party really. There was champagne being sprayed everywhere in the dressing room and a huge celebration."

Robert Huth even drove Watt, Didier Drogba, Lenny Pidgeley, Ricardo Carvalho, and Mikael Forssell around the pitch on a tractor, but that was not to prove the most memorable moment of the week's events for Watt: "I travelled up to the midweek game at Man United a few days after that and narrowly missed out on being on the bench. As Mourinho was walking down the tunnel after the game, I was walking up towards the pitch to congratulate the players. He gave a me hug and said, 'It is your time against Newcastle on Saturday'… Young players will always struggle to become first-team regulars at a top European club. When your competition is [Robert] Huth, [John] Terry, [William] Gallas, and [Ricardo] Carvalho, you know your chances of playing are slim. Understandably, age and experience counts for a lot at the top level. However, Mourinho gave five first-team debuts to young players in the 04/05 season alone so he gave more youngsters a chance than most managers would."

Amid a carnival atmosphere, Chelsea won the game against Charlton through a botched Claude Makélelé penalty - the Frenchman's first goal for Chelsea, after 94 appearances - in the dying moments. Mourinho, though, remained ardently professional to the end: "I drew diagrams before the game and in the dressing room, I wrote that Lampard should take penalties. I also wrote that if we were 2-0 up in the last minute, Makélelé should take one. He has been practicing penalties this week, but they must have been confused because we were not winning."

One man who was to be impressed by this professional attitude was Sir Alex Ferguson and to be fair to the Scot, in third place behind Arsenal, he was gracious in defeat despite being a whopping 18 points behind Chelsea. It was a marked contrast to United's 2–1 defeat to Porto at the Dragão in 2004 and United even handed the Chelsea squad a - then unprecedented - guard of honour after United's 1–3 defeat to the Blues on 10 May 2005. Mourinho, though, was unmoved: "I saw their players and manager go for a lap of honour after losing to us in their last home game. In Portugal, if you do this, they throw bottles at you."

Mourinho would go on to return the favour to Ferguson in 2007 but sourness had long replaced the sparkle. 'Mourinhomania' was now, very much, limited to Chelsea fans.

Chapter 12: The Arrival of the Prince

Rather than resting on his laurels, Mourinho was again looking ahead; using a whiteboard in the closing team meeting of the 2004–05 season, he asked his squad to give him 20 reasons why they were champions. Mourinho would repeat this at the beginning of pre-season, too, but this time, even more powerfully, with a photograph of the jubilant title-winning celebrations.

Even though the last manager to win a top-level English title in their first season was Kenny Dalglish, with Liverpool in 1985-86, Mourinho knew retaining the title would be even more difficult. After all, Chelsea's last title-winning manager, Ted Drake in 1955, naively wrote the following in his programme notes in September of 1955: "I know in my heart that we have the talent to see us through, not only this season but for some considerable time to come. We'll be there at the finish!" With Drake having changed very little of his title-winning squad, Chelsea ended up finishing a dismal 16th in 1955-56.

Mourinho knew complacency could be an issue and in the summer of 2005 - having been awarded a £400,000 wage rise and further transfer backing - he brought in Asier del Horno, Lassana Diarra, Michael Essien and Shaun Wright-Phillips for a combined £56.4 million. Scott Parker, Tiago and Mateja Kežman, meanwhile, departed.

Jiří Jarošík would also leave Stamford Bridge, despite taking part in Chelsea's pre-season tour of America. As the Czech told me: "My time at Chelsea was a great experience for the future, but I was a little bit angry that summer. Before Chelsea, I played every week but this time, I was not such a big star: I didn't arrive for big money. For me, playing every week was much more important. I didn't want it to get to the stage where I was waiting minutes, then weeks, then months. That's why I went looking for the loan to Birmingham City. Chelsea had a big squad and, at some clubs, if you wait for six months or a year, your chance might come. But it was very difficult, because the squad was filled with quality and Chelsea was so big. Also, at this time in the Premier League, only four outfield substitutes were allowed on the bench and it was difficult even just to be in Chelsea's squad for a game... But, in England, it's all about the team and for the first two years that Mourinho was at Chelsea, they were the best and no one can take that away from them."

Hernán Crespo, surprisingly, given his influential role in Milan's progression to the 2005 Champions League final - with six goals in ten European games - returned. The Argentine had witnessed, from a distance, Mourinho's success and how much more progressive the Chelsea project was than it had been under Claudio Ranieri in 2003-04. Having bonded over their love of Italy, Crespo would finally repay the faith Mourinho held in him with 13 goals in 41 games in 2005-06. It must be stressed that this was a decent return as most of Crespo's appearances came as a substitute for Didier Drogba, with Mourinho generally sticking to a 4-3-3 formation.

Despite this extra firepower, from an incredibly harsh viewpoint, Chelsea did not seem the same unplayable force in 2005-06 as they were in 2004–05 – even when recording nine straight victories in their opening nine Premier League games. This was partly due to Premier League teams finally shifting from the somewhat naive 4-4-2 – where they lost a man against Chelsea due to their 'revolutionary' 4-3-3 – and matching them. So, while Chelsea would finish with 91 points, eight points clear of second-placed Manchester United, their league defeats against Blackburn, Fulham, Manchester United, Middlesbrough, and Newcastle proved that they were far from unbeatable. Mourinho, though, was still able to play victim when this happened: "Everybody was waiting for Chelsea not to win every game and one day when we lose there will be a holiday in the country. But we are ready for that."

Still, Chelsea had recorded record points totals in both seasons - 91 points would have broken it but for 2004-05's tally of 95 - and Peter Kenyon was quick to pay tribute to the new regime: "I think what we did was we frightened everyone. Chelsea had been the stylish team that never really got anywhere. Then we came in, new kids on the block, and spent a lot of money. He [Mourinho] came in. We romanced everybody. And then it changed."

Perhaps reflecting a more difficult 2005-06, Mourinho displayed numerous eccentricities. Firstly, when the squad were booked for a photo shoot with their new shirt sponsors, Samsung, on the club's pre-season tour of America, no riders or perks were provided. Incensed, Mourinho cancelled the shoot and so shaken were Samsung's PR department, they then made sure that all the players had an array of gadgets awaiting them when they returned to London.

Then, in initially heeding William Gallas' pleas to play at centre-half, Mourinho dropped Ricardo Carvalho from his first XI for the first game of the season against Wigan on 14 August 2005. Carvalho was dumbfounded, even if the move was influenced by del Horno's arrival; he described Mourinho's decision as "incomprehensible". Mourinho – unfazed and keen to show that an invincible culture had yet to grip the club – fined Carvalho £85,000, suggested that he needed an IQ test, and dropped him for the 1–0 victory over Arsenal in Chelsea's next match a week later.

* * *

A controversial season at Chelsea would not be complete without Barcelona featuring and Mourinho personally intervened in delaying the replacement of the fraught Stamford Bridge turf in the Champions League second-round first-leg tie against Barcelona on 22 February, 2006. Given Barcelona's renowned *tiki-taka* football philosophy, Mourinho believed watering the pitch - as customary pre-match - would only aid the zip of Barcelona's hypnotic passing style. The Portuguese defended his decision in trademark style, claiming: "Sometimes you see beautiful people with no brains. Sometimes you have ugly people who are intelligent, like scientists."

Mourinho's antics against Barcelona did not stop there, though, and the Portuguese criticised Lionel Messi after he was cynically pushed by del Horno, which rightly warranted a red card for the Spaniard in a 1–2 defeat in the first-leg: "How do you say cheating in Catalan? Barcelona is a cultural city with many great theatres and this boy has learned very well. He's learned play-acting." Mourinho then followed this up with this cheeky declaration: "Barcelona have a great club. But in 200 years of history they have won the European Cup only once. I have been managing for a few years and I have already won the same amount."

Such was the animosity these comments stoked, the Chelsea bus was relentlessly taunted by a large group of Barcelona fans as it waited to take off on the eve of the return leg at the Nou Camp six days later and Mourinho, wearing headphones, merely encouraged it as he clapped along. Ultimately, Chelsea were defeated 3-2 on aggregate – with Mourinho exiting the competition at the second-round stage for the first time since his first months as Porto manager, in 2002.

* * *

Still, though, *the Special One*'s Midas touch remained and was plain to see in the pivotal London Derby against West Ham at Stamford Bridge on 9 April 2006. Mourinho, in trademark style, cocooned the squad and eased the relentless pressure in his pre-match press conference by quipping: "Football is nothing compared with life. For me, bird flu is the drama of the last few days. I'll have to buy a mask!" This may have seemed a needless digression, but Manchester United were seven points behind Chelsea – having played an extra game before the match, and had gone nine games unbeaten. As a result, some sections of the media backed a trademark late-season surge by Sir Alex Ferguson - regardless of the fact that Chelsea had won seven of their previous 11 Premier League games.

Before Chelsea faced West Ham, Ferguson likened Mourinho's 'predicament' to Devon Loch, the racehorse who had a five-length lead with just 40 yards remaining of the 1956 Grand National. Owned by the Queen Mother, Loch inexplicably half-jumped and landed on his stomach – failing to finish the race. Mourinho was unfazed: "I know the story, but I'll tell you a Portuguese story because in Portugal there are no Devon Lochs or horses. We're in the sea, in a boat one mile from the beach. I jump, because I'm a good swimmer. And this fellow wants to race me to the beach. I go, using lots of different swimming styles, and get to the beach and walk on the beach. When *he* reaches the beach, he dies. We call it, 'dying on the beach'. He shouldn't chase me! He should say to the boat, 'Take me a little closer.' He's so enthusiastic chasing me, but he has a heart attack. That's our Devon Loch."

When James Collins had given the Hammers the lead ten minutes in, though, apprehension gripped the Stamford Bridge crowd. This was accentuated by Mourinho's cautious, and surprising, use of a 4-4-2 diamond, with Arjen Robben and Joe Cole both on the bench. The situation was made all the bleaker when Maniche, a January loan signing from Dynamo Moscow, was sent-off for a lunge on Lionel Scaloni seven minutes later. Many teams would have caved, but not Mourinho's. Chelsea never lost their belief, even before Mourinho could get access to them with his team-talk at half-time, and this was much owed to the fact they had been unbeaten in the league at Stamford Bridge since February, 2004. As a result, Didier Drogba and Crespo both netted before the half-hour mark and John Terry and Gallas wrapped-up a season-defining three points mid-way through the second-half.

Still, the FA Cup had proved a bogey competition of sorts for Mourinho up to this point and 13 days later, the Portuguese, bizarrely, played Paulo Ferreira in central midfield in the 2-1 FA Cup semi-final defeat to Liverpool on 22 April 2006. Admittedly, Ferreira filled in when the influential Costinha went off injured for Porto in the 2003 UEFA Cup final but this was due to a lack of squad depth.

Just a week later, Mourinho threw his Premier League medal and blazer into the crowd after the 3–0 win over Manchester United. It was after this match that Mourinho, nihilistically, questioned why he had not been awarded a Manager of the Month award once in 2005–06 even though he would go on to win the Manager of the Year award. This had nothing to do with taking the pressure off his players; it was personal. Perhaps, though, given his undoubted inferiority complex with regard to his playing career, this reflected Mourinho's love of accolades. After all, following his induction into the seemingly trivial Madame Tussauds in the same year, he commented that it was a "pleasure to become the first Portuguese person to be inducted in such an important museum."

* * *

Then, though, came the turning point in Mourinho's relationship with Roman Abramovich: Andriy Shevchenko. As one of the world's most prolific finishers and with Drogba beginning to settle as one of the best lone marksmen in world football, following a string of controversies in England over his play-acting, Shevchenko's arrival seemed merely to illustrate that Abramovich would stop at nothing to win the Champions League. Mourinho had hoped to have sold Crespo the previous summer and Shevchenko was an option on his wishlist, along with Samuel Eto'o and David Villa, but Mourinho had eventually grown fond of the Argentine after his determined showing in 2005–06.

Now, however, a two-year loan deal was agreed with Internazionale for Crespo, once Shevchenko signed, and Eidur Gudjohnsen was sold to Barcelona, too. At the time, even though Mourinho would have preferred Eto'o - with the Cameroonian, potentially, acting as the perfect foil for Drogba with his blistering pace - it seemed the Portuguese was more than satisfied. In a rare move in his history of signing players, Mourinho even attended Shevchenko's showpiece contract signing on 31 May and was quick to pay tribute:

"Today is a day when the dream became reality – Andriy has always been my first choice for Chelsea since I arrived. Before it was not possible, now it is for real. He has great qualities: ambition, discipline, tactical awareness and, of course, he is a great goalscorer. I did not need to meet with him to convince him about Chelsea, in the same way we did not need to talk a lot about why I wanted him.

"Everybody knows him as a player; tactically he can play in the Chelsea system no doubt. Milan is a big club, a great club, but for him to leave Milan for Chelsea is a big statement about where Chelsea is. He is a champion and he is joining a team of champions. I have already spoken to some of our players and they are looking forward to playing with him. Great players want to play with other great players."

Given that Shevchenko was used to the tight marking and marshalling of Italy, there seemed few reasons why he would not go on to produce in England. Thus, going by his debut against Liverpool in the Community Shield on 13 August 2006, few would have bet against Shevchenko not living up to his transfer fee and firing Chelsea to their first ever Champions League title. Shevchenko, in trademark, vibrant style, looked full of menace, endeavour, and intelligence. From his brilliant run past Jamie Carragher and Steve Finnan – which required a desperate last-ditched tackle by John Arne Riise – to his excellent lofted pass for Drogba, the Ukrainian was seemingly thriving in

Chapter 12

Mourinho's purposefully-designed 4-4-2 diamond in the first-half of the match.

Shevchenko then scored a fantastic goal before half-time after again skipping past Carragher and Finnan, with a brilliantly timed run, to chest a lofted Frank Lampard pass down and coolly slot home past Pepe Reina. The television cameras immediately cut to a cackling Abramovich in the executive box, who performed a rare double fisted celebration as opposed to his usual nonchalant clap. Shevchenko, unsurprisingly, got caught up in the Millennium Stadium roar and even kissed the Chelsea badge.

It seemed that this would be the beginning of a very fruitful partnership.

Chapter 13: A Crumbling Empire

A dangerous *galácticos*-like policy and pressure was beginning to grip Chelsea, with Peter Kenyon talking of Chelsea becoming the biggest club in the world and winning at least two Champions League titles by 2014. Tellingly, Kenyon neglected to mention Mourinho in the same prophecy. So, while Mourinho certainly sanctioned the superstar signings of Ashley Cole and Michael Ballack in the summer of 2006, the Portuguese's influence at the club was waning in a marked contrast to this cheeky declaration in July, 2004: "Nobody in the club can tell me to buy a player. But they can say to me, you don't buy the player you want!"

Mourinho was no longer the star attraction and even volunteered to sit in economy class if a player was to miss out on business class on a flight. Clearly, Mourinho's carefully moulded 23-man squad of 2004-05 had been turned on its head: "We don't have second-line players like we have had in the last few seasons. Scott Parker, Eidur Gudjohnsen, Tiago, Damien Duff and Glen Johnson have left, meaning a different way to approach the season and prepare for the future. The doors are open for Salomon Kalou and Mikel John Obi. Are they ready like Gudjohnsen and Duff? We will see. They have to be ready to play for 90 minutes. We cannot lose the qualities that made us champions."

Mourinho, naturally, put a brave face on the eroding of his power and structure: "If Roman Abramovich helped me out in training we would be bottom of the league and if I had to work in his world of big business, we would be bankrupt!" However, the arrival of Frank Arnesen, as head of youth development, from Tottenham for an astonishing £8 million in the summer of 2005 and the influence of Piet de Visser – the legendary scout who brought the likes of Ronaldo and Romário to Europe with PSV Eindhoven – worried Mourinho privately. After all, during Mourinho's time in charge of Porto from 2002-04, the phrase on the home dressing room of the Estádio do Dragão read: 'Aqui, ninguém é permitido dentro – exceptonós!' (Here, nobody is allowed in the dressing room – except us!). This not only referred to media dealings and public complaints by players, but, also, interference from club hierarchy. So, while Mourinho had not seen it necessary to go to these lengths with Stamford Bridge's dressing room, control and a lack of interference had been part of his original agreement with Kenyon and Abramovich in taking over at Chelsea in the summer of 2004.

For the squad, though, it was business as usual and Khalid Boulahrouz - who arrived for £8.5 million from Hamburg that summer - told me about settling in under a Mourinho regime: "Mourinho was, and is, a great coach. He knew what he needed to do to win games and prizes. Mourinho was hard with the players but, at the same time, he could be relaxed and make jokes to help you feel comfortable. He was confident within the squad but, one thing's for sure, he liked to win. When we lost, the next day at training was not enjoyable! You knew, straight away, about the importance of winning. He's definitely a winner… He took care of the players like a family, like children. In the squad, you felt really comfortable. At that time, our squad was really close; our players were really close together. The spirit between the players was really strong. I had a really good feeling about that season.

"I arrived after pre-season. There was a lot of ball work to be done, and the squad liked Mourinho's style of training a lot. There were some passing games, some technical games. Training was 90 minutes long and really hard work, but afterwards you felt great and you were done for the day. The training session started with a warm-up, then passing with the ball, some more possessions, and then five vs five situational play. Every time there was a new drill added to the session, so it was never boring.

"This kind of set-up was the logical next step in my career - he didn't need to convince me. After Hamburg, I felt prepared to make the next step and Chelsea was one of the biggest clubs in the world. But, of course, Mourinho being the coach of Chelsea at that moment made it even more special… Also, Frank Arnesen had a great influence on the general things that were going on at Chelsea so maybe he had an influence on my transfer, as well.

"I took the number nine shirt but, for me, it was just a number, not a message. It was not meant to provoke or anything like that. There weren't a lot of numbers available and I didn't want to play with 55 or 67; these were more like NFL or ice hockey numbers. It was actually a mistake, because the number two was still available. It was a bit awkward, actually. After a while, Mourinho came up to me and asked me, 'Why did you take number nine? Number two is still free!'"

* * *

Unfortunately for Mourinho, he never regained the same level of inspiration at the club in their quest to seal an unprecedented quadruple in 2006-07. Andriy Shevchenko, encapsulating this, badly struggled: scoring just 14 goals in 51 games. The Ukrainian was criticised for his attitude, with Mourinho claiming Shevchenko "was treated like a prince at Milan", and was, effectively, dropped from the matchday squad altogether for the crucial Champions League semi-final second-leg match against Liverpool on 1 May 2007. Such was the Portuguese's disdain for the Ukrainian's poor form, Shevchenko had post-season groin surgery brought forward at the behest of Mourinho before this game. Given how insipid this tie proved, and how Shevchenko had made his name at Milan for his intelligence and guile, it had shown just how far the Ukrainian had fallen.

Despite Shevchenko's incredible pedigree as one of the greatest strikers of his generation, he was unable to replicate his goalscoring achievements in English football and this was not simply owed to Mourinho suddenly going off him. Rather, the 31-year-old's pace had naturally flagged and the Premier League's tempo was about to reach an all-time high by the time of his arrival. This is why, far from coincidentally, Shevchenko's greatest moment in a Chelsea shirt – a stunning, standing 20-yard curling finish in the 1-2 FA Cup quarter-final win over Tottenham that season – was owed to Shevchenko's intelligence, audacity, and technique as opposed to his pace.

Boulahrouz echoed these sentiments, as Shevchenko's team-mate in 2006-07: "I can't talk for him [Shevchenko], but it was probably the physical style of English football. He was used to one kind of system at AC Milan, and the league and competition in Italy is not like it is in England. In Italy, it's more tactical; in England, it's much more dynamic and stronger. The defenders are really strong. They go into battles like crazy… He needed time to adapt and that's not easy when you come from the Italian game into the English league. The tempo is much more different than it is in Italy.

"The issue between Mourinho and Shevchenko? I didn't notice that much. It was between the coach and the player, himself. The squad didn't pay attention to what was written in the papers. Most of the things written weren't true. Of course, I don't think Shevchenko was happy about being on the bench, but it's normal: every player wants to play the big games, feel important, and win big prizes."

So, instead of joining successful, peak-aged Serie A strikers exported to the Premier League – such as Fabrizio Ravanelli, Gianfranco Zola, and Gianluca Vialli – Shevchenko's eventual record of nine league goals in 47 Premier League appearances saw the Ukranian join a much less glamorous alumni. Like Shevchenko, Andrea Silenzi, Massimo Maccarone, Bernardo Corradi, Rolando Bianchi, Adrian Mutu and, even, Mario Balotelli all struggled in English football after arriving for big fees from Italian clubs.

* * *

While Chelsea won the FA and League Cups against Manchester United and Arsenal respectively, Mourinho's 'chin-up' gesture to Chelsea's fans after a battling 1–1 draw with Arsenal at the Emirates on 6 May summarised a disappointing season. It confirmed, mathematically, that Manchester United were to be champions. Admittedly, it had been a spirited display by Chelsea - playing 50 minutes of the match without Boulahrouz, who was sent-off - but such was the determination of Mourinho and his staff to not let this setback affect morale, Salomon Kalou was prevented from collapsing to the Emirates' turf in anguish at the result by Steve Clarke and Rui Faria.

Boulahrouz reflected on that somber day: "I had been sent off early in that game and, of course, it was a massive disappointment. For such a long time, we were six points off Manchester United. We were able to maintain this gap, even cutting it to four at one stage, and not let it get bigger. But, at that moment, everyone knew the championship was over and that was a big disappointment because that's what it's all about. Unfortunately, we didn't make it; it was the same for the Champions League, when we made the semi-final. We won two cups, but it could've been an even more successful season for us if we had won the title or reached the final of the Champions League."

In a marked contrast to his finger to lips gesture against Liverpool in 2005, Mourinho's 'chin up' gesture was now addressing his failure to win a league title for the first time in five years. Perhaps, the key psychological blow was not being top on New Year's Day - the hallmark of all of Mourinho's title wins. Augmenting the sense of failure, this disappointment came just five days after Chelsea's defeat to Liverpool on penalties in the Champions League semi-final.

The struggles were not just on the field and it was little surprise that Mourinho, himself, was also suffering throughout that campaign. After all, the Portuguese's inner stress was epitomised when he accused the South Central ambulance crew of arriving 30 minutes late after Petr Čech suffered a fractured skull against Reading on 14 October 2006. Boulahrouz recalls that dark day: "I remember that game very well: it was a really physical game. Mourinho spoke to me beforehand and told me he would give me opportunities to play at centre-back. He gave me a chance there that evening and I was really happy about that.

"The game was horrible. What happened to Petr Čech [lengthy pause]… our thoughts were with Petr and how he was doing. He was not conscious: he left the game by ambulance. Would he make it? Yes or no? I had never felt something like this. It was a huge shock for all of us. At the end of the game, the same thing happened to [Carlo] Cudicini when he came on. It was a corner kick and I remember they had two, big, strong African players [Ibrahima Sonko and André Bikey] at the back and they came up. The ball was heading for the far post and Cudicini was jumping and they both bumped into Cudicini, so he was knocked out as well. All of a sudden, we were out of goalkeepers: [Didier] Drogba and [John] Terry ended up having a chat about who should go in goal!"

Elsewhere, Mourinho, controversially, lamented Raymond Domenech's continued use of the ageing Claude Makélelé: "I think Makélelé is not a football player. Makélelé is a slave. He doesn't want to go but he has to go. In the national team of France they do not have the word liberté." Mourinho was even nearly brought to court by Everton's Andrew Johnson for accusing him of diving, having denouced Gudjohnson for doing the same thing at Barcelona during the same season.

Yet, remarkably, Barcelona were not to prove their annual nuisance for Mourinho when Chelsea met them in Group A of the Champions League. Chelsea, just four days after Čech's horrific injury, faced the Champions League holders and Boulahrouz was 'awarded' the task of man marking the World Player of the Year, Ronaldinho, by Mourinho for both games. Achieving four points in these two games, the 1-0 victory over the Catalan giants at Stamford Bridge on 18 October was particularly memorable for Boulahrouz: "Of course, it was a pleasure to play for a big club: you just want to play. I preferred centre-back to right-back. I didn't feel that comfortable at right-back, because I wasn't used to coming forward all the time on the flank; I couldn't play like modern right-backs should do. I had just played at centre-back for two years at Hamburg and it was a little confusing for me but, at the same time, you're in the starting XI and that's what it's all about. That, and trying to win the game, of course.

"That was a special game, I was really focused. You have different kinds of wingers: some are speedy; some dribble more than others. Every kind of winger has his own quality, so you have to adapt to your opponent's attributes. Ronaldinho was quite unique in that case. He was strong, he was fast – he had all the qualities. He had everything; in that moment, he was the best player in the world. I had to make sure he could not influence the game. I had to stay as close as possible to him, as soon as he touched the ball. But, also, I had to stay close to him as soon as he passed the ball to his team-mate to make sure he didn't have the freedom to be decisive.

"It was really hard to mark Ronaldinho out of the game, but we made it and we had a great result. Everyone had a great feeling after that game and the spirit was unbelievable. I remember, after the game in the dressing room, as always, Mourinho was on the phone to his wife [Tami]. The moment I came into the dressing room, he immediately put the phone down and gave me a big, strong bear hug. That feeling was really special."

Still, this was a rare interlude from the stress Mourinho experienced that season - even receiving a bizarre police caution in May for preventing the quarantine of his un-inoculated Yorkshire Terrier, Gullit. Unsurprisingly, Mourinho would later describe his decision not to leave Chelsea after the FA

Cup triumph over United as the "biggest regret of his career". However, as well as the above-mentioned anxiety, his departure was not simply, as it had seemed, down to Mourinho having already won every trophy in English football – as evident in his six-finger gesture before lifting the FA Cup – or Mourinho's transfer activity suddenly being limited: "The style of how we play is very important. But it is omelettes and eggs. No eggs – no omelettes! It depends on the quality of the eggs. In the supermarket you have class one, two or class three eggs and some are more expensive than others, and some give you better omelettes. So when the class one eggs are in Waitrose and you cannot go there, you have a problem."

Far from a sudden problem, it must be stressed that Mourinho's allusion to limited transfer activity had been a relentless mantra in the previous nine months. This was even evident in Mourinho's sarcastic programme notes before the 4-0 victory against Wigan on 13 January 2007, when Abramovich did not stump up £14 million for the signing of Ricardo Quaresma from Porto: "Are you ready to enjoy us playing with 16-year-olds and 17-year-olds and still be chasing prizes?" Tellingly, this same chord was struck just two weeks later, in Mourinho's post-match press conference after Chelsea defeated Blackburn 3-0: "It is like having a blanket that is too small for the bed. You pull the blanket up to keep your chest warm and your feet stick out. I cannot buy a bigger blanket because the supermarket is closed. But I am content because the blanket is cashmere. It is no ordinary blanket."

Rather, it was backroom personnel that were to prove the final straw for Mourinho's time at Chelsea. While Abramovich had already, indirectly, disrupted the dressing room and Mourinho's tactical dynamics with Shevchenko's signing, the Russian's plans to replace Steve Clarke with Avram Grant – a little-known technical director at Portsmouth – saw Abramovich cross the line in Mourinho's eyes. It was eventually 'resolved', with Grant instead arriving as director of football after Mourinho vowed to resign if Clarke was replaced, but the damage had been done. Even with de Visser and Arnesen already as members of the club's staff, Grant's appointment signalled not only the fact that Abramovich had yet another in-house confidante but, also, that Mourinho's authority and managerial power was rapidly diminishing. This, rather than a lack of backing in the transfer market, was the real reason behind Mourinho's eventual regret.

Boulahrouz, whose loan departure to Sevilla that summer coincided with Grant's arrival, reflected on the Israeli's appointment: "It might have turned out differently for me if I had stayed another year. I was adapting to the lifestyle, the type of game in England - everything. Of course, it was not easy. I was still very young [25] for a defender and still had three years left on my contract, so maybe I could've stayed a little bit longer to give myself a chance and show what I can do.

"I don't think that these kinds of appointments work out for Mourinho. He is someone with a very strong voice. He likes to go his own way. He knows what he needs to make successful teams and everyone around him has to follow him. Mourinho wants to be sure that he can work as he wants, and create his team how he wants to compete for the prizes and championship... I don't think it was a good thing for the club to bring in someone like Avram Grant."

Mourinho remained committed, though, but alongside the markedly cheaper additions of Alex, Juliano Belletti, Tal Ben Haim, Steve Sidwell, and Claudio Pizarro, Chelsea's only double-figure signing in the summer of 2007 would be that of Florent Malouda from Lyon for £13 million. Remarkably, despite this frugal outlay, Abramovich still believed that Mourinho could deliver the attractive football that the Russian so badly craved. It should not have been this way; Mourinho, as early as 2005, genuinely believed his fourth season at Chelsea would be his most successful: "Porto in the last year were a better team from the tactical point of view because it was my third year with them. They knew everything I knew. They knew how to adapt. I could start the game with 4-3-3, switch to 4-4-2, change back to 4-3-3. When we get to my third or fourth year, we can say that this will be my best Chelsea team."

Ben Haim, who started six of Chelsea's eight games under Mourinho in 2007-08, told me that he believed Chelsea were progressing under a still hungry Mourinho: "He was a very charismatic man and a very intelligent coach. This is the memory I keep of him. He met with my father, Emmanuel, and after that conversation, my father told me even in the case of a better offer, I have to join Chelsea because Mourinho's going to make me a better player. Chelsea wanted me 18 months before my eventual arrival but for a variety of reasons, I couldn't join the club...The attraction was already there with Mourinho; the fact that there were Jewish connections, Pini Zahavi and Roman Abramovich, within the club did not make the offer any more appealing.
"What struck me about training under Mourinho and Rui Faria that summer was the intensity. When the ball went out, you had a lot of people bringing it back quickly... Mourinho was very good with the players. When it was the right time, he joked and laughed with us and when it was time to work, he was very serious. Players respect him a lot...It might not have seemed that Chelsea spent much that summer, but I think Mourinho knew exactly the players he wanted. When he first came to Chelsea, not many people knew the players he brought in but after a few games they showed their qualities and, under him, made Chelsea very successful. He built a team for ten years so

even after he left, his successors knew exactly what they had to do. The squad was very strong."

Without Abramovich's continued backing, though, Mourinho struggled and the towering figure of John Terry characterised the turmoil inside the Chelsea dressing room. Terry, who had suffered back, ankle and head injuries through his remarkably valiant exploits in the 2006-07 season, had just signed a then Premier League record £135,000 per week contract extension until 2013. However, having missed much of pre-season through injury, Terry only returned to action when Chelsea played Liverpool in the third league match of the season on 19 August 2007.

Chelsea had won their previous two games without Terry but upon his return, they drew with Liverpool, narrowly beat Portsmouth, and lost to Aston Villa. As a result, before Chelsea were to face Rosenborg on 18 September, Mourinho questioned a noticeably chunkier Terry's fitness, commitment and form, which deeply hurt the Englishman and he, initially, refused to warm-up against Rosenborg. Even if Makélélé's claims in the Frenchman's autobiography, *Tout Simplement,* that Terry actively played a role in Mourinho's eventual departure are ludicrous, the fact that Mourinho had even criticised the man he had handed the captaincy to showed just how chaotic and suspicious the final weeks of Mourinho's reign at Chelsea were.

The strain that Mourinho was feeling in his final weeks at Chelsea was also reflected in his appearance. Gone were the coiffed locks and the Armani overcoat, which was auctioned for €25,800 at a charity fundraiser at Stamford Bridge and later donated to the club's museum. Instead, Mourinho, unprecedentedly, slicked back his hair as if he was, metaphorically, papering over the cracks before the 2–0 defeat against Aston Villa on 2 September, and in a rare move during his time at Chelsea, a grizzly Mourinho wore a tracksuit for the match against Rosenborg 16 days later.

It was the Rosenborg match that was to prove the final straw for Abramovich.

Chapter 14: The Divorce

If one man could empathise with what Mourinho was going through, it was his opponent on the night of 18 September: the 36-year-old Knut Tørum, Rosenborg's affable manager at the time.

It was to be Tørum's first Champions League match of his career, but the build-up to this career milestone had been shrouded in speculation. Rosenborg's newly-appointed sporting director, Knut Thorbjørn Eggen, publicly stated that if Rosenborg's results did not pick up, someone would have to take responsibility. Admittedly, Rosenborg were languishing in fifth place in the Norwegian Tippeligaen, but Tørum had led Rosenborg to the title just 10 months previously and was soon to oversee *Troillongan's* most successful Champions League campaign for seven years.

Far from both managers sharing uncertain futures, Tørum told me that night was strictly about football: "We wanted to take on the clubs with a good tradition in Europe, which was a big motivation for us. The fact that it was in London and it was Chelsea made that motivation even greater. I had my own worries before the match and I didn't think too much about Mourinho. At the press conference the day before match day, the conference room was crowded with people. They just heard a pretty good Mourinho show, with his infamous omelettes rant, but entertainment was not on my mind.

"I didn't meet him during the preparations before the game, so I went over to his bench just before kick-off to say hello and wish him a good game. He had a nice smile, we had a couple of words, and then he joined me back at our bench to shake hands with my assistants. It was a special moment for me and my career. He was polite and didn't seem to be stressed. Mourinho seemed very cool on the bench, with a good dialogue with his players."

Tørum, though, could pick up on a muddled Chelsea side shorn of direction and who lacked a fluid playing style – accentuated by the absence of the missing Ricardo Carvalho, Michael Ballack, Frank Lampard, and Didier Drogba: "Apart from John Terry, who was the boss on pitch? Who was challenging him? What support had Mourinho on the pitch during the game, especially when Chelsea were struggling? When we managed to bring them out of their shape and into our comfort zone, it was a problem for them missing these players - even if their replacements were top-class."

So, while Tørum had expected Chelsea to dominate the opening 15 minutes, Rosenborg thrived at a deserted Stamford Bridge attended by just 24,593 supporters: "I don't know the normal atmosphere at Stamford Bridge, but I remember the missing energy from the stands surprised me at first. I had expected more noise from them. I also felt Chelsea's opening play was less powerful than expected; already, after a couple of minutes, we felt we were able to play our game. Our strength was that we had experienced players, like Roar Strand and Vidar Riseth, who knew how handle the occasion and knew how important it was for us to create trouble for them. We had to show them that they had to take us seriously and not to let them focus solely on attacking us. This was important for building our confidence during the game and we did not need to worry much about the noise from the terraces."

Given that Rosenborg had conceded nine goals in their previous two visits to England, there was no understating what a landmark result this 1-1 draw proved in both Rosenborg's history and Tørum's managerial career. Tellingly, too, a weary Mourinho did not share a glass of wine post-match with Tørum and addressed the Chelsea squad in the dressing room for just two minutes afterwards. So desperate was Chelsea's performance, Mourinho even resorted to the long ball and playing Terry upfront for the final 20 minutes.

These frantic tactics were not lost on Tørum: "When a team like Rosenborg can make results against Chelsea, this, of course, is helped by their opponents not playing their very best football. We could only take some of the credit for that great result, even if we felt pretty good and proud after the match. No other Norwegian teams have even qualified for the Champions League since, which puts our result into perspective. I would never have swapped those epic Champions League nights for more domestic success. When I meet people from Trondheim and other Norwegian cities, they still speak about these nights and their good memories. They hope I will come back and do it again. It is a good feeling and not all managers get these positive feelings from old fans."

In the return match, just 71 days later, in Trondheim, though, both sides were to have new managers.

* * *

Just two days after the Rosenborg match, following the "laws of football" in the Portuguese's own words, Mourinho left Chelsea and his £6.5m annual contract was terminated by mutual consent. Abramovich paid the Portuguese £18 million to cover the final three years of his contact. John Terry and Frank Lampard had been notified, with Mourinho texting the duo on the eve of the public announcement ahead of the premiere of the Chelsea documentary 'Blue Revolution' at the Vue Cinema at Fulham Broadway. Tellingly, neither Terry nor Lampard attended the premiere and the timing was something of a PR disaster for the Chelsea hierarchy, with the documentary eulogising Chelsea's success under Mourinho and Abramovich.

Didier Drogba, Mourinho's other main disciple, was also informed. The tempestuous Ivorian was left heartbroken and, despite having just signed a new four-year deal, Drogba vowed to follow Mourinho wherever he went next: "I'm an orphan who has lost his spiritual father. Certain things were done` that went against everything that this group had stood for. It is perhaps too strong to talk of treasons, but these were real human deceptions. And I can now understand much better why the coach, who was very close to many of his players, told us when he left, 'I want you to know that I am very happy to be leaving this place.'"

Tal Ben Haim – who went on to endure a frosty relationship with Mourinho's successor, Avram Grant – described that morning to me: "I believe he could've turned it around. We had a very strong squad and in football, things can turn very quickly... It was a very emotional morning. Everyone was shocked. Some players cried and some players wanted to leave the club because he was gone. Mourinho was like a father to some players. He made their careers: he bought them and made them the players they are. It was very difficult for them to say goodbye."

It was not all negative, though, and Steven Watt - who had departed Chelsea for Swansea City in January 2006 - explained that Mourinho was one of the main reasons behind his eventual decision to undertake his UEFA B coaching badges: "Mourinho was extremely influential in my decision. Ever since I worked under him, I realised that I wanted to go into coaching after football. I've been fortunate enough to work with some great coaches such as Steve Clarke, Roberto Martínez, and Brendan Rodgers. They all influenced my philosophy, my football and my style of coaching, but Mourinho definitely sparked my initial interest in management and coaching as a career after I eventually retire from football."

Despite his poignant departure, Mourinho had established himself as Chelsea's most successful manager, with six trophies in three seasons and an English league record of 66 home games unbeaten (60 were under Mourinho). Just 14 of these results under Mourinho were draws. To put this into context, Chelsea were to lose 11 home league games in the 111 they contested post-Mourinho between 2007 and 2013. The unbeaten record, too, was to end just 21 league games after his departure, against Liverpool on 26 October, 2008. Thus, there was no disputing the fact that Mourinho's Chelsea legacy was formidable - incredibly, Mourinho averaged an unrivalled 2.33 points from his 120 Premier League games - and, remarkably, that was without the Portuguese claiming that elusive Champions League title. There were agonising knock-out exits to Liverpool ('ghost goal') in 2004–05, Barcelona (Asier del Horno's red card) in 2005–06, and Liverpool (penalties) in 2006–07.

Chapter 14

* * *

Chelsea had to regroup and Fulham's then manager, Lawrie Sanchez, faced Grant in the Israeli's first home game as Chelsea manager on 29 September, 2007. The Northern Irishman told me about that day: "I obviously wanted to face Mourinho in a match. He had a great reputation, having never lost a home league game. But Fulham/Chelsea is a big derby and it was a fantastic time to play them. I was quite hoping that we'd end that home league record that day. I said to the lads: 'If we're going to beat Chelsea, today's the day. Mourinho's gone, today's the day.' We were the better team that day, we should've beaten Chelsea. We drew 0-0, despite the fact we had a couple of chances late on to win it. Paul Konchesky and Diomansy Kamara both had one-on-ones with the keeper [Petr Čech].

"Mourinho will be a big footnote in their history because of what he's achieved. However, he's got a big personality and I think, sometimes, the personality gets in the way of the football team. The man that's funded it, Roman Abramovich, will be the much bigger footnote. At the end of the day, without his money, José Mourinho would never have been there and even if he had been, he would not have had the success he had.

"Everything's a cult these days. Before, the manager was the manager and the team played; you never saw or heard much from him. When I was a player, I did my job whoever the manager was…I didn't know a lot about Avram [Grant], but technical directors should never take over as manager - even as short-term appointments. They have their own job, they know what to do. The manager has every right to suspect that they're after his job in the first place."

While it may have seemed that Mourinho's departure was to prove the final chapter in his love affair with Chelsea, the door had not been shut. After all, Abramovich has, tellingly, not given any other departing Chelsea manager a goodbye gift, which for Mourinho was a rare £2 million 612 Scaglietti Ferrari just days after their parting. Mourinho was a special case and merited such lavishness, having been Abramovich's first winning coach and having been the only Chelsea manager to ever come close to calling the Russian a friend.

Such was Abramovich's undying admiration for Mourinho, his then girlfriend and future wife, Dasha Zhukova, requested that Chelsea's director of communications, Simon Greenberg, get in touch with Mario Rosenstock ahead of Abramovich's 41th birthday on 24 October. Rosenstock was last contacted by Chelsea in 2005 and had become one of the world's leading Mourinho impersonators by 2007, but he told me he had little interest: "She wanted me to write a song sung by me as José. José had left the club, but they were still on friendly terms. I said, even before money came into it, 'I'm not really interested in it.' Then they offered to pay me so, cheekily, I gave them a high number. They came back to me and went, 'That's way too expensive for us!' I thought, 'For God's sake! If the Abramovichs can't afford to pay me for a song, I think we should call the bloody deal off!'"

Nonetheless, it was clear that Abramovich's affection for Mourinho remained as strong as ever.

Chapter 15: Rejection

Mourinho was prohibited - under the terms of his mutually-agreed termination with Chelsea - from working for an English club as his next move. However, aside from his long-term admiration for Sir Alex Ferguson and Manchester United - having held a subscription for MUTV - Mourinho never truly considered another English club. Still, in leaving at such an awkward time in the season, *where* Mourinho would go next was still up for debate. The inevitable managerial merry-go-round in Continental Europe in the summer of 2008 seemed his best bet, with Mourinho eager to prove that his 2004 Champions League victory with Porto was no fluke.

Before then, Mourinho was offered a post that had its personal attractions: the England job. With Steve McClaren having been sacked after England's desperate 2-3 defeat to Croatia at Wembley on 21 November 2007 - which saw the Three Lions miss out on the European Championships for the first time since 1984 - the FA planned to make an appointment that was to shake the football world before Christmas. Fabio Capello eventually emerged as the frontrunner, but this was only after Mourinho ruled himself out of contention on 10 December. Capello, at 61 years of age and having won everything in club football, was ready for international football; Mourinho, even with the immediate opportunity to work with some of his former players again, was not. He said, "I was hours away – I almost signed. But at the last minute I began thinking, 'I am going to coach a national side, there will be one match a month and the rest of the time I will be in my office or overseeing matches.'"

It seems remarkable - in hindsight of the old-school Capello's struggles with international football tactics as England manager, the English language, and the FA's stubborn values - to think how the scenario would have panned out given Mourinho's modern values, unrivalled psychology, and knowledge of the English game and its traditions. However, even in just considering the job offer – despite it coming at such an unsuitable time, with Mourinho only half-way through his club managerial career at the age of 44 and long before his eventual plans to manage Portugal – it shows the high affinity Mourinho still held English football and its players in.

Also, far from resurrecting or boosting his reputation, Mourinho looked at the England job as a project that went far beyond a four-year contract. The Portuguese believed it was an opportunity to truly cement his legacy in English football and having the expectations and dreams of 53 million people on his shoulders certainly tempted him. After all, Mourinho took the FA's overtures incredibly seriously and even put together a strategy called Club England – which was to prove a marked contrast to the eventual Club Wembley focus of the FA on increased ticket incomes.

Chapter 15

Mourinho's plans were outlined in a dossier his agent, Jorge Mendes, delivered to the FA's headquarters at Soho Square on 7 December. Mourinho believed the FA had become too corporate, too focused on incomes and paying back Wembley Stadium's debt. The Portuguese, instead, wanted to revolutionise England's set-up and bring forward the opening of St George's National Park. Mourinho's plans also included having two youthful ex-players as his assistants, with Stuart Pearce, Tony Adams, Gareth Southgate, and Jamie Redknapp among the suggested names; increased tactical discipline with off-season *ritui* (retreats) across Europe, which would not involve friendlies; and larger scouting and medical departments.

Nigel Worthington, who, himself, made a seamless transition from coaching Leicester City to managing Northern Ireland in 2007, told me that Mourinho's rejection of England in 2007 may not spell the end of the Portuguese potentially managing the Three Lions in the future: "International football is probably a long way down the road for Mourinho as he has so much to offer at club level. Still, I am sure there will come a stage where there is another offer of international management for him and not necessarily his own country, Portugal. I actually think he does like a huge challenge, so what I am saying is one day he might just warm to the idea of becoming England manager. The offer just did not come at the right time for him."

Worthington's predecessor at Northern Ireland, Lawrie Sanchez – who managed Sligo Rovers and Wycombe Wanderers in a five-year spell in club management before taking over at Windsor Park in 2004 – echoed Worthington's thoughts: "I'm not sure if he'd like to give up day-to-day involvement. Managing a country is much, much different to managing a club. The amount of time you spend on your own and away from the limelight is, perhaps, something he would not want to give up. I think that tickles him, being the centre of attention, but there might come the time when he'll want to step back from that and, perhaps, be more low-key and not be involved every week of every year. When that comes, I'm sure he'll make a great international manager."

Still, while the FA's interest may have seemed something of a surprise – given Mourinho's boisterous reputation and the fact that they did not appoint Brian Clough in 1977 for similar reasons – there was an even greater shock on the cards: Mourinho was interviewed for the soon-to-be-vacant Barcelona job in February 2008. Mourinho's agent, Mendes, represented both Rafa Márquez and Deco so Mourinho had a relatively seamless process to getting what was, in essence, the unthinkable interview following his antics against Barcelona between 2005 and 2007. Barcelona's vice-president, Marc Ingla, and their director of football, Txiki Begiristain, met Mourinho and his representatives –

namely Mendes – in Lisbon in January, 2008. In this three-hour meeting, Mourinho delivered one of his trademark 27-page PowerPoint presentations and spoke about shifting Barcelona's identity with the use of an all-action 4-3-3.

Much of Mourinho's presentation focused on the dangers of the Gaucho clique of Ronaldinho, Deco, and Sylvinho. Mourinho feared that Lionel Messi could quickly develop the Gaucho's bad habits without the influence of a hard-line manager or assistant. The Portuguese believed Messi's attitude had been on the slide since the no nonsense Henk ten Cate departed as Frank Rijkaard's assistant in 2006. So, for all the talk of Pep Guardiola's brave decision to sell Ronaldinho and Deco in the summer of 2008, Mourinho, too, planned the same drastic action.

Mourinho also wanted to bring the Clarke role to the Nou Camp and use one of Luis Enrique, Guardiola, Sergi Barjuán or Albert Ferrer as his assistant. Coupled with this, the Portuguese planned on appointing Rui Faria, Silvino Louro, and André Villas-Boas as the other members of his backroom staff. Impressed by Mourinho's enthusiasm, Ingla planned to invite Mourinho to meet Joan Laporta, Barcelona's president, and Johan Cruyff, Laporta's unofficial adviser. However, Mourinho - fresh from his experience with a confidante-filled hierarchy at Chelsea, without even addressing his previous barbs with the Dutchman - complained about Cruyff's presence. Also, Laporta was already convinced of Guardiola's managerial ambitions, *tiki-taka* football philosophy, and crucial combination of a placid public persona with the ability to command in-house discipline. Thus, on the 8th of May 2008, Barcelona announced that Pep Guardiola would become the *blaugrana's* next manager.

Undeterred, and less than four months after his February meeting with Barcelona representatives in Lisbon, Mourinho was appointed as manager of Internazionale, on 2 June 2008, on a three-year contract worth €30 million. Faria, Silvino and Villas-Boas (who would depart, for Académica, against Mourinho's wishes, a year later) again joined Mourinho on his latest venture. Giuseppe Baresi, who made 392 league appearances for Inter between 1976 and 1992, took the 'Clarke role' as the in-club assistant. Just a week later, Mourinho was to be unveiled at his fourth club in the eighth year of his managerial career.

Such was Mourinho's confidence and aptitude in his opening press conference, he spoke in Italian. It must be stressed that this was a language Mourinho had never learnt as a translator but after three weeks of mainly five-hour days of cramming, Mourinho spoke near-effortlessly at his press conference. Zlatan Ibrahimović, Inter's talisman, was impressed: "During the

2008 European Championship I was told that Mourinho was going to phone me, and I thought: 'Has something happened?' He just wanted to say: 'It'll be nice to work together, looking forward to meeting you,' – nothing remarkable, but he was speaking in Italian. I didn't get it. Mourinho had never coached an Italian club. But he spoke the language better than me! He'd learned the language in three weeks, I couldn't keep up. We switched to English, and then I could sense it: this guy cares."

Just like at Chelsea, it was to prove a revealing press conference and Mourinho was, clearly, itching to put his Chelsea departure behind him and start the next chapter with renewed ambition and vigour: "The president gave me a beautiful book about Inter's history, but we need to write a new book. I like to win and forget the past. I have arrived at a special club and I believe I am a great coach but I don't want to be special. I am Mourinho – that's all." There was little evidence that Mourinho would later go on to have strained relations with the Italian press, either, with the Portuguese charming his audience with his colloquial use of *pirla* (plonker) and the big knot of his tie being keenly analysed by Milanese fashion experts.

While it may have seemed something of a leftfield managerial move for Mourinho, this was far from a rash decision and Inter had always intrigued him. After all, the Portuguese had considered *I Nerazzurri* alongside Liverpool before leaving Porto for Chelsea four years previously. This time, though, Mourinho could not resist and Inter's president, Massimo Moratti, had made contact as soon as Roberto Mancini tended his resignation after the 0-1 defeat to Liverpool in the Champions League quarter-final second-leg on 11 March, 2008. Even though Mancini withdrew his resignation the morning after, and was Inter's most successful coach since the great Helenio Herrera, 40 years previously, Mourinho had already been contacted.

Mourinho knew that an offer was on the table from as early as mid-March and, as a result, the Portuguese wasted no time in drafting his plans for Inter's playing squad with technical director, Marco Branca. This would prove one of Mourinho's most disastrous transfer windows. Mancini (Alessandro Faiolhe Amantino), the Brazilian winger, was recruited for €13 million from Roma. Ricardo Quaresma, who Mourinho wanted at Chelsea in January, 2007, was signed against Moratti's initial wishes from Porto for €18.6 million and Pelé in part-exchange. Sulley Muntari arrived from Portsmouth for €16 million. Even Mourinho's prodigal son, Hernán Crespo, signed on a free transfer.

With Mourinho looking to replicate the dynamic 4-3-3 formation he had used at Porto and Chelsea, though, his main target had been Frank Lampard. In all his years of management, it was Lampard who left the most profound effect on Mourinho with his professionalism and willingness to learn. The

Englishman was more than a footballer in Mourinho's eyes, reflected in the fact that Lampard scored a whopping 150 in an IQ test Mourinho conducted after John Terry's head injury against Arsenal in the 2007 League Cup final. Mourinho even believed Lampard would have won the Ballon d'Or in 2005 if Chelsea had lifted the Champions League. Far from this being a one-sided bond, when Lampard was told by Mourinho that the Portuguese believed that he was the best player in the world in 2005, Lampard immediately rang his mother, Pat: "I felt ten feet tall and trained harder than ever. Everything I tried came off."

With Chelsea's new manager, Luiz Felipe Scolari, having signed Deco from Barcelona, Lampard had been chased by Mourinho and Chelsea rejected a £7 million bid from Mourinho in the summer of 2008. Still, Lampard and Mourinho originally had an informal agreement, which would lead to Lampard following Mourinho to Inter on a free transfer in the summer of 2009 if he decided/was forced to see out the final year of his contract with Chelsea. However, following the death of Lampard's mother in April, 2008 and Chelsea's admirable support of the Englishman, Lampard instead decided to stay in SW6 and signed a new five-year contact in August, 2008.

To this day, Lampard remains one of the few footballers to ever turn down Mourinho's overtures and the Portuguese never forgot this: "Frank is in my heart for everything we have done together. But I'm left with a bitter taste in the mouth. He said to me 'I will go with you to Inter, if it's not possible now, then in a year we will be together'. Afterwards he changed his mind. What would have disillusioned me is if he had gone to another club. He renewed with Chelsea. Okay, we're friends as before."

Little did the pair know, though, that they would, eventually, be reunited.

"Please don't call me arrogant, but I'm European champion and I think I'm a special one."

[The Frisk Incident] "When I saw Rijkaard entering the referee's dressing room, I couldn't believe it."

[On not quitting Chelsea after the 2007 FA Cup triumph over Manchester United] "It was the biggest regret of my career."

[The manette] "You can take me away, arrest me, but my team is strong and will win anyway, even if we are reduced to nine men."

Chapter 16: Doubt

To put into context the seemingly easy environment Mourinho entered, Internazionale - from the end of Helenio Herrera's reign in 1968 to the Portuguese's arrival in the summer of 2008 - won just six league titles and failed to replicate the 'Golden Age' under president Angelo Moratti from 1962–66.

The club's lack of success provided a tangible inferiority complex for Angelo's son, Massimo, who brought the Moratti name back to the presidency in 1995. After all, AC Milan had won two Champions League titles, in 2003 and 2007, which eclipsed Inter's UEFA Cup victory in 1998; and Inter were only awarded the 2006 Serie A title due to the *Calciopoli* match-fixing scandal.

Regardless of Inter's three Serie A wins between 1995 and 2008, a dearth of Champions League success – just one semi-final appearance (2003) before Mourinho's arrival – left Moratti restless in the shadow of his father. It was one of the main reasons behind Moratti's somewhat harsh sackings of managerial talent such as Giampiero Marini, Luigi Simoni and, of course, Roberto Mancini. Also, this lack of a meaningful impact on the Champions League led to record-breaking amounts of money being spent on the likes of Christian Vieri (£31 million in 1999), Ronaldo (£19 million in 1997), Francesco Toldo (£17 million in 2001) and Hernán Crespo (£17 million in 2002). Such was this ground-breaking strategy in Italy, even Pope John Paul II would condemn Moratti's frivolousness for being an "insult to the poor".

Moratti's theory was that if Inter could break the world transfer record – as they did with the Vieri and Ronaldo deals – the ingredients of his father's landmark success could be found. After all, Angelo Moratti also broke the world transfer record twice, with the signings of Luis Suárez (£152,000 from Barcelona in 1961) and Harald Nielsen (£300,000 from Bologna in 1967). Following Inter's nine years without a domestic title - and with the club having never won the European Cup - Suárez went on to inspire Inter to three league titles and two European Cups between 1963 and 1966. The prolific Nielsen was seen as the heir to the 32-year-old, but a back injury soon scuppered his chance to live up to the fee.

Now, though, a world record salary for a manager was required. So, with Mourinho's appointment, Moratti was clearly hankering for not only a return to the glory days in Europe, but also a shift back to the profile of a disciplined manager, like Herrera, who had delivered such incredible success. Herrera – with his confrontational style, revolutionary psychology, bed checks, rapport with the club's fans, and deflection of media attention from his players to himself – was the man who delivered these three titles and two European Cups.

Over four decades later the parallels were stark. Mourinho was, like Herrera, about to generate near-unprecedented controversy in Italian football for his brutal disrespect towards fellow Serie A managers, namely Claudio Ranieri, Luciano Spalletti and Carlo Ancelotti. Even though Mourinho would go on to accuse the Italian press' support for Spalletti and Ancelotti being akin to "intellectual prostitution" - and lambasted his rivals for their *zeru tituli* (zero titles) - Mourinho's rivalry with Ranieri was the most intriguing.

The seemingly fragile Italian remained haunted by his dismissal at Chelsea four years earlier and as manager of Juventus in 2008–09 and, eventually, Roma in 2009–10, Ranieri was well aware that he was soon to come up against Mourinho's trademark tirade of mind games towards his title rivals. Therefore, the Italian struck the first blow: "I think the opposite to Mourinho. I don't need to win to be sure of what I do. I think that if I would have been the one to ask [Roman] Abramovich for [Frank] Lampard, he would have come to Juventus."

The attack was aimed at pricking Mourinho's remaining sensitivity: Lampard turning the Portuguese down, the breakdown in Mourinho's football relationship with Roman Abramovich, and Mourinho's win-focused playing style. Mourinho, though, was unmoved and, within days, seized the initiative. On 4 August, he said: "Ranieri? He's actually right – I am very demanding with myself and I need to win to be sure of things. For that reason, I have won so many trophies in my career. He, on the other hand, has the mentality of one who does not need to win and, at almost 70 years of age, has won a Super Cup and another small cup. He is too old to change his mentality."

Mourinho's early barb with Ranieri was a telling precedent of what was ahead at Inter: brilliant efficiency on the field, but chaotic relations off it. The press were the first victims, having been banned from attending Mourinho's pre-season training sessions at the Angelo Moratti Sports Centre as early as 25 July - amid fears that details of Mourinho's and Rui Faria's revolutionary ball-playing sessions were being leaked. Clearly, just like when Mourinho took over from Ranieri at Chelsea in 2004, his approach in training – away from the Italian staples of cardiology and double sessions – was having an impact.

So, while Mourinho's early suspicion of the Italian media was a stark contrast to his time in England, this was in many ways owed to the fact that Mourinho was well aware of the increased detail and sophistication of Italian sports' coverage at the time. There are three daily sports papers in Italy: *La Gazzetta dello Sport*, *Tuttosport*, and *Corriere dello Sport*. Without even addressing radio, there are also five television stations – RAI, Mediaset, Sky Italia, SportItalia and La7 – and local television stations cover training every day. It truly was 24/7 for Mourinho and far from it solely being based on transfer gossip - Mourinho's tactics, substitutions, salary, endorsements, religious devotion, and training sessions were all dissected by numerous sports newspapers and pundits daily. Even Mourinho's ritual of hugging his son, José Jr, 15 minutes before kick-off at every home game was scrutinised. Perhaps, amid compulsory hour-long post-match press appointments after every match, it was little surprise that Mourinho's hair was to turn completely grey during his first season at Inter – even if Hernán Crespo had prepared Mourinho for this cauldron: "When we are in Italy, we are tired of Italy. When we are not in Italy, we miss Italy."

These commitments had become a nuisance for Mourinho as early as 24 September, with the Portuguese accused of showing a lack of respect by Lecce's manager, Mario Beretta, after missing the post-match press conference following Inter's 1-0 win over Lecce. Beretta was not the only figure in Serie A to be offended by Mourinho's abrasive attitude. For example, after Inter beat Catania 2-1 eleven days previously, Mourinho boasted: "I could have played in goal and we still would have won." Catania's managing director, Pietro Lo Monaco, was incensed: "Mourinho is the kind of guy who deserves a smack in the teeth." Mourinho replied in trademark fashion: "As for Lo Monaco, I do not know who he is. With the name Monaco, I have heard of Bayern Monaco and the Monaco GP, the Tibetan Monaco and the Principality of Monaco. I have never heard of any others."

Perhaps, the reason why Mourinho was particularly prickly at the beginning of that campaign was owed to the fact that Inter had not wholly impressed. After all, in Mourinho's first eight games as Inter manager, *I Nerazzurri* conceded eight goals – winning just four matches in the process. A 3-1 humbling away to lowly Torino on 21 September and the 1-0 *Derby della Madonnina* defeat to Milan a week later were particularly worrying results. Compared to how Mourinho had begun his reigns at Porto and Chelsea, in particular, the Portuguese was already facing scrutiny about whether he could deal with the tactical minefield of *catenaccio*. Even Mourinho's commitment was questioned, with the Italian press already tiring of his constant references to his time in England and criticising Mourinho for advising Gianfranco Zola to appoint Steve Clarke as the Italian's assistant at West Ham United.

However, something changed after Inter's 4-0 win at Roma on 19 October, which was Roma's heaviest defeat against Inter for 40 years. A gauntlet had been thrown down and a message sent, with Mourinho's inclusion of the raw Victor Obinna an inspired move which won him much acclaim in the press.

Chapter 16

Tellingly, after the match, Inter were to go on an 11-match unbeaten run in the league. Among those defeated included Ranieri's Juventus, with Inter edging a narrow encounter 1-0. It seemed Mourinho was finally at ease, with his foundations - including utilising youngsters Davide Santon and Mario Balotelli regularly and reviving the short-term fortunes of Adriano - and gameplan established.

In fact, for all the criticism Mourinho received for his reliance on older players at Inter, he demanded four players from the Academy be a part of his 23-man squad when he took over. Mourinho constantly involved youngsters in first-team training sessions, too, and tellingly, five players - Giulio Donati, Cristiano Biraghi, Luca Caldirola, Matteo Bianchetti, Mattia Destro - from Inter's Academy went on to make Italy's Under-21 squad at the 2013 European Championships. Also, in Balotelli's first season under Mourinho, the 18-year-old made double the number of appearances (31) that he had previously under Mancini (15).

Rene Krhin was eventually promoted by Mourinho into Inter's first-team squad at 19 years of age in 2009 and the Slovenian was praised by Mourinho for his "ambition, discipline, and talent". Krhin told me this still ranks as a career highlight: "I think he is one of the best managers of all time. He's the best manager in the world. I had the honour to work with him for one season and it was really fantastic. I can't explain to you all the reasons why I think he is the best; a person must work with him to truly understand what makes him so special. I know a lot of people criticised him in Italy, but I think they were a little bit jealous… Receiving praise like that from him really was a dream come true. I couldn't imagine something like that ever happening and yet it did. It really gave me a lot of will to continue and train even harder to impress him."

* * *

Even the press were to eventually benefit from the Portuguese's time in Italy taking off, with Mourinho serving Christmas cake and champagne to those journalists who gathered to watch the Champions League second-round draw on 19 December. The draw saw Mourinho renew acquaintances with two old friends, Sir Alex Ferguson and England, after finishing a narrow second in a Group B featuring Panathinaikos, Werder Bremen, and Anorthosis Famagusta. Mourinho was to relish coming up against Ferguson for the first time in 18 months and sharing a bottle of wine after a two-legged knockout tie for the first time since this utterance after the League Cup semi-final first-leg in 2005: "After the game, after the press conference, we were together in my office. We laugh, we spoke, we speak, we drank and, to be fair, when we go to Man United, I will bring a very good bottle of wine because the wine we drank was very bad and he was complaining. So, because when we go there it's my birthday, I will go with a beautiful bottle of Portuguese wine to enjoy with him at the end of the game. I have a lot of respect for the big man. I call him 'boss' because he's our [the other managers'] boss. He's the top man, a really nice person and he deserves to be the boss. Maybe when I am 60 the kids will call me the same."

The tie would be the ultimate test of how far Mourinho had come with Inter in just eight months, with the holders, United, unbeaten in 19 Champions League matches. Even though Mourinho had lost just once in his previous 12 encounters with Ferguson, this Inter side was still very much a work in progress. Encapsulating just how raw Mourinho's team were, the 25-year-old Nelson Rivas put in a nervy performance in the biggest match of his career, the 0-0 draw in the first-leg at the San Siro. It led to the Colombian defender being substituted for his more experienced compatriot, Iván Córdoba, at half-time.

Mourinho did not lambast Rivas, though, and delivered the news delicately as the defender told me: "Mourinho did not really need to calm my nerves before the match. We all knew this was an important game against a strong Manchester United side and we were all focused on doing everything to get the win. You're always a bit disappointed to leave the game at half-time; I wanted to play the full match. The coach told me I was returning from a long-term injury and that it was better for me to step out and make sure I was fit for the next game, which, for me, was against Sampdoria in the Coppa Italia semi-final. Mourinho told me that I had a lot of potential and to continue working hard."

Despite hitting the woodwork twice in the second-leg, Inter were clearly not ready and lost 2-0. An over-reliance on the mood of Zlatan Ibrahimović, sloppy defensive organisation, and wastefulness in front of goal were not the hallmarks of a Mourinho team in Europe – let alone European champions. So while Mancini had left the perfect foundations for Mourinho to continue Inter's dominance of Serie A, Europe was another matter. Thus, Mourinho, as expected, led Inter to the 2008-09 Serie A title – with a comfortable ten-point lead over Juventus.

Still Mourinho deserved much credit, following that hollow exit to Manchester United, for not losing his passion domestically in the eyes of Ibrahimović: "He built us up before matches. It was like theatre, a psychological game. He might show videos where we'd played badly and say: 'So miserable! Hopeless! Those guys can't be you. They must be your brothers, your inferior selves,' and we nodded. We were ashamed. 'I don't want to see you like that today,' he would continue. 'No way,' we thought.

Chapter 16

'Go out there like hungry lions,' he added. 'In the first battle you'll be like this…' He pounded his fist against the palm of his open hand. 'And in the second battle… 'He gave the flip chart a kick and sent it flying across the room, and the adrenaline pumped inside us, and we went out like rabid animals. I felt increasingly that this guy gives everything for the team, so I want to give everything for him. People were willing to kill for him."

Even though Mourinho had become the first foreign manager since Sven-Göran Eriksson, in 1999, to win Serie A, the Mourinho factor, on its own, would not be enough in Europe. So, while Moratti's €47 million splurge in the summer of 2008 had yielded little reward – with Quaresma and Mancini making just a combined 33 appearances on the way to Inter's title win – Mourinho needed further investment: "Three of the four Champions League finalists – Arsenal were the exception – were simply stronger than us. Yet if we managed to sign those three or four players that we are chasing then we can be as strong as them."

It would prove a prophetic statement.

Chapter 17: The Mourinho Model

Mourinho knew he had another two seasons to fulfill Massimo Moratti's objective of delivering Inter's first European Cup since 1965 but judging by Moratti's eventual backing in the transfer market, the pressure was on Mourinho to, at the very least, guide Inter to their first Champions League semi-final for seven years in 2009-10.

Given how Mourinho had delivered Porto's 2004 Champions League title unexpectedly and had struggled with the pressure of Roman Abramovich's obsession with the tournament at Chelsea, doubts lingered about Mourinho's supposed Midas touch in Europe in the Italian press. Thus, the Portuguese realised, in order to achieve European success, Roberto Mancini's foundations – which had again disappointed in Europe – needed to be dismantled somewhat.

Mancini stalwarts like Adriano, Olivier Dacourt, and Julio Cruz were all released. Mancini's lieutenant, Patrick Vieira, followed the Italian to Manchester City, in January 2010. Mourinho's first signing, the Brazilian Mancini, was loaned to Milan. Nicolás Burdisso moved on loan to Roma. David Suazo was loaned to Genoa. Nelson Rivas would also move on loan, to Livorno, but the Colombian told me he only had positive memories of Mourinho – having also played under his predecessor, Mancini: "I've always thought that José Mourinho was a great coach and a great person to me. It was a privilege to play for him. Mourinho and Mancini were two very different coaches, most notably in the way that Mourinho has the players reacting to various situations and his hands-on approach… I had plenty of one-on-one discussions with Mourinho throughout my career, not just at Inter. They were about family a lot of the time, something that was very important to him. We also talked about the play on the pitch, individually and as a team. I was very fortunate to play for him and with great players in the squad."

The telling departure was that of the one-time invincible, Zlatan Ibrahimović. This was the man who Mourinho referred to, in 2008-09, as the best player in the world. In fact, even though Ibrahimović was open to moving to Barcelona, the initial contact even surprised the Swede - with Barça's original dialogue with Inter a smokescreen centred on buying Maxwell for a mere €5 million. Ibrahimović was to cost Barcelona a club-record €49.5m plus Samuel Eto'o.

While Mourinho and Ibrahimović held a close bond, with the Swede declaring that he would have been willing to kill for Mourinho, the Portuguese had lingering doubts. Sure, Ibrahimović had scored 29 goals in 47 games for Mourinho in 2008-09, but just one of those goals came in Europe. Far from it being an isolated drought, either, Ibrahimović had scored only 18 goals in 68 European games for Ajax, Juventus and Inter in eight seasons.

Mourinho knew the Swede had his uses – a near-unrivalled ability to lead the line and, also, to come deep and connect play – but Ibrahimović's moods were a problem. After all, just days after Ibrahimović won Serie A's best foreign player award at the Calcio Oscars, the Swede put in a desperate first-half showing in the Coppa Italia quarter-final against Roma on 21 January, 2009. Mourinho was incensed at half-time, declaring that Ibrahimović may as well give the award to someone who deserves it, such as his mother. Riled, the Swede came out in the second-half possessed and scored the winning goal, a fantastic kung-fu volley, in the 2-1 win. Mourinho, though, did not have the patience to repeat this ritual every time Ibrahimović failed to turn up.

Then, there was the small matter of the Ibrahimović fee and Eto'o. €49.6 million would allow Marco Branca and Mourinho to comfortably bring in their two primary targets, Diego Milito and Thiago Motta from Genoa, and with Moratti's backing, also, Lúcio, Wesley Sneijder and, eventually in January, the fairly sizable wages of Goran Pandev. Thus, the four or five players Mourinho had desperately sought to take Inter to the next level would be provided and it must be stressed what a huge fan of Eto'o Mourinho was, having chased him with Chelsea in the summer of 2006. The big-game temperament, European experience, and near-unrivalled striking instincts of Eto'o would be welcome compensation for Ibrahimović's departure. In fact, such was Mourinho's bond with Eto'o, the Cameroonian would display the selflessness - in playing on the right-wing - that Ibrahimović never came close to. Much of this was owed to the fact that Mourinho, personally, phoned Eto'o to convince him to come to Internazionale after the Cameroonian had, previously, told Moratti that he had given his word to Mark Hughes and Manchester City.

Far from focusing solely on expensive imports, though, Mourinho also continued his work with Inter's Academy and promoted Giulio Donati, Alen Stevanović, and Rene Krhin into the first-team for 2009-10. Krhin was attracting much attention, with Chelsea, Manchester City, and Liverpool all interested in the Slovenian before he signed a contract extension with Inter in November, 2009. The Mourinho factor had again worked its magic - with Krhin going on to make six first-team appearances that season - as he told me: "Of course I was glad that all these clubs were interested in me, but Inter gave me everything and I didn't think too much before signing the five-year contract. Mourinho made my choice even easier. One example was after I made my debut for Slovenia against England at Wembley just two months previously. During one training session a few days after, he told me he watched the match and said he was very happy with my performance. He rewarded me, days later, and I made my Inter debut against Parma… I think he did very well with young players; he really gave me more courage. But, of course, he couldn't let us play more because there was such pressure and everybody wanted to win trophies, which I think is normal. For young players, like me, it was an honour just to be a part of that team."

After discussions with two of his youth coaches, Marco Monti and Paolo Migilavacca, Mourinho also gave his blessing to *Football's Next Star*. This was a competition broadcast on Sky1 that saw ten young footballers from Britain and Ireland move to Milan and compete for a professional contract with Internazionale in 2010. The eventual winner, Ben Greenhalgh, 17, was told to "never lose his passion" by Mourinho upon first meeting the Portuguese as he revealed to me: "Mourinho was a busy man and it meant a lot to have a slot in his schedule and to be presented with the Inter shirt. The whole way through the show and my time in Italy, I kept very level-headed and just took every moment as it came, thinking nothing of it. But with all the attention and publicity from it, at the time, you can only think that you've made it when you meet a man like that. To be given personal advice from one of the most successful football managers meant a great deal and it's definitely a quote that has helped me through my past few testing years in football. It will always play on my mind.

"I had spells training with the first-team when José was on the sideline watching and sometimes taking the sessions. At that time, Inter were winning everything and the players had great respect for him so it was a great experience to be part of it all. Mourinho isn't a manager who is against young players; he believes in a lot of older players due to their experience in the game. At Inter, none of the younger boys felt like they weren't being given a fair chance because of the incredible results he was producing with the first-team… I'll never know what might have happened without my time at Inter, but I do know it was a great experience and I learnt a lot from it. I think just being involved helped me develop as a player."

* * *

While it seemed that everything had gone to plan for Mourinho in the summer of 2009, the Portuguese was to be rocked by the news of 31 July. Sir Bobby Robson had lost his battle with lung cancer, which had been confirmed as terminal 11 months previously, at the age of 76. Given everything the duo had been through – not just on the coaching bench at three different clubs, but, rather, regarding the tragedies of Serhiy Scherbakov, Rui Filipe, and Mourinho's sister, Teresa – it was particularly tough for Mourinho and he did not attend the Englishman's memorial service: "I hadn't spoken to him in the last two months because it was hard for me because I didn't want to think that he was dying. That wasn't the image I wanted to keep with me forever… that wasn't the voice I wanted to hear."

* * *

Despite not being highly-rated by Inter's fans, Sulley Muntari's services would be retained. The Ghanaian, though, began fasting for Ramadan in August, 2009 and Mourinho was unimpressed: "Muntari had some problems related to Ramadan, perhaps with this heat it's not good for him to be doing this [fasting]. Ramadan has not arrived at the ideal moment for a player to play a football match." Mourinho's comments infuriated Muslim leader Mohamed Nour Dachan, who responded: "I think Mourinho could do with talking a little less. A practising [Muslim] player is not weakened because we know from the Institute of Sports Medicine that mental and psychological stability can give a sportsman an extra edge on the field."

Already, it seemed 2009-10 would be one of the most controversial campaigns in Mourinho's career but, arguably, it would prove the Portuguese's greatest ever season. Inter were incredible, displaying the three hallmarks of Mourinho's philosophy - resilience, efficiency and ruthlessness - throughout. As early as October, 2009, this was evident, with Sneijder's last minute winner against Udinese only the third time that Inter had won a game in the dying minutes under Mourinho up until that point. Mourinho's reaction to the Dutchman's winner echoed that of his celebration after Dmitri Alenichev's third goal in Porto's 2004 Champions League victory, with Mourinho's tongue unfurled as he pounded his chest with his fists amid an ecstatic finish. Moratti, though, was unmoved: "The reaction was a bit strange but the important thing is that we won."

Inter would lose just three competitive games from a possible 27 in all competitions by the time they played Milan in the crucial *Derby della Madonnina* on 24 January, 2010. This game, with Inter going down to ten-men after Sneijder's dismissal by Gianluca Rocchi before the half-hour mark, would offer a telling precedent. After all, when Inter went on to defeat Milan 2-0 with nine men after Lúcio was sent-off in injury time, the seeds of Mourinho's war with Serie A's referees were sown: "Everything was done for us not to win. We were perfect. We would have won this game even with seven men. Maybe with six we would have struggled, but we would have won with seven." Mourinho was fined €18,000 for the outburst.

This fine would not censor Mourinho, though. During Inter's ill-tempered 0-0 draw with Sampdoria a month later, referee Paolo Tagliavento sent-off Walter Samuel and Iván Córdoba - as well as harshly booking Eto'o for an alleged dive in the first-half. Mourinho was suitably unimpressed: turning towards the television cameras and media photographers to brandish a *mandette*, a handcuffs gesture, just before half-time. It was an act of defiance; rather than being awarded champions' luck, Inter were being victimised in Mourinho's eyes: "You can take me away, arrest me, but my team is strong and will win anyway, even if we are reduced to nine men." Such was the furore, there were even reports that the Italian Football Referees Association would go on strike if Mourinho was not suitably punished.

Having already served two separate one-match suspensions that season, Mourinho was banned from the touchline for three games and fined €35,000. While the handcuffs gesture was typical Mourinho bravado, there was no doubting that the Portuguese was feeling the strain of a stronger title challenge from Roma and Milan in 2009-10. It even led to a paranoid Mourinho prohibiting Andrea Ramazzotti – a *Corriere dello Sport* journalist who Mourinho had clashed with previously, leading to Mourinho being fined €13,000 – from hanging around Inter's team bus despite the fact he was within his right to do so. Mourinho even lambasted Italy's captain, Fabio Cannavaro, for "speaking like a coach" after the defender pleaded with Davide Santon to leave Inter to further his international career.

Still, outbursts of defiance from Mourinho were key to taking the pressure off the players, in Milito's opinion: "There's no coach like him when it comes to sticking his neck out and defending everyone, that way reducing the tension within the team when things aren't going well. It's no fluke that after a defeat, Inter gets straight back on its feet. That's thanks to Mourinho." Such was Mourinho's mastering of easing the pressures on his players, he would even award them short breaks if he felt they were over-worked as Sneijder testified: "He said to me, 'Wesley, you look tired, take some days off, go to the sun with your wife and daughter.' All other coaches just talked about training… so I went to Ibiza for three days and, when I was back, I was ready to kill and die for him."

With an incredibly motivated squad, Inter, ultimately, secured the title by two points and would go on to defeat Roma 1-0 in the Coppa Italia final to complete an impressive double. What would really seal Mourinho's place in the pantheon of greats, though, was Inter's performance in Europe.

Chapter 18: His Greatest Achievement

Just like with Porto in 2003-04, Mourinho's performance in a tricky Champions League group was impressive and his team would again finish second. Despite daunting away trips to Barcelona, Rubin Kazan, and Dynamo Kyiv in Group F, nine points were claimed from six games. Just one loss was recorded, in the final group game against Barcelona, but like in 03-04, finishing second was far from a disaster for Mourinho. Inter, after all, were drawn against Chelsea – who may have been about to record a historic double under the wily Carlo Ancelotti, but were far from a daunting opponent for Mourinho. Still, as a result of finishing top of their group and having home advantage in the second-leg, Chelsea went into the tie as slight favourites. It was the perfect scenario for Mourinho: an opportunity to claim a scalp of sorts and send a message across Europe.

Still, it must be stressed what a difficult tie it was for Mourinho. Aside from Ross Turnbull, Branislav Ivanović, Yuri Zhirkov, Daniel Sturridge and Nicolas Anelka, Chelsea's first-team squad and foundations remained identical to the one Mourinho left in 2007. It would, undoubtedly, work in Mourinho's favour in targeting the flagging mobility of John Terry, for example, but the Portuguese took no pleasure from facing his old club again.

Interacting with the English media and Chelsea's indebted fans for the first time in two-and-a-half years, on the other hand, was exactly what Mourinho needed. After all, it must be noted that the first-leg of the Chelsea tie at the San Siro on 24 February came just days after Mourinho's *manette* gesture against Sampdoria. The effect of seeing familiar friends and journalists from England at his press conference on the eve of the game - and speaking English in front of the Italian press for one of the few times while he was at Inter - cannot be understated. It all relaxed Mourinho ahead of that crucial 2-1 victory in the first-leg.

The second-leg would follow suit: 'Mourinhomania' returned to London for what, at times, felt like a testimonial for the Portuguese. From Mourinho declaring his love for Custard Creams during his pre-match press conference to having his image cheered by the capacity home crowd on the big screen in the minutes before the match, this felt a world away from Mourinho's final game as Chelsea manager, against Rosenborg, in front of 24,793 people. Crucially, even though he was to hug every single Chelsea player before the warm-up, Mourinho did not get too caught up in the adulation: "The warm-up is the warm-up they did in our time. The way they defend set-pieces is exactly the same. Sometimes they play a 4-4-2 diamond, sometimes they play 4-3-3, which are exactly the systems we worked when there. Chelsea have suffered in the last two years and it's no coincidence that their decline happened after I left."

Inter went on to record an impressive 0-1 victory thanks to Samuel Eto'o's fine finish late in the second-half to win the tie 3-1 on aggregate, following Diego Milito and Esteban Cambiasso's goals in the first-leg. *I Nerazzurri* were particularly outstanding in the second-leg: their fitness, resilience, and physicality a level above Mourinho's prototype that night: the Chelsea of John Terry, Frank Lampard, Michael Ballack, Didier Drogba, *et al.* The precedent for incredibly valiant defending - in tandem with some sweeping counter-attacking - had been set and after Inter eased past CSKA Moscow 2-0 on aggregate in the quarter-finals, Mourinho was to face Barcelona, again. The drought was over: it was to be Mourinho's first Champions League semi-final for three years. Five months on from their previous encounter in Group F, there was no disputing the fact that Mourinho had regained his European Midas touch and was better prepared for Barcelona.

Just like in 2004-05 and 2005-06, mind games were going to dominate proceedings. Barcelona's 14-hour coach trip, via Cannes, to the San Siro due to the Eyjafjallajökull volcanic ash cloud would only accentuate the cabin fever atmosphere of facing Mourinho again. Barcelona, too, would resent that a Portuguese official, Olegário Benquerença, was to referee the first-leg and that Mourinho, unsurprisingly, had prohibited the San Siro pitch being watered for the first-leg. It was as if the holders were already preparing the excuses for what seemed an inevitable defeat.

There was also the small matter of Samuel Eto'o and Zlatan Ibrahimović facing their old clubs again, but, encapsulating how their respective moves had worked out, the Swede was to be subbed on the hour mark in both legs of the semi-final. Ibrahimović was left furious: "Guardiola looked at me as if it was all my fault and I thought: 'That's it. I've played my last card.' After that match, it felt like I was no longer welcome at the club. I felt like s*** when I sat in the locker room, and Guardiola glared at me as if I was a disturbance, an alien. It was mental." Ironically, despite having a focal point, Ibrahimović's static movement counted against Barcelona and played into the slower Walter Samuel and Lúcio's hands. So, despite Barcelona going 0-1 up through Pedro after just 19 minutes, Inter rallied – freed from the shackles for one of the rare times of Mourinho's reign.

Barcelona were unable to dominate possession, with Inter's incessant pressing and closing down even eclipsing that of their fine display at Stamford Bridge just a month previously. It left Barcelona, always sumptuously fluid under Guardiola up until that point, flustered and their rhythm out of time: Xavi misplaced passes and Lionel Messi was caught in possession on numerous occasions. Mourinho had Barcelona rattled and Inter's 3-1 victory - with fine goals from Wesley Sneijder, Maicon, and Diego Milito - was well deserved. Such was the achievement, Inter became the first team to defeat Guardiola's Barcelona by more than a one goal margin. To put this into perspective, Barcelona had won 82 of the 114 matches they played in all competitions under Guardiola - losing just ten games - before their defeat to Inter. It was only Barcelona's fourth defeat from a possible 24 European games under the Catalan. Mourinho, though, could not resist a dig, post-match: "The way they are, tomorrow, we will probably read I am to blame for the volcano. Maybe I have a friend in the volcano and I am responsible for that."

* * *

The only moment to overshadow Mourinho's fine victory was that of Mario Balotelli flinging his Inter shirt to the ground at the final whistle after a poor cameo performance. The Italian came on for Milito for the final 15 minutes, but stormed down the tunnel to a chorus of boos while his team-mates celebrated at the final whistle. It was the perfect encapsulation of a mutually frustrating relationship for Balotelli and Mourinho. Previously, Balotelli had been sent-off for a double-booking - despite Mourinho's warning at half-time - for an injury-ridden Inter against Rubin Kazan in September, 2009; and the Portuguese made Balotelli cry after awarding him a 0/10 mark for his performance against Roma on 8 November, 2009. Mourinho, tellingly, made no public comment about the incident against Barcelona but Inter's captain, Javier Zanetti, condemned Balotelli: "I am disappointed that a celebration was ruined with something like this. If the fans whistle at him he's got to understand that it could depend on a lot of different things. We've always stood by him."

* * *

While Guardiola, purposefully, delayed Mourinho's press conference before the second-leg by 40 minutes, the Catalan refused to get involved in Mourinho's mind games: "We aren't playing against Inter, we're playing against ourselves. We are going to see if we are capable of being ourselves in the most important, transcendental game of our lives. Inter Milan don't even exist. We are an exemplary institution. We have lost and won a few times in the past 20 months, but we have always retained respect."

Mourinho, though, had smartly turned the status quo - the Portuguese's undoubted obsession with Barcelona - on its head regarding Barcelona's thirst to become the first side to retain the Champions League, at the Santiago Bernabéu: "For Barcelona it's an obsession. Our dream is more pure than obsession. A dream is about pride. Our players will be proud to reach the final in Madrid. It's an obsession you can see and feel. I was here in 1997 and

Chapter 18

I lived a Spanish Cup final at the Bernabéu between Real Betis and Barça. It seemed like we won the World Cup. To have a Catalan flag in the Bernabéu is an obsession. It's anti-Madridismo."

Mourinho had drawn the battle lines: Inter were ready for a Barça onslaught at the Nou Camp and content to sit back and hit Barcelona on the counter. In truth, the latter never came to fruition: Thiago Motta's sending-off, amid Sergio Busquets' theatrics, saw Inter camped in their own half for more than an hour. Remarkably, Inter would record just a single shot during the game and had only 24% possession. Samuel Eto'o even played at right-back. Yet, it was, without question, a sensational defensive performance with Inter holding out – aside from Gerard Piqué's consolation goal five minutes from time – and reaching their first European Cup final since 1972.

The one-time *El Traductor*, typically, revelled in triumphing in adversity in the cauldron of the Nou Camp. From mischievously listening in on Guardiola handing Ibrahimović instructions - with Mourinho telling the Catalan it was not over - and darting onto the pitch in an echo of his exploits at Old Trafford in 2004, it really was Mourinho's most beautiful defeat. Inter left blood on the field, as Mourinho proclaimed, and it was, perhaps, fitting that Barcelona turned on the sprinklers to, inadvertently, cleanse Mourinho's battered troops.

After weeping and giving thanks in the Nou Camp's in-house chapel, Mourinho paid tribute to Guardiola and Barcelona in typical style post-match: "It is always difficult to lose, especially for those who are not used to it. This is my most beautiful defeat." Guardiola, still, would not be drawn into Mourinho's minefield: "I respect him a lot and I won't spend a single second answering things like that. Criticising him would be looking down on Inter and that is not fair."

For all the criticism Mourinho received for Inter recording just 24% possession and completing only 67 passes in the second-leg, being reduced to ten-men perfectly suited that approach – as Chelsea would also showcase in the Nou Camp two years later. Also, in contrast to his team's 50% possession in the first-leg, having Motta sent-off in the second-leg forced Mourinho's hand: "We did not park the bus, we parked the plane. Do you really want me to compete for possession with them and lose? If you have a Ferrari and I have some small car, I have to puncture your tyres or put sugar in your petrol tank."

With Bayern Munich having defeated Lyon 4-0 on aggregate in the other semi-final, a reunion was now in store with an old friend, Louis van Gaal.

Chapter 19: The Long Goodbye

Following the chaos of the semi-final against Barcelona, the warmth of the pre-match build-up to Inter's final against Bayern Munich, at the Santiago Bernabéu, was welcomed by Mourinho. It would be the first time he was to face Louis van Gaal in a competitive match and having never met his other mentor, Sir Bobby Robson, on the touchline either, the contest took on even further significance for Mourinho.

So, while Mourinho was his typical jovial self in his pre-match press conference, he was also quick to pay tribute to van Gaal: "We had a really special rapport. He showed faith, gave me confidence and responsibility. It's been 12-13 years but I never forget those times and that person who was fantastic for me. But when my friend, Louis van Gaal, says he wouldn't have celebrated the same way as I did in Barcelona, he couldn't anyway because he is too slow. He can't run the way I can. I'm fast like a lion! Voom! Did you see that run?!"

Of course, following the ordeal of the Barça bloodbath, Mourinho always seemed destined to win that final against his mentor. However, it was testament to Mourinho's achievement that he got so much out of one of the oldest average aged winners of a club competition in history. After all, Inter's Champions League final XI's average age was 29.63 years and *I Nerazzurri's* seven substitutes, plus the suspended Thiago Motta, averaged 29.57 years. These were players with engrained tactical quirks, yet Mourinho was able to unite them under his system.

Still, in trademark style, again it was clear that Mourinho had other matters on his mind. Amid the Inter squad's euphoric celebrations after the 2-0 triumph - through two clinical counter-attacking goals from Diego Milito - Mourinho's thoughts were already focused on the managerial post at Real Madrid, ahead of the inevitability of Manuel Pellegrini's sacking.

Mourinho's mind had long been made up and even though he had a year left on his contract, the Portuguese had previously declared that it would be an honour to manage Real Madrid ahead of playing the final at their stadium, the Santiago Bernabéu. This was not meant as an act of disrespect or hankering but the Italian media, naturally, saw this as a come-and-get-me plea from Mourinho. The Portuguese was unimpressed by this supposed misinterpretation and imposed a ban on media commitments - other than television or radio where he had full control over what was recorded - in May.

Thus, for yet another final - be it the Champions League in 2004 or the FA Cup in 2007 - Mourinho's future was to dominate proceedings. Given how Mourinho's initial intentions were, effectively, leaked before each of these finals, there was no doubting the fact that Mourinho was deflecting attention from his pressurised players right until the end – even in the ironic, and fateful, surroundings of the Bernabéu in this instance. With each of these three finals resulting in a positive result, no one can fault Mourinho's somewhat curious thinking.

Yet this was different to the emotionless aftermath of Porto's victory in 2004 and while Mourinho stood on his own with the match ball away from his most of his players, the Portuguese was openly emotional with the elder statesmen of his squad. Remarkably, the likes of Francesco Toldo, Javier Zanetti, and Marco Materazzi had never played in a Champions League final despite glittering careers spanning two decades. The enormity of this fact was not lost on Mourinho as he delivered Inter's first European Cup for 45 years and the first treble in Italian football history. An inseparable bond had been established and Zanetti, *Il Capitano*, would give the Portuguese his captain's armband in one final plea for Mourinho not to depart. Mourinho and Materazzi even shared an incredibly moving 22-second embrace in the car park post-match, with the usually unflappable Italian remarking: "What am I to do? Retire? After you, I can't have another coach." Mourinho would never forget that night: "When I say forever, I mean forever. I can't say that the players I had at Chelsea, Porto and Inter are my ex-players, they continue to be my players. And they don't talk about their former boss, they say: 'You are the boss'. They are ties forever."

With Mourinho – alongside Ottmar Hitzfeld and Ernst Happel – becoming only the third man to win the Champions League with two different teams, the tributes continued to pour in over the next six months, with Massimo Moratti proclaiming: "Mourinho is the best coach I have ever had. He is perfect in the ways he works, with both seriousness and dedication. You don't measure this on his attacks on Italian football, but in the way he applies himself to his work. It's a shame he was not awarded in Italy. I have had many coaches, but he was the best." Wesley Sneijder would dedicate his UEFA best midfielder award to Mourinho, which led to the Portuguese welling up in the audience, in September, 2010. FIFA even recognised Mourinho's achievement, with the Portuguese winning the inaugural managerial Ballon d'Or – which he would go on to donate for auction to the Sir Bobby Robson Foundation and Breakthrough Breast Cancer nine months later – in December, 2010.

One matter had irked Mourinho, though, in the aftermath of his departure from Inter and that was the conduct of Rafa Benítez, his controversial successor at the San Siro. In truth, despite their differences, the pair are cut from the same cloth: both of their playing careers ended in their mid-20s and they have compensated for this with incredible attention to detail and undoubted tactical genius as managers. Jerzy Dudek - who played under Benítez at Liverpool in 2004-07 and under Mourinho at Real Madrid in 2010-11 - told me about the two managers: "Both Mourinho and Rafa Benítez were extremely professional and they knew how to do their job very well. Mourinho was a charismatic leader and psychologist, and had a great relationship with his players; Rafa had a more analytic mind."

From the moment Luis García's 'ghost goal' stood in 2005 and Liverpool became Mourinho's bogey team in cup competitions, the pair never saw eye-to-eye. As a result of this fall-out, Benítez resented the eulogising of Mourinho upon succeeding the Portuguese in June, 2010. From, supposedly, taking down photos of Mourinho's Champions League triumph to aiming to change Inter's playing style radically in placing premature first-team pressure on youngsters such as Philippe Coutinho and Jonathan Biabiany, Benítez clearly resented the fact that Mourinho had laid the foundations. While Benítez would always deny, vehemently, that he took down the photographs, Mourinho was still unimpressed: "I don't need photos to make those around me love me. They carry me in their hearts."

Benítez's behaviour was akin to Howard Wilkinson - regarding the ongoing legacy of Don Revie at Leeds United, even 14 years on from his departure, in 1988 - and a marked contrast to Mourinho's acknowledgement of the work Roberto Mancini had done between 2005 and 2008. However, rather than struggling in the shadow of Mourinho, Benítez will always point to the fact that he won the Supercoppa Italiana and the Club World Cup without any summer investment and only departed because Moratti did not back him in the winter transfer window. Yet, in contrast, Claudio Ranieri - who managed Inter for seven months in 2011-2012- admitted that Inter might as well build a statue of Mourinho outside the Angelo Moratti Sports Centre to reflect his ongoing presence.

Rene Krhin, who became the first ever Slovenian to receive a Champions League medal and left for Bologna after Mourinho's departure, told me about the difficulties Benítez faced in succeeding Mourinho as Inter manager: "I think Mourinho will remain forever in the hearts of every fan and every person that works for Inter. He is a legend there and I think everybody is waiting for that one day he returns to the San Siro…I met **Benítez before I left** and he made a really good impression on me. But, now, I can't say whether staying would have been better for me. Maybe, I would have played some more matches in that period with Rafa but the dynamic and team wasn't quite the same with Mourinho not being there anymore."

Chapter 19

César Peixoto, who witnessed the arrival of five managers at Porto within two years of Mourinho's departure in 2004, told me how tough it is for a manager to maintain Mourinho's momentum: "It is difficult for a new coach to equate the work done and left by Mourinho. His legacy greatly increases the pressure. For players, it is a new mindset, with new training and new ideas. Sometimes, it becomes difficult to adapt to a new formula because the previous formula worked so well. But it is a question of time. One thing is for certain: Mourinho's replacement has to have a great personality and conquer the players to convince them that he is armed with everything to win."

The fact that Chelsea were also to have four managers within two years of Mourinho leaving Stamford Bridge in 2007 and Inter were to have five in the same post-Mourinho period was far from a coincidence. Real Madrid, though, were banking on Mourinho's short-term success to usurp a familiar foe, Barcelona.

Chapter 20: Entering the Cauldron

Before Mourinho's unveiling to the Spanish press, Florentino Pérez, Real Madrid's president, paraded Madrid's nine European Cups and told Mourinho how much he craved re-living the ecstasy of the 2002 victory, to which Mourinho remarked: "I only won my last one ten days ago and I already miss it!" It was the perfect anecdote to reflect a movement away from Pérez's, and Madrid's, past. In appointing Mourinho, Pérez realised that in order for Madrid to regain their mantle as the world's biggest club, a new approach was required.

After all, in his first spell as Madrid's president, from 2000–06, Pérez employed six different managers. This was a period that included the unjustified and unforgivable sacking of Vicente del Bosque, who was second only to the mighty Miguel Muñoz as the club's most successful ever manager with eight trophies. Added to this was Pérez's meddling in transfers, which led to brilliant yet seemingly 'unmarketable' talents like Claude Makélelé, Esteban Cambiasso, and Samuel Eto'o leaving the club. Gone, too, was Pirri - the legendary Madrid midfielder and technical director - who drove home the unfashionable signings of Makélelé and Flávio Conceição in a bid to build a team rather than a group of globetrotters. Thus, the predominantly flawed *galácticos* policy and the insistence that players were selected based on sentimentality rather than form – such as an out-of-form Raúl being picked ahead of Michael Owen in 2004–05 – led to an unstable and inconsistent first presidency for Pérez, with a fairly paltry return of two league titles and one Champions League in six seasons.

Pérez's return in the summer of 2010, amid the fanfare at the arrival of the second era of *galácticos* and the appointment of what seemed a weak appointment in the placid Manuel Pellegrini, suggested that the Spaniard had learnt little from his previous mistakes. After all, the nature of modern day football meant that it was very unlikely a successful team could be moulded on the back of selected spending - €204m of Madrid's €272.5 outlay that summer was spent on attacking superstars such as Kaká, Cristiano Ronaldo, and Karim Benzema - under a meek manager.

Thus, while eventually appointing a superstar manager, like Mourinho, may have seemed the perfect way of taking the *galácticos'* brand to the next level - with the Portuguese on a world-record €14.8m annual contract and having a life-size cut-out of himself in his office - Mourinho was not about to lose track of what had made him such a successful manager: discipline, teamwork, and structure. Mourinho would even allude to this in his unveiling press conference: "I am José Mourinho and I don't change. I arrive with all my qualities and my defects."

Chapter 20

So, unlike Pellegrini's regime - when Pérez and Madrid's director general, Jorge Valdano, handled transfers and sanctioned the signings of commercial assets - money was more wisely spent in the summer of 2010 and several signings clearly had Mourinho's signature. After all, for 2010–11, Ricardo Carvalho offered Madrid the defensive maturity, experience, and solidity that they had been badly missing since Fabio Cannavaro left the club in 2009. Sami Khedira gave the midfield balance and energy. Ángel di María lessened the dependence on the right flank and on Ronaldo. And the diminutive Mesut Özil provided an unrivalled creative outlet in the final third. So, in not massaging individual, peak-aged brilliance - instead importing hungry, high quality young players - Mourinho looked to have found a sustainable middle ground in the once ill-fated *Zidanes y Pavones galácticos'* policy of the past.

David Mateos - a *Madrista* who Mourinho, personally, promoted from Real Madrid B into the first-team in 2010-11 - told me about two very different regimes: "Mourinho and Pellegrini were two completely different coaches who represented two totally different styles. Mourinho used an offensive tactic; Pellegrini was focused on playing possessive football. Personality wise, Mourinho was much more quick-tempered than Pellegrini, who has a calm personality. Like other coaches all over the world, Mourinho kept the 'one step' distance away from his players, but, crucially, he took away the responsibility from the players' shoulders.

"Training wise, I didn't see any major differences between Pellegrini and Mourinho. With Mourinho and Rui Faria, we were always training with the ball. The sessions had a physical part, too, but mainly we were dealing with the tactics... I owe a lot to José: he made me a European-level qualified player. It was a big honour for me to play for him and receive praise. I didn't get a first-team place for such a long time under three previous managers, but he released [Christoph Metzelder] from the team to give me a place... Before my debut against Ajax, he simply told me: 'If you do what you've been doing before, you'll be successful.'"

Jerzy Dudek - despite training more under the goalkeeping coach, Silvino Louro - was also impressed by the arrival of Mourinho: "José was a very nice man, who brought out the very best from us. If you had a problem, he was the first person who tried to solve it. This kind of understanding was very important to him... Working with him was unforgettable; time passed very quickly, because it was a fantastic experience... In my life, I have worked with many great coaches, but I'd be lying if I said that the first meeting with Mourinho in 2010 did not make a huge impression on me.

"Mourinho had such authority that, even with the stars at Madrid, he had a great impact. Funnily enough that was despite the fact that, during my days at the Bernabéu, he was not a coach with a huge amount of charisma. Of course, Mourinho could be very funny when he wanted but once he made a gesture, in that one moment, the joke was over; it was time to get back to hard work… He had no problems with communication, because he spoke Spanish very well. Don't forget, he worked previously in Barcelona with [Sir Bobby] Robson and [Louis] van Gaal. Because of that, all conversations took place without an interpreter; the messages were worded very clearly.

"Training sessions were very intense. Each session, even the smallest fragment, took place with the ball. It was quite amazing; I have never seen a coach for whom the exercises with the ball were so important. You could tell that even the most sophisticated training drill without the ball would not appeal to him; he was talking endlessly about the ball. Stamina and speed were also very important to him."

* * *

Just like at Inter, there were few signs at the Portuguese's unveiling that Mourinho and Madrid's press were to endure a difficult relationship. Although the issue of Mourinho's effective playing style was always going to be a stickler - along with Mourinho's half-knot tie, which bizarrely had a half-page analysis in *Marca* - Mourinho pointed to the fact that in three European finals, his teams had scored eight goals. Already Europe, Madrid's obsession, was dominating column inches and given Mourinho's continental pedigree, it was felt that Mourinho could finally deliver *La Décima* (Madrid's 10th European Cup) – particularly after knocking Madrid's eternal rival, Barcelona, off their perch with Inter previously. It was, arguably, the biggest job and challenge of Mourinho's career: "If you don't coach Real Madrid, then you will always have a gap in your career."

Far from Mourinho and Pep Guardiola stoking the flames from day one, though, the pair actually interacted amicably at UEFA's annual coaches' conference in Nyon in September, 2010: "Mourinho will improve me as a manager. It is important that he works in Spain, because he is one of the best in the world. He will make us all better." Even after Mourinho's first duel with Guardiola – the humiliating 5-0 defeat, *una manita*, at the Nou Camp on 29 November when Mourinho, ironically, was criticised for a lack of passion on the bench by Madrid's fans – the Portuguese did not make any controversial excuses or claims: "This is the first time I have ever been beaten 5–0. It is a historically bad result for us. It is not a humiliation, but I am very disappointed. It is sad for us, but it is not difficult for me to swallow. What's difficult to swallow is when you lose a game because you have hit the post or the referee has been bad. I have left here in that state before with Chelsea and

Inter Milan but that was not the case tonight. It is easy for me to take because it is fair. We played very, very badly and they were fantastic. We gifted them two goals that were bordering on the ridiculous. It is our own fault."

It was Guardiola's fifth consecutive *El Clásico* victory, with an astonishing 17-2 aggregate score. However, the season, up until this point, had been encouraging for Mourinho: Madrid were free-scoring and unbeaten in 19 games in all competitions. The Portuguese felt that this momentum could carry through into the Nou Camp and that Madrid could take on Barça at their own game, with Madrid making a decent 381 passes compared to Barcelona's 684. Now, though, Mourinho had to rally his weary troops, in the words of Dudek, substitute goalkeeper that night: "There was chaos in the locker room. Some players were crying, others were arguing, some looked to the ground. Mourinho then entered the locker room. He knew what had happened was awful for the team. We looked at him and he said, 'I know this hurts you. Perhaps for most of you it is the worst loss of your entire career. They are happy now and seem to have won the championship, but they have only won one game. This is just the beginning. There is still a long way to get the title. Tomorrow I will give you the day off, but do not stay in your houses. Go with your families, children or friends for a walk around the city. Let people see that you can overcome this. Perhaps people talk about the significance of this defeat, but do not hide behind it. You must show your manhood. After this defeat, we must fight for the title.'"

However, this humbling actually gave Mourinho an opportunity to take his plans to the next level. Mourinho forbade his players from facing the media after that match – a tactic designed to humiliate them privately and make them think about their performance, as opposed to solely protecting them – and planned to shift Madrid's playing style to serve as an antidote to Barcelona's brilliance rather than complimenting and imitating it.

From then on in, something clearly changed in Mourinho's approach, with Xabi Alonso and Sergio Ramos' purposeful yellow cards against Ajax and Mourinho's vigorous criticism of referee Carlos Clos Gómez's supposed 13 errors in an ill-tempered 1-0 victory against Sevilla on 19 December only the tips of the iceberg. Incidentally, Dudek was the man who passed on Mourinho's message to Casillas – who, in turn, told Alonso and Ramos. The Pole, though, has no regrets: "No one from UEFA even asked me for clarification [before the fine]. I have always worked as hard as I could and tried to help Real Madrid… I would rather have given that €5000 to a charity instead of UEFA's account. I did not, and do not, feel guilty."

Sure, Manolo Preciado, Sporting Gijón's late manager, had called Mourinho a *canalla* (scoundrel) after the Portuguese criticised Gijón's weak team selection against Barcelona on 24 September 2010 but Mourinho's spikiness was to reach an all-time high after that 5-0 defeat to Barça two months later.

Such was Mourinho's renewed hostility, it would even be felt within the safe haven of Madrid after Gonzalo Higuain seemingly picked up a fairly routine back injury in the winter of 2010. Madrid's medical department felt that the injury could be treated without surgery. Mourinho - who had only brought Rui Faria, Silvino Louro and José Morais with him to Madrid - had to put his faith in Madrid's medical staff but the ultimate result of this was that Higuain's back did not recover through non-surgical methods. Higuain was ruled out until May following surgery in Chicago, leaving Mourinho furious.

However, little did Mourinho know how important this injury would prove to the destiny of his reign; with Benzema as his only recognised striker, Mourinho's options were incredibly limited. Therefore, in the January window, the Portuguese requested that Jorge Valdano sanction the signing of a striker, with Ruud van Nistelrooy, Miroslav Klose, Emmanuel Adebayor, and, particularly, Hugo Almeida suggested by Mourinho. Valdano was weary: not only was Almeida Portuguese, the striker's representative was Jorge Mendes – the agent of Mourinho, Pepe, Carvalho, and Ronaldo. Also, Valdano, as the theoretical middle man between Mourinho and Pérez, needed to keep the peace.

The Argentine knew how much Benzema meant to Pérez, with Pérez having met the Frenchman's family in Lyon to convince them that Benzema should join Madrid in the summer of 2009. Valdano, who scored 56 goals in 120 games with Madrid from 1984-87, felt Benzema was more than qualified to lead Madrid's line. However, in Mourinho's eyes, Benzema was out of sorts: overweight, petulant, and out of form. Mourinho knew he could use the €35 million Frenchman as a pawn and even dropped him for the 1-1 draw with UD Almería on 16 January, 2011. It was an echo of when Mariano García Remón had dropped Ronaldo, the Brazilian great, in 2004 - and Mourinho was well aware that Remón had been sacked by Pérez within two weeks of that decision.

Something had to give and after Mourinho banned Valdano from travelling with the team, being in the dressing room, and attending the team's training sessions, the situation reached crisis point. Somehow, though, Mourinho managed to cocoon the dressing room. In the words of David Mateos: "Jorge was a good coach and a fantastic personality. He loved talking with the players… To be honest, at the Bernabéu, a lot of players and officials are always arriving and leaving the club, so I can't give a definitive opinion on what happened. All I can say is, I didn't feel any tension in the dressing room…"

Chapter 20

The chaos even led to Esperanza Aguirre, the president of Madrid's parliament, declaring, chillingly, in one of her first speeches after cancer recovery: "I'm with Mourinho to death." Tellingly, Pérez backed Mourinho – not just with the six-month loan signing of Adebayor from Manchester City, but, crucially, the removal of Valdano. It was an unprecedented move in Madrid's history - even dwarfing the monumental managerial power Fabio Capello was awarded by president Lorenzo Sanz in 1996-97 - with a landmark shift towards the English managerial model and, with it, increased power for Mourinho.

Little did the Portuguese know, though, that the real battle was just around the corner.

Chapter 21: Morbo

Laced in propaganda - and owing much to George Orwell's sympathetic account, *Homage to Catalonia* - popular history, wrongly, paints the Spanish Civil War in an extreme way. Barcelona was a city seemingly in ruins, while Madrid stood tall as General Franco's pet project. In actual fact, Madrid, not Barcelona, was the last city to gruesomely fall. It is one of history's great misconceptions to this day.

The traditional narrative reads as follows: Real Madrid, Franco's supposed centralist propaganda avenue, facilitated the immoral and repressive Nationalists and cheated their way to success 'with' the establishment's aid. Barcelona, the people's club of Catalonia, were the incredibly marginalised minority, the Republicans, who retreated to the safehaven of the Nou Camp and chanted, and triumphed, through adversity against the vast riches of Madrid.

For all the talk of Franco influencing Spanish football in favour of the capital, Barcelona won eight titles and nine Copa del Reys during Franco's 36-year dictatorship. This haul is only slightly eclipsed by Real Madrid's 14 titles and six Copa del Reys. Thus, it was not until the late '60s - when the Catalan club were, far from coincidentally, enduring a lengthy La Liga title drought - that FC Barcelona began to cultivate their image of being anti-Francoist.

Football and politics firmly overlapped in the Franco era, whether it was the shooting of Barcelona's martyr president, Josep Sunyol i Garriga on the front line in 1936, or the tapping up of Alfredo Di Stéfano - under Barcelona's nose - by Madrid in 1953. Fascism against democracy; nationalism opposing republicanism; good versus evil. These clubs could not help but get caught up in the passionate divide they embody in their respective regions. Even the meek Sir Bobby Robson, manager of Barcelona in 1996-97, was mobilised: "Catalonia is a nation and Barça its army."

Yet, it was no coincidence that it was under Mourinho that this *morbo* (hatred) re-surfaced and boiled over. After all, Madrid had been the epitome of a gentleman's club in the previous three decades. It must be stressed, too, that Madrid once shared a similar passion for the *cantera*, with four members of *La Quinta del Buitre* - Emilio Butragueño, Manolo Sanchís, Martín Vázquez, and Míchel - firing Madrid to five La Liga titles in a row between 1986 and 1990. Perhaps, it is worth noting that this glorious crop - which was the envy of clubs throughout Spain - broke into Madrid's first-team just seven years after the death of Franco.

Also, it is far from an exaggeration to suggest that these youth products inspired Johan Cruyff even further - in turning to the likes of Guillermo

Amor, Pep Guardiola, Albert Ferrer, Sergi Barjuán, Óscar García, Iván de la Peña, and Roger García - as Barcelona manager between 1988 and 1996. Indeed, even when Barcelona's vice-captain, Luís Figo, secretly signed a golden handshake with Florentino Pérez before crossing the divide in 2000, Real Madrid still paid the *la cláusula de rescisión* (release clause), a world-record fee of €60m. Also, Figo, a Portuguese, was not a *cantera* product.

Mourinho's plan of action, however, centred on reversing those decades of attacking football, crisp white shirts, and steadily improving relations - *señorío* - with Barcelona. David Mateos put it to me simply: "Mourinho approached the *Clásicos* like a boxer would a big fight… His antics surrounding them were all about taking the immense pressure away from the squad."

The fact that Pep Guardiola was to be involved, again, made it all the sweeter – despite the pair, seemingly, being on amicable terms following that UEFA conference in September. What accentuated the eventual fall-out and ill-feeling between the pair was the fact that Madrid were to play Barcelona a record four times in three different competitions in what Guardiola called "18 tremendously hard days" in April and May, 2011.

- La Liga game 16 April, 2011

- Copa del Rey final 20 April, 2011

- Champions League semi-final (first leg) 27 April, 2011

- Champions League semi-final (second leg) 3 May, 2011

If Guardiola had thought the 14-hour coach ride to Milan was the worst possible dose of Mourinho cabin fever in 2010, this was to set a new precedent.

So, while the first meeting, in the league on 16 April, may have seemed meaningless – with Madrid eight points behind the Catalans with only six games left – it was to prove landmark. The pressure at the Santiago Bernabéu was building, with Mourinho having lost his incredible nine-year 151 league home match unbeaten run against Sporting Gijón just two weeks previously. Thus, in a curious move, Mourinho let his assistant, Aitor Karanka, handle the press conference on the eve of the league game against Barça and, bizarrely, sat alongside him mute – leading to many of the attending journalists walking out.

Clearly, Mourinho was feeling the strain and just three hours before the first Barcelona game, the Portuguese's plans to play Pepe alongside Xabi Alonso and Sami Khedira were leaked. This was Mourinho's master plan for nullifying Xavi and the leak could only have come from within the club. Mourinho was incensed: "You are traitors. I asked you not to leak information about the line-up and you have betrayed me! It's obvious you are not on my side! The only friend I have is [Esteban] Granero, but I can hardly trust him! You have left me alone. You are the most treacherous squad I've had in my life!"

Tellingly, though, the dressing room rallied and followed Mourinho's niggling containment instructions to a tee – even when Raúl Albiol was sent-off early in the second-half. The influential and legendary Alfredo Di Stéfano - who was part of, arguably, the most attractive Madrid side of all-time, in the '50s - was left crestfallen, with a deep-lying Madrid having completed just 179 passes compared to Barcelona's 740 in 'earning' their 1-1 draw. The onlooking Argentine, Madrid's honorary president, even likened the contest to being akin to a lion facing a mouse. Mourinho, though, was unmoved and it seemed the Portuguese had found a way of adapting elements of his Internazionale strategy from 2009-10 with Madrid.

The second instalment, the 1-0 Copa del Rey victory just four days later - which saw Mourinho prevent Guardiola from winning a full set of trophies for the second time in three seasons - proved that Barça were not invincible and that Mourinho's style of football would continue to pay dividends. Having lambasted his seemingly treacherous squad only the previous weekend, Mourinho was now catapulted into the air in ecstasy by his team – capturing Madrid's first Copa del Rey for eight years.

It was Jerzy Dudek's first trophy at Madrid for three years and the Pole told me about Mourinho's preparations during those 18 days: "José can cope very well at the highest level; he loves the prestigious games. Mourinho showed what a great strategist he is during that final. He perfectly set out our team in that match, and the Copa del Rey trophy confirmed his genius. In previous years, the Copa del Rey was treated less seriously, but Mourinho did not want to hear those thoughts. That night, we saw once again that Mourinho possesses a great hunger for football and winning; none of his predecessors had it... I remember that during the pre-match briefings or during half-time in the games against Barcelona, he was predicting the scenario of the game. He said something like, 'If we don't play in this way, this [negative] *will* happen".

However, it must be stressed that while Madrid were far from proactive in the Copa del Rey final, they pressed high up the pitch in contrast to their ultra-defensive tactics in the previous encounter. Still, the victory gave Mourinho immense confidence and while he had been relatively quiet in the build-up to those two matches, this was to change radically for the Champions League

Chapter 21

semi-final a week later. After all, with Madrid, again, having finished the Copa del Rey final with ten men - after Ángel di María's sending off deep into extra-time - Mourinho taunted: "I have to train with ten men, how to play with ten men, because I go there with Chelsea, I finish with ten, I go there with Inter, I finish with ten and I have to train to play with ten men because it can happen again."

Coupled with this, Mourinho criticised Guardiola for supposedly lamenting correct referee decisions after Pedro's goal was correctly disallowed in the Copa del Rey final by Alberto Undiano Mallenco: "A new era has begun. Until now, there were two groups of coaches. One very, very small group of coaches who don't speak about refs and then a big group of coaches, of which I am part, who criticise the refs when they make mistakes – people like me who don't control their frustrations but also people who are happy to value a great job from a ref. Now there is a third group, which is only Pep, that criticises referees when they get decisions right! In his first season, [Guardiola] lived the scandal of Stamford Bridge, last year he played against a ten-man Inter. Now, he is not happy with refs getting it right. I'm not asking the referee to help my team. If the referee is good, everyone will be happy – except Guardiola. He wants them to get it wrong."

Amid the glare of the *Caverna mediática*, Madrid's media cave, Guardiola finally snapped. Remarkably, this was even before the pre-match press conference, at the Bernabéu, had officially begun ahead of the first-leg: "In this room, he is the chief, the f****** man. In here he is the f******man and I can't compete with him. I just want to recall that we were together for four years. I know him and he knows me. And that's what I hold onto. If he wants to hold onto the comments made after the Copa del Rey final….then he has every right to do so… José, I don't know which is your camera, but there you go."

Mourinho must have finally thought that he got under the skin of the otherwise calm Barcelona coach, but a rare public outburst from Guardiola was to invigorate Barcelona. The Barça squad even awarded the Catalan a standing ovation when he returned to the team's hotel. Thus, Madrid - with Mourinho returning to his deep-lying defensive tactics - had just 28% possession in a desperate 0–2 first-leg defeat and the flaws of Mourinho's containment strategy were brutally exposed. After all, Madrid's key creative outlet, Mesut Özil, would complete just two passes in the first-half and Cristiano Ronaldo constantly threw his hands up in the air in a lament of Madrid's caution. Pepe was sent-off on the hour mark, leaving Madrid without their crucial crux. And frustrated with Barcelona's play-acting and the referee, Wolfgang Stark, Mourinho was dismissed for complaining about

Pepe's red card. It was not supposed to be this way: Barcelona, not Madrid, were the team expected to crack.

Pepe was the sixth player to be sent-off in Mourinho's 13th career game against Barcelona. It led to Mourinho's most ludicrous post-match press conference of all-time, with his Barcelona obsession laid out for all to see in his impeccable recollection of Barcelona benefiting from certain refereeing decisions in Europe since 2009: "If I tell UEFA what I really think and feel, my career would end now. Instead, I will just ask a question to which I hope one day to get a response: Why? Why? Why Øvrebø? Why Busacca? Why De Bleeckere? Why Stark? Why? Because every semi-final the same things happen. The question is why? I don't know if it is the Unicef sponsorship or if it is because they are nice guys. They have power and we have no chance.

"Josep Guardiola is a fantastic coach, but I have won two Champions Leagues. He has won one Champions League and that is one that would embarrass me. I would be ashamed to have won it with the scandal of Stamford Bridge and if he wins it this year, it will be the scandal of the Bernabéu. I hope that one day he can win a proper Champions League. Deep down, if they are good people, it cannot taste right for them. I hope one day Guardiola has the chance of winning a brilliant, clean championship with no scandal."

It was a desperate monologue but, crucially, it was clear that Mourinho's siege mentality had taken off within his squad. Even Ronaldo, who was so vehemently against the fact that Madrid were playing the majority of the game in their own half, echoed his manager's conspiracy sentiments: "No, I don't like it but I have to adapt to what is asked of me. This is the way it is. We have a strategy. I feel bad for us and for Mourinho – because it always happens to him. Barcelona are a great team but these guys have a lot of power off the pitch too. Chelsea, Inter, Arsenal. It's always the same. Is that a coincidence?"

Madrid went on to draw the second-leg 1-1 and while it passed off without much incident - much owed to Mourinho's suspension, amid a wrongfully disallowed goal against Gonzalo Higuain - another low point against Barcelona was imminent. Remarkably, that was to come after Sergio Ramos dropped the Copa del Rey trophy under the wheels of the team's open-air bus celebrations on 13 May. Conveniently, and wistfully, it was the same date that Barcelona wrapped up the La Liga title.

* * *

Super Cups are rarely anything but curtain raisers: the final pre-season outing before the tenacity and aggression of competitive league fixtures return.

However, occasionally, they throw up anomalies – particularly when the country's two top teams are involved. Take the 1974 Charity Shield between Leeds and Liverpool, for example, when a horrified Brian Clough looked on as his boisterous captain, Billy Bremner, traded punches with Kevin Keegan. As long as there is a historic rivalry, even supposed friendlies can instigate moments of madness.

Still, Real Madrid's 2-2 draw with Barcelona in the Supercopa de España first-leg, at the Santiago Bernabéu, on 14 August 2011, would have been the perfect one-off tie. It was a much more encouraging result for Mourinho than the sides' encounter 109 days previously in the first-leg of the Champions League. Of course, it was not a competitive match but Madrid played without fear and, clearly, Mourinho had eradicated the scars of that desperate 0-2 defeat on 27 April. Remarkably, this was despite the fact that Mourinho did not start any of his new signings, namely Nuri Şahin, Hamit Altintop, José Callejón, Fábio Coentrào or Raphaël Varane. Karim Benzema, particularly, looked reinvigorated – having spent much of the summer in a health spa in the Dolomites to shed excess weight. The pattern of the game suggested a new chapter, too, with the tie devoid of late challenges, play-acting, and red cards.

However, three days later, the *morbo* returned, with eight yellow cards and three red cards being the mere tip of the iceberg in Barcelona's 3-2 second-leg victory. With 30 seconds of the match remaining, Marcelo's ugly scissors kick on Barcelona's prodigal son, Cesc Fàbregas, instigated it all in injury-time. It led to the two benches brawling, with the usually placid Mesut Özil and David Villa - who had both been substituted earlier - being shown red cards by David Fernández Borbalán. Although the result saw Pep Guardiola claim his 11th trophy as Barcelona manager - thereby surpassing Johan Cruyff as the club's most successful manager - it was Mourinho who was to steal the headlines.

As both benches emptied following Marcelo's tackle, Mourinho sneaked around the periphery of the 30-man brawl. The Portuguese made a beeline for Tito Vilanova, Guardiola's assistant, with Guardiola, wisely, having stayed out of it. Vilanova was the next best thing, with Mourinho having also taunted Dani Alves and Lionel Messi. Mourinho, revelling in the role of the 12th man as always, jammed his finger into Vilanova's right eye as his players continued to clash. Artfully, Mourinho aimed to slip away but Vilanova, and the television cameras, witnessed it and the Catalan reacted by pushing a smirking Mourinho in the back.

It was all so schoolboy, but there was something sinister about it. Mourinho could not plead the 'in the moment' defence; it all seemed pre-planned as he lurked at the back. Mourinho then referred to Villanova as *Pito* (penis) in a further act of disrespect in his post-match interview. Yet, unlike any other manager in world football, few seemed surprised by Mourinho resorting to such a heinous action. The fall-out was predictable: Gerard Piqué - echoing UEFA referees' committee chairman, Volker Roth, and his criticism of Mourinho following the Anders Frisk fiasco - described Mourinho as the "enemy of football". In contrast to that night in 2005, though, Mourinho would apologise – albeit one year later: "I should not have done what I did. The person who messed up there was me. I work a lot with my players precisely on this: control the emotions, only think about playing, and work well. The key thing is the negative image. As Tito said a few weeks ago, the footage will be there forever. There are no problems between him and me. The story is over and what needs to be done now is to make sure nothing similar happens again."

Philippe Montanier, the Frenchman who managed Real Sociedad between 2011-2013, told me that Barcelona brought the worst and best out of Mourinho in equal measure: "In the first two years, I think there was a real communion between Mourinho and his players as they felt he could help them put an end to Barça's hegemony… I don't think Mourinho has a complex about Barcelona. There are huge tensions around the events between Real and Barça, which - as unforgivable as it was - can account for such a gesture [eye gouge]. This was not to be helped by the coverage of the Spanish press, as they can be very harsh with the coaches and especially harsh with foreign coaches as I experienced at times. As far as I am concerned, I keep a very good memory of Mourinho. He always shows consideration towards less famous coaches like me; moreover, he is a very friendly person."

While it seemed that Mourinho had a squad that had wholeheartedly bought into the outrageous antics that were synonymous with his cult of personality, it was not to prove the most straightforward season for the Portuguese.

Chapter 22: The Only One

Iker Casillas, Spain's captain, was eager to ensure that his nine Spanish colleagues at Barcelona - who he had won the World Cup with only 13 months previously - did not hold Mourinho's antics against him. As a result, Casillas telephoned Barcelona's captain and vice-captain, Carles Puyol and Xavi, after the Supercopa debacle. When Mourinho discovered this, he immediately called a team meeting. The Portuguese pleaded with his Spanish players to keep faith with him, as the promise of Madrid's first major piece of silverware in four seasons dangled in front of them. Mourinho's captain, Casillas, was furious and unimpressed with the Portuguese's conduct: "Everybody in the same direction? What does that mean? All of us go in the direction that you want to go? That's the last time you make a s***of me in front of my *compañeros!*"

Despite this outburst - and Mourinho and Casillas not being on speaking terms for another month - this was just written off by the squad as a typical training ground disagreement. It did not affect morale greatly and the first crack in the dressing room was not to appear until after the 1–0 defeat to high-flying Levante on 19 September, when Mourinho criticised Sami Khedira for getting himself sent-off just before half-time. The red card was the turning point, as Arouna Koné put Levante ahead 30 minutes later, and Mourinho was furious. This irked the Madrid dressing room, who felt they had given a committed display. Then - in a bid to strengthen his position and warn the Madrid hierarchy of his undying popularity, amid being named *Rock Star of the Year* by the Spanish version of *Rolling Stone* magazine - Mourinho declared in an interview with the BBC on 26 December that he "would love to come back to England". Madrid's press saw this as Mourinho unethically - it was during the Christmas break in Spain - hankering for a move in the summer of 2012.

Within the confines of the squad, however, the most shocking episode of Mourinho's time at Madrid had not occurred. It was to come two days after the 1–2 Copa del Rey quarter-final first-leg defeat to Barcelona on 18 January 2012. Yet again, Barcelona were to be at the root of a fall-out for Mourinho. Having employed a press officer to compile a broad mix of newspaper cuttings every morning, Mourinho headed to Valdebebas, for training, the morning after the defeat in the knowledge of what his players had said to the press. Sergio Ramos, for example, declared post-match: "We follow the coach's tactics. Sometimes it works and sometimes it doesn't." Also, before Mourinho, himself, analysed the match, the Portuguese had a broad set of weaknesses to work on; weaknesses that the press had highlighted. One was Ramos' set-piece positioning:

Chapter 22

Mourinho: "You [guys] killed me [with your quotes] in the mixed zone."

Ramos: "No, boss, you have only read what it is in the press, not everything we said."

Mourinho: "Of course, as you are world champions and you are protected by your friends in the media… like the goalie."

Casillas [30 metres away, shouting]: "Boss, here things are said face-to-face."

Mourinho [ignoring Casillas]: "Where were you in the first goal, Sergio?"

Ramos: "Marking [Gerard] Piqué."

Mourinho: "But you had to mark Puyol."

Ramos: "Yes, but Piqué was blocking in the set pieces, so I decided to change the markings."

Mourinho: "What is going on now? You are now the manager or what?"

Ramos: "No, but depending on the situation of the game, there are times where the markings have to be changed. And as you were never a player, you don't know that these situations take place."

It was an incredible sequence of events, arguably the first time that Mourinho had so publicly - the transcript was leaked - been undermined and appeared so vulnerable and mortal. Mourinho believed the leak had come from Casillas, whose girlfriend, Sara Carbonero, is a sports reporter. Regardless, here was a man who never played the game at the highest level and while this was an irrevocable setback for Mourinho, the Portuguese delicately handled the situation. After all, Madrid were clearly united in rallying in the 2–2 second-leg draw at the Nou Camp a week later. Even Casillas was, briefly, back onside – belittling the referee, Fernando Texeira Vitienes, post-match: "I suppose you'll be going to party with the Barcelona players now." It was a key moment and Mourinho, even with his incessant media blackouts due to the immense pressure, went on to lead *Los Blancos* to the title with a league-record 100 points, a league-record 121 goals scored, a league-record 13 away wins and 32 wins overall, and a satisfying nine-point lead over Barcelona.

Manuel Pellegrini's prophetic grumbling, following his dismissal from the Santiago Bernabéu in the summer of 2010, that his successor would need to rack up 100 points was fulfilled. Mourinho, clearly, had united his players and staff under one flag and this was not lost on Philippe Montanier when his Real Sociedad side visited the Santiago Bernabéu on 24 March. Since he had been sent-off in a fiery 1-1 draw away to Villarreal three nights previously, Mourinho was suspended for the match so his meek assistant, Aitor Karanka, took his place on the bench. Far from sensing an advantage, Sociedad were humbled 5-1 and Montanier told me that facing a motivated Mourinho side was incredibly challenging – even without the Portuguese's unrivalled presence on the bench: "Mourinho's teams are very difficult to face as they play with such high intensity, both offensively and defensively. From a physical point of view, it is always hard to recover from those games. This was even the case when we played them when Mourinho was suspended in 2012. Even though Mourinho was not sitting on the bench, his team remained efficient as the match is the result of the work he did in training during the week. It said a lot that Mourinho could transmit his instructions through his assistant with the same vigour."

Sure, it was Barcelona's worst season under Pep Guardiola – with Barça winning just one trophy, the Copa del Rey – but Madrid's football was sumptuously consistent. Mourinho's exploitation of his obsession - transitions - led to some breathtaking results. Karim Benzema's fantastic goal against Getafe on 10 September 2011, for example, was owed to just six touches from five different players. Madrid counter-attacked with incredible menace that season and Cristiano Ronaldo's fine finish against Valencia on 19 November was another profound example, with touches from seven different players culminating in an incredible 15-second end-to-end finish. By the 17-game mark of 2011-12, Madrid had scored 61 goals and conceded just 16.

Clearly, *Los Blancos* had found their groove, a far cry from 2010-11, and it was the 1–2 victory over Barcelona at the Nou Camp on 21 April 2012 that turned the tide. After all, Madrid finally overcame their five-year hoodoo against Barcelona in La Liga. Ronaldo silenced his doubters with, arguably, the most important brace of his career up to that point. And, it was only Mourinho's second victory against Barcelona as Madrid manager in 11 attempts, as well as being Madrid's first win at the Nou Camp since 2007. Even Johan Cruyff could not help but pay tribute in his own unique, backhanded way: "The main problem for this version of Real Madrid has been to coincide with Guardiola's Barcelona. If this Barça didn't exist then Real Madrid would continue to reign supreme."

Mourinho had become the first manager in history to win titles in England, Spain, and Italy and it earned the Portuguese a new four-year contract, amid Mourinho's very public visit to Belgravia to look for houses in London after his daughter, Matilde, began studying at the Camberwell College of Arts.

Tributes flowed in from his squad with Ramos, the man who so audaciously questioned Mourinho's playing career, commenting: "We all knew this was coming under Mourinho. Very few coaches bring about change in the way he does. Real Madrid really needed an inspirational figure – someone with Mourinho's character and personality. We're lucky to have him. I learn something from him each day. He pays attention to every detail and that helps you to keep improving." The team's posterboy, Ronaldo, was also quick to pay tribute: "The boss is, first and foremost, my friend. Secondly, he's my coach. And, thirdly, he's a guy I admire and from whom I continue to learn a lot every day. I'm delighted to be working with him."

The stars were aligning: Mourinho's adversary, Guardiola, announced that he was to resign just a week before Madrid officially clinched the title, on 27 April. Guardiola was to be replaced by his unassuming assistant, Tito Vilanova. As Mourinho - decked out in a crisp white shirt and black slacks to match Madrid's colours - bowed to his squad as they lifted Madrid's first title in four years, it seemed the Portuguese was about to oversee his very first football dynasty.

Chapter 23: The Unravelling

As glorious as the La Liga campaign was, 2011-12 proved to be Mourinho's greatest opportunity to become the first manager to win three European Cups with three different teams.

Madrid were irresistible in Europe: cruising to the top of Group D with six victories, 19 goals, and just two goals conceded against Lyon, Ajax, and Dinamo Zagreb. *Los Blancos* then went on to defeat CSKA Moscow 5-1 on aggregate in the second-round and hammered APOEL 8-2 on aggregate in the quarter-final to set up a meeting with Bayern Munich. Avoiding Barcelona in a two-legged semi-final had been Mourinho's preference and even though the Portuguese fancied his chances in a one-off final with Barcelona - having defeated the *blaugrana* 1-2 in a one-off league match at the Nou Camp on 21 April - he held out a hope he would meet his old club, Chelsea, at the Allianz Arena on 19 May. Was it written in the stars?

Of course, it did not work out that way. Twice, Mourinho made questionable, negative decisions over the two legs. The first was to sit on Madrid's away goal equaliser from Mesut Özil on the hour-mark in the first-leg against Bayern Munich. Madrid had failed to deal with the towering Mario Gómez in the first-leg and Mourinho's contentment with a 1-1 draw meant that Madrid invited further swathes of penalty box bombardment from Bayern. This was accentuated by the fact that little threat was offered in response, particularly with Cristiano Ronaldo struggling with his counter attacking. The result was Gómez striking deep into stoppage time, to make the tie 2-1 in Bayern's favour - meaning Madrid had to race out of the blocks in the second-leg.

Yet, just like when Chelsea went 3-0 up inside 19 minutes against Barcelona in 2005, Madrid started similarly clinically and Ronaldo – who had unperformed in the first-leg – struck twice inside 14 frantic minutes. Madrid allowed Bayern to settle, though, and when Arjen Robben converted his penalty just before the half-hour mark, Mourinho seemed more concerned with the possibility of Bayern scoring another away goal than Madrid finishing the tie in normal time. The eventual penalty defeat - as Mourinho always does, despite Madrid missing three of their four spot-kicks - was put down to penalties being a mere lottery. Little did Mourinho know that this was his greatest chance of tasting European ecstasy with Real Madrid.

Still, Mourinho believed he would have, at least, two more cracks at the tournament with Madrid. Having guided *Los Blancos* to two successive Champions League semi-finals – which had not been achieved since 2003 – progress was, clearly, being made. Florentino Pérez - for all the focus on his plans to open a $1 billion Real Madrid theme park in Dubai - recognised this and Mourinho's power was to grow even further in the summer of 2012 after a new four-year deal was inked. Reflecting this, Mourinho personally met Michel Bruynickx, Standard Liege's acclaimed academy director, to devise the best way forward for Castilla. Also, following Gonzalo Higuain's injury misdiagnosis in 2010-11, Mourinho sought closer co-operation with Sanitas La Moraleja Hospital to improve the club's medical department – pointing to the legacy of the Milan Lab in prolonging players' careers, which AC Milan still enjoys today.

Thus, everything about the summer of 2012 seemed dynasty-focused, with Mourinho even refusing the cut-price €5m signing of his former Internazionale right-back, the 31-year-old Maicon. Little of Mourinho's traditional scorched-earth tendencies were evident and it must be noted that Hamit Altintop, Michael Essien, and Ricardo Carvalho were the only outfield players aged 28 or above that Mourinho recruited in six transfer windows with Madrid. Subsequently, with the signing of Luka Modrić – who had just enjoyed a stellar season with Tottenham – Mourinho's focus had shifted towards players aged 26 and under. An enquiry was even made for Gareth Bale, the 23-year-old who was about to become a world superstar.

Excitement was building and squad morale was at the highest it had been during Mourinho's reign as the players assembled for pre-season – influenced, undoubtedly, by the fact that Pep Guardiola was not to return to Barcelona. After all, Mourinho had recorded just two wins against Guardiola in 11 matches as Madrid manager. Far from this being just a problem at Madrid, Mourinho won only one game against Guardiola out of a possible four as Internazionale manager. Thus, there was a sense that without the Catalan present, Madrid - for the first time since Vicente del Bosque - would have a stable path and philosophy for an extended era of glory and dominance. Mourinho, in short, looked at peace with Spanish football and within himself.

Rejecting the idea of selling Sergio Ramos or Iker Casillas after that training ground clash five months previously, Mourinho's bond with the other Spanish members of the squad was never closer, too. After all, the Portuguese even spontaneously watched Spain play Italy at the Gdansk Arena in Euro 2012 on 10 June. Of course, for Mourinho, it was yet another way of antagonising the Catalonia/Castile tensions: "They talk about the national team and Barcelona but there are also five players from Real Madrid. I don't understand why they mix them because they are two distinct things. Spain isn't Barcelona. Barcelona were the champions of Spain. And I repeat, *were* the champions because now they are not."

With Madrid having defeated Barcelona on away goals in a good-spirited 4-4 aggregate Supercopa de España it seemed that everything was in place. So, with this harmony seemingly established, no one envisaged Mourinho having his worst ever start to a league season: claiming just four points from the 12 on offer in the first four league games. To put this into context, Mourinho had a record of 40 wins, 13 draws, and just 2 defeats in the first four league games of each of the previous 12 years of his managerial career. Therefore, given how Mourinho teams race out of the blocks, the signs were worrying: set-piece goals were conceded, Casillas made some uncharacteristic goalkeeping errors, and Mourinho's tactical aptitude was questioned, after desperately deploying six forwards for the final 15 minutes against Getafe.

In short, just 27 days into the season, the pressure was already on – with Madrid a whopping eight points behind Barcelona. *Los Blancos* had never overcome such a deficit.

Of course, with nine members of Madrid's squad having reached, at least, the semi-finals of Euro 2012, fatigue was an issue – with a four-game tour of the United States in August doing little to help matters. Mourinho, though, was not going to point to this as an excuse as each of the world's leading clubs had a similar number of players playing at the tournament and they, too, had overseas pre-season commitments.

Something else was not quite right and Ronaldo was to embody this with the declaration that he was sad after not celebrating his two goals during Madrid's 3-0 victory over Granada on 3 September. Far from this being owed to Madrid failing to acknowledge the Portuguese's dressing room status - with Kaká on the same salary as Ronaldo, despite not being an indispensable player anymore - it all came down to the upcoming Ballon d'Or. Ronaldo ranks his 2008 Ballon d'Or victory as his proudest career moment and felt Madrid were not supporting his 2012 campaign enough to overthrow the favourite, Lionel Messi. After all, Pérez did not even attend the prelude event, the Champions League draw and UEFA awards, with Ronaldo in Monaco on 30 August.

Ronaldo would point to Mourinho's precedent – his bold backing of Zlatan Ibrahimović for the Ballon d'Or in 2008 – but Mourinho had little time for what he saw as triviality: "Cristiano is doing a brilliant job. The symbiosis between the way the team plays and the technical and psychological strengths of this fantastic player means we are creating something which, God willing, will result in trophies. And team trophies are obviously more important than things like the Ballon d'Or or the Golden Boot."

Mourinho, himself, would not attend the ceremony in December – even though he was nominated for Manager of the Year – and he would go on to claim this was owed to the fact that several international captains, including Macedonia's Goran Pandev, voted for him but their votes did not go through amid Vicente del Bosque's victory. It was also a way of making a point to

Ronaldo, massaging the forward's ego in the press: "When someone with the same responsibility as me comes out and says: 'Mine is the best on the planet' then I have to say: 'Mine was not born in Madeira, he was born on Mars; he is not from planet Earth, he is the best in the universe.'"

Ronaldo's vanity did little to help the dressing room's focus, though, and after Madrid returned from a two-week international break, they were defeated 1-0 by Sevilla on 15 September. Mourinho was furious, having hauled off the desperately disappointing Özil and Ángel di María at half-time: "I made two changes at half-time; I could have made seven. There are very few whose heads are focused on football. Right now, I do not have a team." It was a disastrous opening to the season for Mourinho, with dissent growing and doubts creeping in the dressing room.

While the rigours of the Nou Camp led to Pep Guardiola losing his hair, enduring sleepless nights and suffering a spinal disc herniation, by the autumn, Mourinho had, on average, overseen an *El Clásico* match once every two months in two years at Madrid. The pressure was beginning to tell. Mourinho was bloated and greyer, favouring shapeless shell-suits instead of his usual demure fashion offerings.

Dressing room murmurings continued to stir, with Madrid's captain, Casillas, not taking part in a Happy Birthday video for Mourinho for Real Madrid TV and Ramos wearing Özil's shirt underneath his own against Deportivo La Coruña on 30 September in support of the dropped German. Mourinho was increasingly tetchy, too, even reading a 40-player list of quality *cantera* players who had left Madrid before he arrived in response to his failure to utilise young players. There was resentfulness in Mourinho's voice in recognising that Madrid had provided more players for other La Liga clubs than any other team. Among those mentioned included numerous one-time Spanish internationals, such as Álvaro Negredo, Diego López, Luis García Fernández, Juan Mata, Borja Valero, Roberto Soldado, and Javi García.

By the time of the 2-2 draw against Espanyol two months later, Mourinho had given up on the title. Madrid would go on to finish a mammoth 15 points behind the eventual winners, Barcelona - which was the largest gap between first and second in La Liga history. The rest of the season, and how Mourinho's time at Madrid would be viewed, therefore depended on the Champions League. Mourinho realised he could not afford for these games to be overshadowed by his rapidly diminishing grip on the dressing room, so he sought to send a message: dropping Casillas for the first time in a decade. It was always planned and, tellingly, only executed after conceding the title - following that draw with Espanyol on 16 December, 2012 - in the 3-2 defeat to Malaga six days later.

Mourinho, instead, preferred Antonio Adán – the 25-year-old who had started just three league games for Madrid in the previous two-and-a-half years. Mourinho was always going to die by this decision - even with Casillas' patchy form up to that point - and Madrid's defence looked even shakier than usual with Adán in goal. After all, in Adán's second appearance of the season, against Real Sociedad 15 days after that Malaga defeat, the nerve-stricken goalkeeper was sent-off after just five minutes. The Bernabéu erupted, knowing that Mourinho had no other choice but to send on Casillas – and he did.

Jerzy Dudek, who was backup goalkeeper to Casillas between 2007 and 2011, reflected on Mourinho's decision: "Mourinho has incredible strength, but I don't think he told the truth when he claimed that Adán was in better form than Casillas. Adán seemed, to me, at least a class below Casillas. But, in that season, Iker didn't save Real as often as he did when I was at Madrid. Back then, he was a hero in nearly every second match."

The parallels with Newcastle United's Ruud Gullit dropping Alan Shearer, a man who also embodied the club, in 1999, were stark and regardless of the result of the next 32 games of the season in all competitions, Mourinho would have to continually defend his decision to drop Casillas. Unlike Gullit, though, Mourinho was to see out his bold decision - with the press mischievously talking of Mourinho calling-up his 12-year-old son, José Jr, from Madrid's Canillas Academy ahead of Casillas - and the Portuguese even signed the 31-year-old goalkeeper Diego López on a free transfer in January. Remarkably, though, there was no open opposition from the squad to Mourinho's bold move as David Mateos - who arrived at Real Madrid as a 12-year-old in 1999 - told me: "I'm not sure if it was a good idea to drop Iker. He is a legend of Real Madrid, but it was Mourinho's choice. The coach always has to take the responsibility and nobody can question him after his decision." Still, perhaps, it was telling that Mourinho's eventual successor, Carlo Ancelotti, would also prefer López – albeit 'only' for La Liga matches.

Regardless, Mourinho seemed to relish establishing a siege mentality within a siege mentality, being well aware of the fact that Casillas and Ramos had stormed into Pérez's office in the New Year and declared that if Mourinho remained as manager in 2013-14, they would walk. There was even talk that Mourinho would be sacked over the Christmas break, with a world-record compensation fee being readied.

Yet, one matter could save Mourinho's legacy and patch the squad together to focus on those final five months of 2012-13: *La Décima.*

[Losing 1-0 at the Nou Camp but defeating Barcelona 3-2 on aggregate]
"It was my most beautiful defeat."

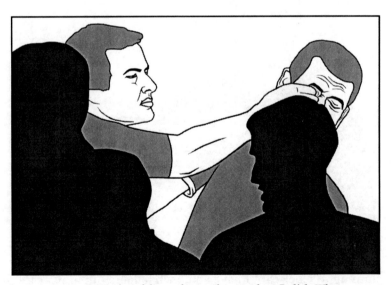

[On the eye gouge] "I should not have done what I did. The person who messed up there was me."

[On his travails with Madrid in 2012-2013]
"Right now, I do not have a team."

[On returning to Chelsea] "I have some white hairs but in my case that's a
good sign. It means I am better now than before."

Chapter 24: The Outsider

One thought was going to get Mourinho through those testing five months: Luis Carniglia, the man who led Madrid to European Cup triumphs in 1958 and 1959.

Carniglia, in 1959, was, arguably, the last man to mastermind a European Cup victory amid uncertainty and in-fighting. After all, the Argentine had lost the Madrid dressing room – dominated by the egos of world-class talents such as José Santamaría, Francisco Gento, Raymond Kopa, Héctor Rial, Alfredo Di Stéfano, and Ferenc Puskás – due to his conduct with the mighty Puskás.

The popular, but burly, Puskás was still one of the world's greatest forwards at 32 years of age. However, Puskás had not played football professionally for two years after receiving a two-year ban from UEFA for refusing to return to Hungarian heavyweights, Honvéd, after a friendly in Brussels amid the Hungarian Revolution. Thus, when Puskás' signature was sanctioned by Madrid's then president, Santiago Bernabéu, at the beginning of the 1958-59 campaign, the Hungarian was 15kg overweight. Carniglia, at the very least, saw Puskás as a vanity signing by Bernabéu and knowing that his treatment of Puskás was already going to cost him his job, the Argentine, nonetheless, decided to drop Puskás for Madrid's 2-0 European Cup final victory against Stade de Reims.

Similarly, Mourinho knew that not even *La Décima* could save his job. Sure, the Portuguese had already won a battle with one Madrid alumnus, Jorge Valdano, but Iker Casillas was another matter in Florentino Pérez's eyes. Not only is Casillas the greatest goalkeeper in Real Madrid's history, he symbolises so much more. The Spaniard broke into Madrid's first-team at just 18 years of age in 1999 and even when he lost his place, Casillas reclaimed it in spectacular fashion. Coming on as substitute for the injured César Sánchez for the final 25 minutes of the 2002 Champions League final against Bayer Leverkusen, Casillas made a series of astonishing saves to help Madrid win the trophy. Casillas then went on to become Madrid's captain, figurehead, and most capped goalkeeper, which was a running parallel to the goalkeeper leading Spain to their historic golden age between 2008 and 2012. Put simply, Mourinho had struck at the heart of *Madristas* with his treatment of Casillas, the greatest Castilla Academy graduate since Raúl González in 1994.

So, while Mourinho had become the first ever Real Madrid manager to have his name chanted at the Bernabéu, in 2011-12, this practice was only continued by Real Madrid's *Ultras Sur* as Casillas' treatment worsened. In fact, such was the state of affairs by the time Madrid played Atlético Madrid, on 1 December, Mourinho strutted out onto the field 40 minutes early and challenged *Los Blancos'* supporters to jeer him; remarkably, they did not. It seemed, therefore, that the club could pull together going into the New Year, with the carrot of a Champions League tie against Manchester United dangled in front of them.

Thus, just as a cloud was hanging over Mourinho regarding his conduct in Serie A - when Inter met Chelsea in the Champions League in 2010 - a second-round tie against Manchester United would bring yet another chance for welcomed English rejuvenation. Sure, Mourinho had met Manchester City at the Etihad Stadium only two months previously in his 100th Champions League game, but Old Trafford, and Sir Alex Ferguson, hold special significance for Mourinho – particularly when it comes to knockout football.

Neither side had greatly impressed in the group stages, with Manchester United having scored just nine goals and conceded six in claiming 12 points from a possible 18 against Galatasaray, CFR Cluj, and Braga in Group H. Madrid, in contrast in Group D, had a much more difficult group, facing three different league champions in Borussia Dortmund, Manchester City, and Ajax. Nothing suggested Madrid could differentiate their patchy form in La Liga with Europe, though, and this chaos was epitomised by the fact that Mourinho's team conceded nine goals in just six group games.

Qualification was achieved, but now Mourinho had to rally his weary troops for an assault on Europe. To think, Mourinho had once taunted Rafa Benítez, in 2007, by suggesting Liverpool were favourites for their semi-final tie against Chelsea because they were able to pool their resources for one major competition. Now, unashamedly, Mourinho had to do the same, with Diego López, Michael Essien and the precocious Raphaël Varane coming into the first XI for the final months of the season.

Hosting Manchester United at the Bernabéu for the first-leg, Mourinho knew Ferguson would attack and the eventual 1-1 draw was far from a disaster in the Portuguese's eyes. This was despite the fact that Madrid had never overcome such a scoreline, and not since Dynamo Kyiv in 1999 had a home team progressed in the Champions League after drawing the first-leg 1-1. Still, Mourinho relished the unlikely odds and knowing that Ferguson would seek another goal, eventually, played into Mourinho's hands.

Madrid had lost eight of their previous 20 away games that season and a common theme had emerged: Mourinho's counter-attacking tactics proved futile when Madrid had to be on the front foot against the opposition. Here, at Old Trafford, that was not the case. In fact, it appeared that the proactive United were very comfortable – with Nemanja Vidić hitting the post in the first-half – and relished being on the front foot. The fact Vidić's header did not go in – regardless of Sergio Ramos' own goal after half-time, which did not change the fact that Madrid still had to score – gave Mourinho encouragement, though. After all, the last time the Portuguese had visited Old Trafford, with Internazionale in 2009, a Vidić header from a corner had ended the tie before it ever really began, just three minutes into the second-leg.

Then, with Nani's fairly harsh sending-off by referee Cüneyt Çakır before the hour mark, it seemed that Madrid were to have the luck that all, eventual, European champions require. Nonetheless, it is often forgotten how bold and decisive Mourinho was that night: the Portuguese immediately threw on Luka Modrić for Alvaro Arbeloa after Nani's sending-off and Madrid had just three defenders on the pitch. What a contrast this was to Mourinho's timid response to facing a Bayern side who were on the ropes in the semi-final second-leg a year earlier.

Just seven minutes later, Modrić struck a fantastic 20-yard finish and, near-immediately, Cristiano Ronaldo slid in Gonzalo Higuain's cross against his former club. In Mourinho's conveniently humble eyes, the better team had lost but, ultimately, Ferguson was outfoxed as much as outraged by the sending-off.

* * *

It is rare that anyone outside the football club enters Mourinho's circle but he made an exception for Abel Rodriguez, a metro station cleaner from Los Angeles. Rodriguez, a massive football fan, had flown over to Spain in February in a bid to get a ticket for *El Clásico* at the Bernabéu. Having worked as an unpaid ball boy for Madrid during their pre-season tour in Los Angeles the previous summer, Rodriguez headed to their Valdebebas training ground upon arrival in the hope of being recognised. Security turned Rodriguez away, but one man noticed him out of the corner of his eye when leaving the training ground in his Range Rover with Rui Faria: Mourinho.

The Portuguese immediately booked Rodriguez into the team's hotel, invited him to dinner, and gave him VIP tickets for the game, which Madrid went on to win 2-1. Mourinho then invited Rodriguez into the dressing room post-match, where Rodriguez posed for photographs with Cristiano Ronaldo and the attending Diego Maradona. While these were already a series of extraordinary gestures, Mourinho then offered Rodriguez the job of kit man for Madrid's second-leg clash against United at Old Trafford. Rodriguez was so overwhelmed that he burst into tears.

Rodriguez returned to Los Angeles with an incredible experience, having bagged a match ball as well as shirts worn by Javier Hernández, Mesut Özil, Kaká, and Michael Essien following that 1-2 victory at Old Trafford. More memorably, though, Mourinho declared that Rodriguez had become Madrid's good-luck charm, with his stomach having been rubbed by each of Madrid's squad before that momentous win at the Theatre of Dreams.

* * *

It, wrongly, seemed Madrid had turned a corner and this buoyant atmosphere continued for Mourinho when *Los Blancos* were drawn with Galatasaray in the quarter-finals. It was a chance to catch up with Wesley Sneijder, Fatih Terim, and Didier Drogba. Such was the warmth of the run-up to this tie, Terim made a point of giving Mourinho several convivial embraces when he realised the Portuguese was in the stands scouting Galatasaray's game against Kayserispor on 17 March. Madrid, though, failed to impress: defeating Galatasaray 5-3 on aggregate but only ever just doing enough and lacking the urgency and hunger required to make a strong challenge for the trophy. It was as if most of the Madrid dressing room were going through the motions - with Sergio Ramos and Xabi Alonso picking up purposeful yellow cards, yet again - and merely counting the days until Mourinho inevitably departed.

Thus, Madrid would have to raise their game considerably in facing Borussia Dortmund in the semi-final, having failed to defeat the German side in two attempts in Group D five months previously. Mourinho had become the first manager to lead four different teams to the Champions League semi-finals but Dortmund – with their attractive playing style, progressive structure, and quality young side – were far from out of their depth. Also, with Jürgen Klopp at the helm, a shift in dynamic was established in the run-up to this match. In essence, the German is one of the few remaining tracksuit managers, who only dons a suit for Champions League games. So effortlessly charismatic, quirky, and good-natured, Klopp had established himself as one of football's most likable coaches – who also possessed a dangerous tactical brain.

Klopp's refreshing enthusiasm and quick-wit reminded the football world of the charm and lustre Mourinho seemed to have lost, despite equalling Sir Alex Ferguson's record of seven Champions League semi-finals. After all, Klopp's cheeky comment that a Dortmund victory would be like Robin Hood taking from the rich echoed Mourinho taunting Ferguson and his superior budget as Porto manager in 2004. Thus, just as Mourinho guided Porto to their first European Cup final for 17 years, in 2004, Klopp would follow suit in defeating Madrid 5-4 on aggregate to help Dortmund reach their first Champions League final for 16 years. It seemed, echoing Mourinho outfoxing Ferguson in 2004, that a relatively new name was to upset the established order.

Given how news of the talismanic Mario Götze's departure to Dortmund's bitter rivals, Bayern Munich, was leaked on the eve of the first-leg, Klopp's achievement was made all the more astounding. It appeared that the Mourinho Bible would need some revisions but, admittedly, Mourinho's preparations for the 4-1 first-leg defeat on 24 April were not helped by the benched Ángel di María's fatigued state of mind – following the birth of his son in Argentina – and the ineffectiveness of the blunted Özil on the wing. However, Mourinho had few excuses, and Madrid's limp showing in the first-leg defeat proved a bridge too far.

Deep down, Mourinho knew the tie, and his time at Madrid, was over, and the Portuguese refused to take part in a rabble-rousing video for Real Madrid TV before the second-leg: "I did not want to do the video because I think the best way to motivate the fans is with football. People work in other areas at the club and they think [a video] is good. I am a football coach, that is how I motivate them. They do videos, I do football."

Mourinho had reached three Champions League semi-finals with Madrid, a personal best given that he led Porto and Internazionale to just one each and Chelsea to two. However, this campaign had been the most difficult of Mourinho's career, with 15 of Madrid's players voting that Mourinho be sacked at the end of the season in an anonymous survey conducted by Florentino Pérez in April. The Portuguese looked in desperate need of a sabbatical in his post-match press conference after the 3-1 victory in the second-leg six days later. His once glowing olive complexion was now peaky and leathered; his once slicked salt and pepper locks now shorn and white; bags hung under his eyes, with his enthusiasm for football seemingly eroded.

A once unthinkable avenue for rejuvenation remained, though: Chelsea Football Club.

Chapter 25: Home

"I want to be where people love me."

It was a cliff-hanger. With Mourinho's post-match interview with ITV's Gabriel Clarke having been tantalisingly cut short due to advertising obligations, the world could only speculate about whether this was a desperate final roll of the dice by Mourinho or if a return to Stamford Bridge really was on the cards. Just a week before Sir Alex Ferguson was to shock the football world with the public announcement of his retirement, it could not have been better calculated by Mourinho. This was the man, after all, who appeared so stale in comparison to Jürgen Klopp's wit and charisma in the run up to these games.

Would Madrid sack him? Had things been patched up with Roman Abramovich? Was it proverbial bait for Manchester United, with Mourinho later claiming that he was told of Ferguson's retirement in advance? Or was Mourinho, merely, using Chelsea's speculated interest as a bargaining position for a move to Paris Saint-Germain or Manchester City? It was media box office: a return to form from Mourinho but, also, a reflection of his desperation and vulnerability as he stared down the camera longingly. Yet again, at his time at Madrid, Mourinho looked mortal and, again, his fate was out of his hands. After all, during the previous three summer occasions that the Chelsea job had become available, since the Portuguese's departure in 2007, Mourinho's name had always been optimistically touted by Chelsea's fans. Now, it was different – Mourinho was the one to issue the come-and-get-me-plea. Mourinho, like Chelsea, had run out of options.

With the timing of Mourinho's declaration coming after the confirmation that it would be 11 years since Madrid last made a Champions League final, it certainly was a narcissistic act. However, Mourinho knew he had to rectify that blot - not winning *La Décima* - with another club as soon as possible. The Portuguese is a tireless worker, whose longest period out of the game was a mere nine months between September 2007 and June 2008. A voluntary sabbatical, like Pep Guardiola in 2012-13, was never an option.

Instead €200 was spent in IKEA on cardboard boxes to pack his belongings, and given that he was willing to put his Chelsea legacy on the line, clearly, Madrid had affected Mourinho deeply. Unlike the occasions when he had left União de Leiria, Porto, Chelsea, Internazionale and, even, Benfica, few tears were wept upon Mourinho's departure. In fact, so ignominious were the final days, Iker Casillas, Pepe and Cristiano Ronaldo cited 'back pain' in their refusal to take part in Mourinho's final game, against Osasuna on 1 June. In contrast to when Marco Materazzi cried on Mourinho's shoulder in 2010, Ronaldo - who Mourinho believed was too precious to take criticism - would smirk as he stared an emotionless Mourinho down in the catacombs of the Bernabéu pre-match. The press, though, were loving the drama of it all and the match was even stopped at one point because 20 over-zealous photographers surrounded the snarling Mourinho as he prowled the Bernabéu's touchline one last time. It epitomised a hollow end for Mourinho, with the Portuguese only waving to the *Mourinhistas*, the *Ultras Sur*, in the south end and not addressing the media post-match.

The consolation of the Copa del Rey trophy had not even been provided after a 1-0 defeat in the final to Atlético Madrid 15 days previously. It was Real's first defeat to Atlético for 14 years and a frustrated Mourinho was sent-off for arguing with the officials deep into the second-half. So exasperated was Mourinho, he even refused to collect his runners-up medal from King Juan Carlos. It was moments like these that led to Andrés Iniesta declaring that Mourinho had damaged Spanish football. Iniesta's assessment was an echo of his team-mate Xavi's comments in 2010: "Mourinho is a great coach, but he will not enter the history of football. To go down in history you must do different things, and he does not bring new things to the game."

Still, one cannot help but look back on that 2011-12 campaign without some admiration; Madrid played some of the most ruthless counter-attacking football that had ever been seen in Spain. Barring Casillas, Mourinho had the dressing room wholeheartedly on side; the cult of personality had long been established against the enemy, Barcelona. Failing to defeat Bayern in the semi-finals, though, allowed doubts to creep in.

Also, in truth, Mourinho had not, and has not, yet proved himself as a manager who can elevate a team into a three-year spell and given the unsustainable flames he stoked as Madrid manager, it was never a feasible long-term project. Sure, Madrid's squad had an average age of just 25 and Mourinho was, remarkably, La Liga's longest-serving manager at the time, but these were just superficial facts. A stubborn, superstar-filled squad - particularly with the self-centred egos of the likes of Casillas, Pepe, Sergio Ramos, and Ronaldo, who were already long at the club before Mourinho arrived - meant a stable partnership with a superstar manager was never going to be enjoyed.

It may seem a similar story with Mourinho's second act at Chelsea but there is one crucial difference. The key dressing room figures – namely Petr Čech, John Terry, and Frank Lampard – are already indebted Mourinho disciples. The same can be said of the other members of the squad to have played under Mourinho, namely Hilário, Ashley Cole, Michael Essien, and John Obi Mikel. These seven players make up an influential bloc of Chelsea's squad and when one considers that the future of the club - Thibaut Courtois, David

Luiz, Nathaniel Chalobah, Wallace, Ryan Bertrand, Juan Mata, Oscar, Marco van Ginkel, Ramires, Eden Hazard, André Schürrle, Kevin de Bruyne, and Romelu Lukaku - have yet to reach their peaks, this is an even more intriguing project.

Of course, with Mourinho having only signed a new four-year deal at Madrid in May 2012, the Portuguese's return to Chelsea seemed a sudden opening of convenience rather than a typical, Mourinho-plotted ploy. Yet, there was something fateful about Roman Abramovich returning to Mourinho after the chaos of Rafa Benítez's seven-month interim reign. After all, what attracted the Russian to Benítez – who he very nearly appointed instead of Roberto Di Matteo in February, 2012 – was the fact that the Spaniard often thwarted Mourinho. Between 2004 and 2007, Chelsea met Liverpool 16 times and Mourinho recorded just seven victories – failing to progress past the Reds in the Champions League semi-finals twice in the process.

Yet, turning to a man who served as Mourinho's antithesis – with Benítez having claimed he would never take the Chelsea job after criticising Chelsea fans' use of plastic flags in 2007 – was a PR disaster. Admittedly, a Europa League win and third place in the Premier League was an admirable return amid the vitriol Benítez received from the majority of Chelsea supporters. Also, in fairness to Abramovich too, he had always planned for Pep Guardiola to take over in the summer of 2013 and it was far from a coincidence that recent signings - such as the likes of the dimunitive Mata, Oscar, and Hazard - all fell under Guardiola's *prueba de la muneca* (doll's test) profile. Thus, Abramovich naively felt, if Guardiola could not be convinced - perhaps Benítez's pedigree might have, somehow, won the fans around to merit a permanent appointment. Of course, with the shadow of Mourinho still looming over Stamford Bridge – and in replacing a club hero like Di Matteo – Benítez never stood a chance as such a passionate Liverpool figurehead from 2004-10.

Events saw Abramovich's popularity – while not affecting Chelsea's fans gratitude towards him for his £2 billion investment since 2003 – take a hit for, arguably, the first time since Mourinho's departure in 2007. The Russian knew that while a Chelsea manager lasting longer than three-and-a-half years has never happened under his ownership, having six different managers in the previous five years was a shocking statistic and an unsustainable pattern to continue with a young squad in the coming years. Thus, turning to one of the best managers in the world, Mourinho, was far from a ploy of sentimentality or a way of solely eradicating the bizarre interlude of the Benítez era.

Also, unlike similar Second Comings such as Sir Matt Busby, Kenny Dalglish, Howard Kendall or Kevin Keegan when they returned to Manchester United,

Chapter 25

Liverpool, Everton and Newcastle United respectively, Chelsea and Mourinho are of similar statures when judged against the start of Mourinho's first spell. Therefore, the idea of Mourinho resuming the instant success he first delivered as Chelsea manager does not seem anywhere near as delusional as the above-mentioned.

Sure, it may have seemed that Chelsea have moved on considerably since Mourinho's departure in 2007 - with the historic double under Carlo Ancelotti in 2010 and, finally, the Champions League under Di Matteo in 2012 - but the club has lacked a tangible identity due to the constant turnover of figureheads. That is why Abramovich desperately sought Guardiola as the man to finally deliver the attractive blueprint - which could also be implemented within Chelsea's Academy at Cobham - that would make the rest of Europe envious.

While Mourinho's playing style is not as proactive as Guardiola's - when on song, Mourinho has an unrivalled ability to impose his identity on a squad. Given his history at Chelsea, this will be a lot easier to convey than as a Portuguese at Spain's most divisive club, Real Madrid. This is why the free-roaming Hazard partly-quipped that he would be intimidated by Mourinho in his first few training sessions. Mourinho, more than any other manager in the world, is a stickler for the smallest details and has an unrivalled managerial aura. For mercurial talents like Hazard, the thought of their natural game being adapted by Mourinho's methodology and tactics is, initially, disconcerting. Yet, at the same time, it would be far from a coincidence to see a bulkier Hazard's consistency, defensive work, and goalscoring progress onto the next level in the coming seasons and for Mourinho to mould him into a player he may never have become without the Portuguese's unique tutelage.

The same can be said for an experienced player like Fernando Torres, who has thrived under Mourinho's methodology as a much more aggressive threat. Having played under five different managers at Chelsea since 2011, Torres has finally settled at Stamford Bridge – owed much to Mourinho – and recovered strands of his once trademark change of pace. Also, not since that infamous pre-season in the summer of 2004, has a Chelsea squad looked so happy in pre-season – owed much to the undying popularity of Mourinho's ball-playing double sessions. This was just one of the reasons why Abramovich had no qualms in awarding Mourinho an £8.5m annual salary, a four-year contract, and buying Rui Faria, Silvino Louro, and José Morais out of their staff contacts with Real Madrid. Clearly, Abramovich trusts Mourinho and his staff to lead this Chelsea – which has finally emerged from a delicate transition stage after a fairly inconsistent three years – to mount the club's first sustained title challenge since winning the double in 2010.

Regarding the title race, too, it has never been a better time to make a radical u-turn in appointing Mourinho again; the top three English sides have undergone the most chaotic period of upheaval since 1974. That summer saw Don Revie depart the champions, Leeds United; second-placed Liverpool's legendary manager, Bill Shankly, retired; and third-placed Derby County's former manager, Brian Clough, replaced Revie at Elland Road for his ill-fated 44-day spell.

However, as well as a more tactically adept Premier League compared to 2004, it must be noted that this is the first time Mourinho has returned to a club as a manager and, far from coincidentally, Mourinho is entering a club on the back of failure for the first time in his career. To think Mourinho once lambasted his Madrid predecessor, Manuel Pellegrini, for finishing as runners-up: "Second place is just the first loser. If Madrid were to fire me, I wouldn't go to Malaga. I'd go to a top-level team in Italy or England."

Ironically, Mourinho has proven to be a man of his word in this instance, but compromises have had to be met. Mourinho has agreed to work alongside Michael Emenalo - the abjectly-qualified technical director who even tendered his resignation in the wake of Mourinho's arrival - at Chelsea and, while lavish, the Portuguese has had his lowest transfer outlay, £58 million, since that infamously frugal summer in 2007.

As always, too, Mourinho has tweaked his persona upon being appointed, and calmness will be required amid the politics and pressures of Stamford Bridge. Reflecting this new 'Happy One' persona, Mourinho has talked continually of stability, legacy, and dynasty. Thus, Mourinho's, seemingly, 'unrevealing' unveiling press conference at the Harris Suite on 10 June was perfect evidence of the above-mentioned, with Mourinho using the word happy 18 times and the word stability on 22 occasions. It is clear, following Sir Alex Ferguson's retirement, that Mourinho is relishing the opportunity to become the Premier League's Godfather.

Regarding taking Ferguson's place, one only has to look at the fact that the Scot did not win his first English title - Manchester United's first for 26 years - until the age of 51 after seven testing seasons in English football. Also, Ferguson won 'only' 18 of his eventual, mammoth career haul of 49 trophies by the age of 52 in his 19th year of management; Mourinho, by contrast, lifted 20 trophies at the same age in just 13 years of coaching. This puts into context the startling reality that world football may not have yet seen the best of Mourinho. There remains a hunger deep in the Portuguese to oversee a five to ten-year project with his "beautiful young eggs", and to match Bob Paisley's record of three European Cups.

* * *

Chapter 25

One matter that has not changed since 2004 is Mourinho's suaveness as Lauren Cochrane, fashion writer with *the Guardian*, told me; "I'm not sure if he's set a new trend for what managers wear since coming back - though it does seem even Paul Lambert has even taken up his V-neck this season! AVB [André Villas-Boas] - Mourinho's apprentice, as some call him - is kind of like Mourinho mark II. Although, that may be down to both men coming from Southern Europe, where men traditionally tend to dress better and take more care of their clothes… If you think about most managers in the Premier League, it's still either the standard suit or tracksuit affair. David Moyes has even gone a bit retro with his monogrammed suit… Pep Guardiola is probably Mourinho's closest rival in fashion terms and, obviously as an Arsenal fan, I think Arsène Wenger has always looked suave!

"In terms of style, I would score Mourinho 7/10. He has, definitely, subtly changed his look as time has gone on and become more Dad friendly - like with that collared jumper [against Norwich]. We've yet to see *the* coat though – that's what I'm intrigued by!"

* * *

Still, even if his marked restraint does not last, it certainly is a different Mourinho to the brash figure who waltzed into an unnatural environment, Stamford Bridge, in 2004. After all, would the Mourinho of 2005 not have bid for Wayne Rooney before a crucial match against Manchester United because of ethical concerns? Indeed, for all the talk of Mourinho and Chelsea gazumping Tottenham with their 11th hour bid for Willian – who had already held a medical at Tottenham's Enfield Training Centre – Abramovich had targeted the Brazilian since the summer of 2011. Chelsea, technically, did nothing wrong and Abramovich, clearly, has briefed Mourinho about the importance of maintaining Chelsea's improving image around the world. Following the horrors of the Anders Frisk incident and the tapping-up of Ashley Cole during the Portuguese's first reign, it was essential that Mourinho grew into this calmer persona.

Mourinho has even built bridges with Arsène Wenger, the man he once referred to as a voyeur: "I had a chance to meet him much, much better when I left England and I started meeting him in UEFA [coaching meetings], at the Euros, the World Cup. I think I met him a few times, we had dinner and so on. And when you are not in the same league and when you are not playing against each other, it is easier to get to know people, it is easier to go deeper. It is easy to speak about football. He's a very nice guy. I wouldn't bet for one single problem between us."

Refreshingly, too, the Portuguese has also talked at length about the need to comply with Financial Fair Play - which is partly why the cheaper, but proven, Rooney and Samuel Eto'o were chased ahead of Falcao and Edinson Cavani - and utilise the fantastic young players that Chelsea have mass-imported since 2011. This is far from Mourinho being out of his comfort zone or compromising greatly, either, as the Portuguese has always held an ambition to oversee a dynasty and deviate away from the criticism he has received for creating a scorched earth environment in leaving older players at the club upon departure.

As early as 2005, when Mourinho had led a Chelsea squad with an average age of just 25 to their first title in 50 years, the Portuguese had alluded to this thirst: "I started my career in the youth academy at Barcelona so I know perfectly how to work with young players, their strengths and weaknesses. I won the Champions League with Porto thanks to the first goal scored by an 18-year-old [Carlos Alberto]. He started that season with the reserve team but in December, for several reasons, I called him into the side."

Still, this is a Chelsea side that will desperately require Mourinho's paternal instincts and need even more tactical harnessing than the class of 2004-07. After all, suffering the worst start to the Abramovich era - with just seven points from a possible 12 in the Premier League and losing Chelsea's first home game in the group stage of the Champions League, against Basel, for ten years - was hardly part of the script. Also, initially, Mourinho sidelined figures who, far from coincidentally, thrived under Benítez – namely César Azpilcueta, David Luiz, Fernando Torres and, particularly, Juan Mata. Even though this Chelsea side have gone on to thrive and enjoy harmony under Mourinho, Abramovich had, already, sounded the dreaded knock on Chelsea's dressing room door after the Basel defeat.

Yet, it seemed fitting that Mourinho's triumphant return at Chelsea, against Hull City on 18 August, overlapped with the celebration of the ten-year anniversary of Abramovich's ownership. Arguably, the two most influential figures in Chelsea's recent history were back together. From Mourinho - wearing a two-piece suit and tie for one of the first times in three years - blowing kisses to the Chelsea fans after their raucous welcome, to Abramovich's image being cheered on the big screen, there was a rare sense of serenity and shared popularity at Stamford Bridge. Egos were in check and Mourinho did not milk the adulation – gesticulating to Chelsea's fans to chant for their team, rather than their manager.

Nearly a decade on from first working for Abramovich, the conditions may seem different. Mourinho has white hair, uses an iPad in training, bears a tattoo of his family's name on his wrist, and Chelsea have since won the

Chapter 25

Champions League. However, Mourinho's desire will only have increased in his 14th year of management. The passion he displayed in rousing Chelsea's fans in the dying moments of the 'meaningless' 2013 European Super Cup against Guardiola's Bayern Munich was a perfect illustration of this. Clearly, the cult witch doctor is again back amongst his tribe, with a delirious Mourinho having even leapt into the crowd after Torres' last minute winner against Manchester City on 27 October.

How long this stable dynamic lasts remains to be seen, but the idea of Abramovich upsetting Mourinho's work environment with botched experimental appointments again seems unlikely - given that Frank Arnesen and Avram Grant have long departed - and the Russian's last major appointment in the club hierarchy was Emenalo in 2011. Thus, the chance to rejuvenate at the 'safe haven' of Chelsea will only strengthen the possibility of Mourinho becoming, statistically, the greatest manager of all-time by the time of his planned retirement at the age of 65 in 2027. As well as further club success, the idea of Mourinho winning the 2026 World Cup with Portugal is hardly far-fetched.

Madrid has wounded him, but a better, battle-hardened Mourinho will emerge.

Appendix A - List of multiple European Cup winners

Name	No. Of EC's	Age at first EC win	Year	Team
Bob Paisley	3	58	1977	Liverpool
Béla Guttmann	2	62	1961	Benfica
Sir Alex Ferguson	2	57	1999	Manchester United
Helenio Herrera	2	54	1964	Internazionale
Jupp Heynckes	2	53	1998	Real Madrid
Stefan Kovács	2	51	1972	Ajax
Nereo Rocco	2	50	1963	Milan
Dettmar Cramer	2	50	1975	Bayern Munich
Vicente del Bosque*	2	49	2000	Real Madrid
Ottmar Hitzfeld *	2	48	1997	Borussia Dortmund
Ernst Happel	2	44	1970	Feyenoord
Carlo Ancelotti *	2	43	2003	Milan
Brian Clough	2	44	1979	Nottingham Forest
Arrigo Sacchi	2	43	1989	Milan
José Mourinho *	2	41	2004	Porto
Luis Carniglia	2	40	1958	Real Madrid
Miguel Munoz	2	38	1960	Real Madrid
Pep Guardiola *	2	38	2009	Barcelona
José Villalonga	2	36	1956	Real Madrid

*= still managing

Appendix A

Age at last EC win	Year	Team
62	1981	Liverpool
63	1962	Benfica
66	2008	Manchester United
55	1965	Internazionale
68	2013	Bayern Munich
52	1973	Ajax
56	1969	Milan
51	1976	Bayern Munich
51	2002	Bayern Munich
52	2001	Bayern Munich
67	1983	Hamburg
47	2007	Milan
45	1980	Nottingham Forest
44	1990	Milan
47	2010	Internazionale
41	1959	Real Madrid
44	1966	Real Madrid
40	2011	Barcelona
37	1957	Real Madrid

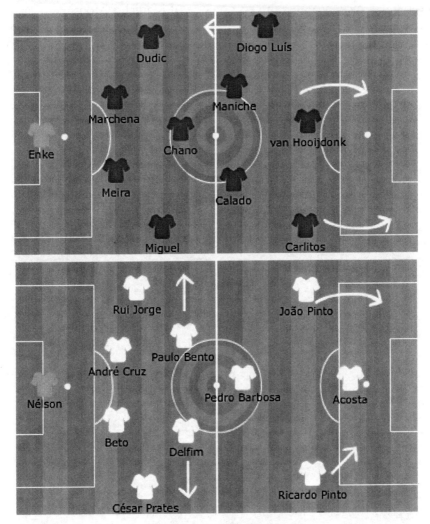

Benfica 3 -0 Sporting

Van Hooijdonk (p) 41' - João Tomás 77', 82'

3 December, 2000. A result still eulogised by *Benfiquistas*, particularly given the fact it was Mourinho's last game in charge and was against the champions. Having worked with Sir Bobby Robson and Louis van Gaal for a combined eight years, it was little surprise that tactical ingenuity came naturally to Mourinho as a manager. The Portuguese pinpointed Cesar Prates and Ricardo Pinto as Sporting's dangermen so made a point of bringing in the defensive-minded 20-year-old Diogo Luís to neutralise these marauding flankers' threat.

Appendix B

Sporting's manager, Augusto Inácio, in contrast to Mourinho, allowed his full-backs to press high up the pitch with the cover of Delfim and Paulo Bento. However, Sporting's midfield was left stretched - particularly by the emerging technical qualities and composure of Maniche. Mourinho - sensing that the leggy veterans, André Cruz and Beto, were vulnerable on the run - encouraged his team to launch quick balls over the top and in behind. This proved inspired.

***

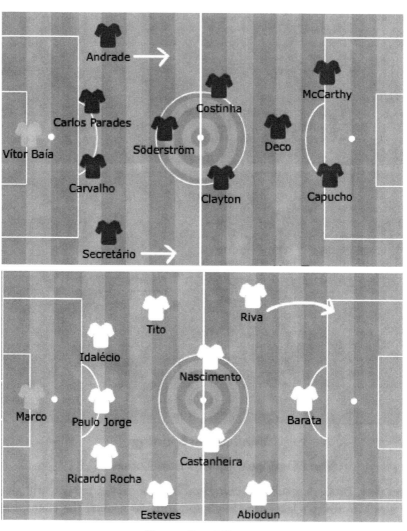

Braga 0 – 4 Porto

McCarthy 33', 39', 74', Postiga 89'

20 April, 2002. Leiria had been an important foundation in the tactical evolution of Mourinho, particularly with regard to honing one of his future trademarks: attacking full-backs. So, while Nuno Valente and Paulo Ferreira had not yet arrived, Carlos Secretário and Jorge Andrade were hugely important to giving Porto's narrow midfield width in 2002. It had defensive purposes, too, with Secretário neutralising the nimble Riva's threat by pushing him back into his half. Elsewhere, the free-roaming Deco, at the tip of Mourinho's diamond, repeatedly pulled Paulo Jorge and Ricardo Rocha, in particular, out of position. This allowed McCarthy to continually beat the offside trap, with Braga's outnumbered midfield offering little cover.

**

Celtic 2 – 3 Porto

Appendix B

Larsson 47', 57' - Derlei 45+1', 115', Alenichev 54'

21 May, 2003. Aside from the imminent arrivals of Pedro Mendes and Carlos Alberto, this would go on to be the first XI that would win the Champions League a year later. Celtic, though, were an incredibly dogged side and with 80,000 Celtic fans having made the trip to Seville, the passion and roar of Parkhead was replicated. Mourinho saw a weakness in Alan Thompson, who was an out of position left wing-back not wholly comfortable under the high ball. As a result, Ricardo Carvalho and Jorge Costa continually hit long diagonals, with Capucho and Maniche constantly double-teaming on the Englishman. Elsewhere, while Martin O'Neill had wisely tasked the tireless Neil Lennon with picking up Deco, the often underrated Dmitri Alenichev was left free and the Russian played a part in two of Porto's three goals.

***

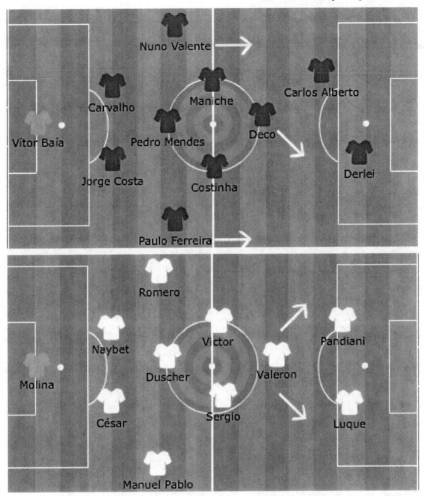

Deportivo 0 – 1 Porto

Derlei 60'

4 May, 2004. Given how one-sided Porto's 3-0 victory against Monaco in the Champions League final proved, this was the real test. Mourinho is always content with a draw at home in the first-leg – a 0-0 in draw in this instance – but Deportivo had won all six of their previous games at the Riazor in the Champions League that season and had kept clean sheets in every single one. They had also hammered Milan 4-0 in the previous round. As a result, Benni McCarthy and Dmitri Alenichev were sacrificed, with Pedro Mendes shackling Juan Carlos Valeron. In the battle of the number 10s with Valeron, it was Deco who dazzled and continually got inbetween the lines. The Portuguese's quick use of the ball proved pivotal to Porto dealing with Deportivo's incessant pressing and even when Porto lost possession, Mendes,

Appendix B

Costinha and Maniche were so well-drilled by Mourinho that it rarely resulted in Deportivo even getting into the final third.

***

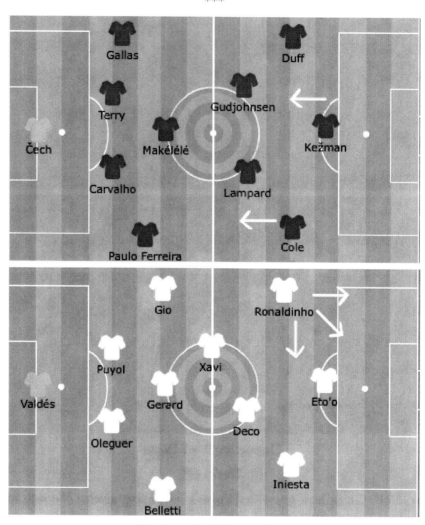

Chelsea 4 – 2 Barcelona

Gudjohnsen 8', Lampard 17', Duff 19', Terry '76 - Ronaldinho (p) 27', 38'

8 March, 2005. Ironically, despite missing the suspended Didier Drogba – who would go on to prove a constant thorn in Barcelona's side as a focal point – Chelsea were well set up for taking on the might of Barça. The blunted Mateja Kežman often came deep to close down Deco alongside Eidur Gudjohnsen, while Joe Cole's improved defensive ability was crucial in limiting Ronaldinho's threat somewhat. Having so much pace in abundance allowed Chelsea to race out of the traps, target Giovanni van Bronckhorst

and storm into a commanding lead, which proved pivotal to their eventual victory. The most intriguing tactical aspect of this match, though, was Mourinho's back four, which mirrored the key component of Helenio Herrera's *catenaccio* playing style at Internazionale. Mourinho, wary of the free-roaming of Deco, Andrés Iniesta and Ronaldinho, did not let Paulo Ferreira or William Gallas cross the half-way line and, in fact, Gallas often moved centrally to form a three-man defence with John Terry and Ricardo Carvalho.

***

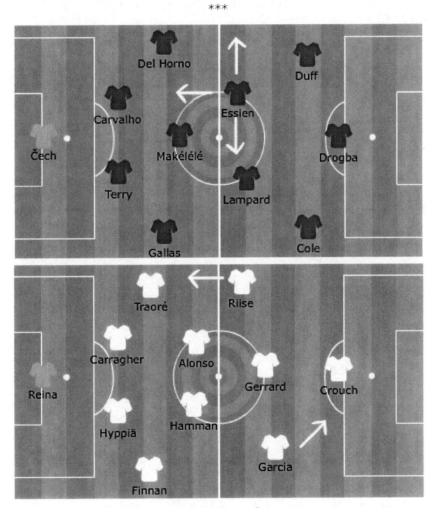

Liverpool 1 – 4 Chelsea

Gerrard 36' - Lampard (p) 27', Duff 43', Joe Cole 63', Geremi 82'

2 October, 2005. Considering this match was just four days after Chelsea had failed to break down a dogged Liverpool outfit in a 0-0 draw at Anfield in

Appendix B

Group G of the Champions League, the result may seem something of a surprise. Remarkably 19 of the 22 who started that game would, again, start this one. The difference? As well as Liverpool having had their worst Premier League start for 13 years, a possessed Didier Drogba. The Ivorian came of age in English football during this match, playing a part in all four of Chelsea's goals. Coupled with Michael Essien's man marking of Steven Gerrard – which would be, again, echoed to great effect under Guus Hiddink in 2009 – Chelsea ran riot and brutally exploited Liverpool's weak, defensive left flank.

***

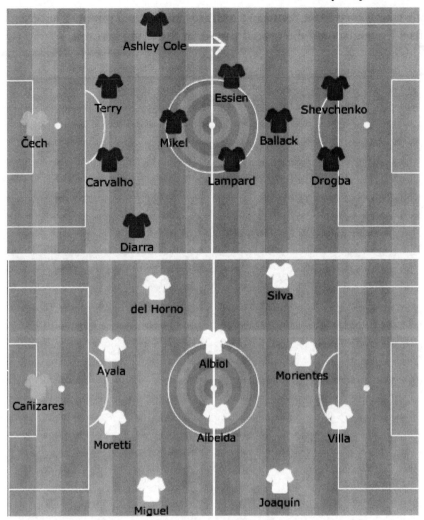

Valencia 1 – 2 Chelsea

Morientes 32' - Shevchenko 52', Essien 90'

10 April, 2007. Just like when Porto played Deportivo in 2004, Mourinho faced a daunting away leg: Valencia had lost just three Champions League games at the Mestalla out of a possible 32. Chelsea, having drawn the first-leg 1-1, would need goals. With David Silva having effortlessly roamed in the first-leg, Mourinho set his team out to frustrate Valencia, with John Obi Mikel tasked with shackling the Spaniard in a bid to disrupt Valencia's rhythm and create a scrappy game. Valencia striking first in the second-leg actually suited Chelsea and having an extra man in central midfield – as opposed to Salomon Kalou on the flank – allowed Chelsea to dominate possession. It seemed fitting, therefore, that after one midfielder, Michael Ballack, forced a

breath-taking save from Santiago Cañizares in the final minutes, another, Michael Essien, scored the crucial winner in the dying seconds.

***

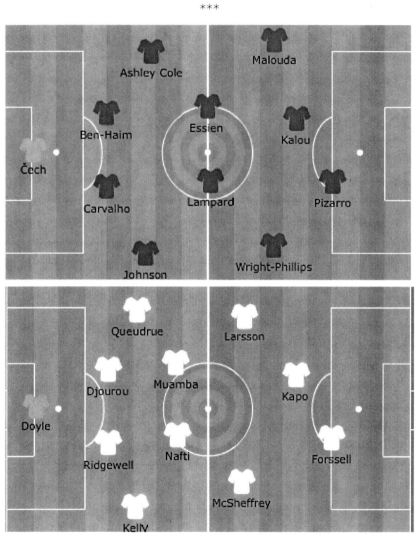

Chelsea 3 – 2 Birmingham City

Pizarro 17', Malouda 31', Essien 50' - Forssell 15', Kapo 36'

12 August, 2007. This was the result that sealed Chelsea's English top-flight record for most home league games unbeaten, 66 games. However, it was far from a fitting result for a Mourinho team with Chelsea having conceded two goals at home in the Premier League just six times previously from a possible 58 league games under the Portuguese. Admittedly, Chelsea were under-strength and Roman Abramovich's thirst for more expansive football saw

Mourinho shift to an attacking 4-4-2 formation. However, the newly-promoted Birmingham would go on to finish 19th that season. Worryingly, too, despite dominating swathes of this match, a blunt Chelsea conceded two goals against the run of play. None of the Mourinho hallmarks – wingers tracking back, defensive cover from central midfield or timed full-back runs – were evident and it was clear that Mourinho was unable to strike a delicate balance with Chelsea's new philosophy.

***

Manchester United 2 – 0 Internazionale

Vidić 4', Ronaldo 49'

Appendix B

11 March, 2009. Following Inter's poor performance in the first-leg, Mourinho rung the changes. Gone were Nelson Rivas, Cristian Chivu, Sulley Muntari, and Adriano; in came Iván Córdoba, Davide Santon, Patrick Vieira, and Mario Balotelli. Inter's shape stayed the same but Mourinho felt that the pace and exuberance of Inter's teenagers, Santon and Balotelli, could hurt United on the counter. Of course, when Nemanja Vidić headed United in front so early on, the onus was now on Inter to attack. Even though Mourinho had lost just once in his previous 13 encounters with Sir Alex Ferguson, this was always going to be a big ask of his still-evolving Inter project. Inter's spine lacked the pace, quick-wit, and finishing required to penetrate a strong United side and despite hitting the woodwork twice, Ronaldo's goal after half-time ended the contest.

***

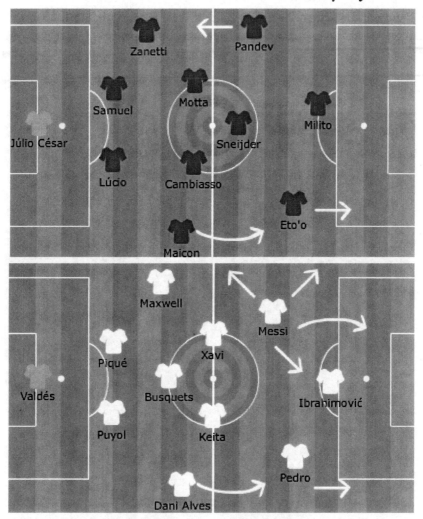

Internazionale 3 – 1 Barcelona

Sneijder 30', Maicon 48', Milito 61' - Pedro 19'

20 April, 2010. While Inter's heroics in the second-leg seemed even more impressive, going down to ten-men forced Mourinho's hand in shifting to an ultra-defensive shape. Therefore, the first-leg was a much more intriguing tactical battle and Mourinho made every single one of Pep Guardiola's usually dynamic threats look somewhat predictable. Goran Pandev prevented the usually dangerous Dani Alves from shuttling down the flank, thereby reducing Barca's width greatly. Esteban Cambiasso diligently harried Lionel Messi. And, of course, Walter Samuel and Lúcio double-teamed on the static Zlatan Ibrahimović. While this sounds an incredibly simple assessment of how Inter stopped Barcelona, it was testament to Mourinho's drilling and

Appendix B

Inter's incredible tactical discipline. Given Inter's dramatic increase in effectiveness on the counter, it was, perhaps, little surprise that there were only five survivors from the toothless display against Manchester United 13 months previously.

***

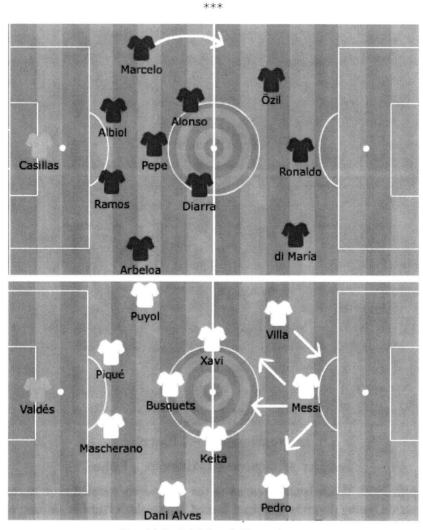

Real Madrid 0 – 2 Barcelona

Messi 76', 87'

17 April, 2011. Arguably, the ugliest match in Champions League history with unseemly play-acting, horrific tackling, and petulance marring the sides' first meeting in Europe for nine years. Madrid played incredibly deep, targeting a 0-0 draw, and an ambitious 35-yard strike from Cristiano Ronaldo in the first-half was their only notable attack. With Xabi Alonso so pre-occupied with his

defensive duties, Madrid had no creative threat or even a platform to retain possession. Still, somehow, Madrid held out until Pepe's red card on the hour mark - which gave Barcelona an extra man in midfield and allowed a free-roaming Lionel Messi to exert even more influence. Tellingly, therefore, both of Barcelona's goals were owed to spectacular runs from deep by the talismanic Argentine.

***

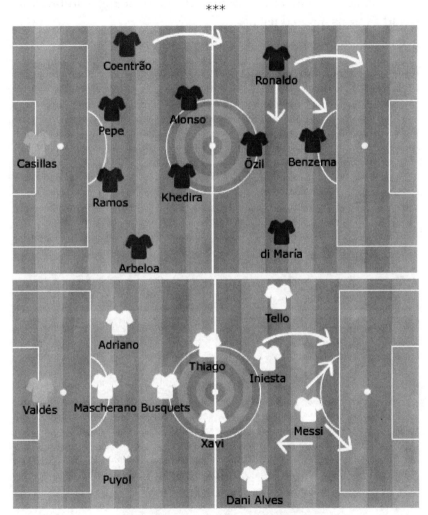

Barcelona 1 – 2 Real Madrid

Sánchez 70' - Khedira 17', Ronaldo 73'

21 April, 2012. Far from the title already being over, had Barcelona won this match, they would have moved within just one point of Madrid with four games to play. Madrid had the tougher run-in, too, with games against Sevilla and Athletic Bilbao to come. Therefore, this was a momentous result for

Madrid and given how both sides had endured difficult away trips in their respective Champions League semi-final first-legs days earlier, both were on a level footing. Just one year after the Bernabéu debacle in the Champions League, Madrid's evolution under Mourinho was plain to see. Madrid pressed high and took full advantage of Pep Guardiola's surprising shift to a 3-4-3 when numerous chances presented themselves. In fact, Madrid had six shots on target, double the number that Barça did, and their ability to break so swiftly and clinically proved telling.

***

Borussia Dortmund 4 – 1 Real Madrid

Lewandowski 8', 50', 55', 67'(p) - Ronaldo 43'

24 April, 2013. Having brought Luka Modrić in for the benched Ángel di María – owed to his fatigued state of mind after the birth of his son in Argentina – Mourinho clearly wanted to dominate this game. After all, this was one of his most attacking line-ups in his time at Madrid. Mourinho felt, with Madrid's added composure in midfield, Dortmund would be frustrated and would struggle to win the ball. It was as if Mourinho was trying to address the failings of the semi-final in the previous year, which was also against a German team, Bayern Munich. Dortmund, though, played without fear and Madrid's central midfield was constantly snapped and double-teamed by a hungrier Dortmund outfit. The shrewd rotation and inter-change of Mario Götze and Marco Reus proved particularly difficult for Madrid to marshal, with Mesut Özil and Cristiano Ronaldo offering little protection to a noticeably shaky and leggy defence.

***

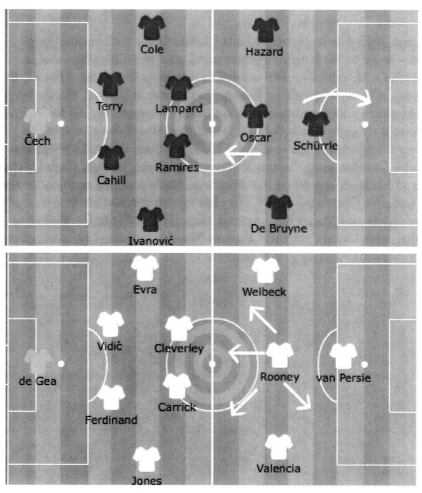

Manchester United 0 – 0 Chelsea

26 August, 2013. While much was made of Mourinho, supposedly, fielding no striker in a 4-6-0 formation – given that Samuel Eto'o had not yet arrived – it is important to stress that André Schürrle played right on the shoulder of Rio Ferdinand and Nemanja Vidić. Mourinho, clearly, felt – compared to the slower Fernando Torres and Romelu Lukaku – that Schürrle had the mobility to get in behind United's formidable defence and drag them out of position. With Oscar coming deep to assist Frank Lampard and Ramires, this, theoretically, seemed a smart tactic – given the pace and pattern of Chelsea's evolving counter-attacking play under Mourinho. However, the fact that both these sides faced each other so early in the season – and were both desperate not to lose – meant that they ended up cancelling each other out. Epitomising this, ironically, it was Wayne Rooney – who had an incredibly disrupted pre-

season, amid Mourinho and Chelsea's interest – that looked the most committed, on-song, and fit.

"After being on the Barça coaching staff, nothing else measures up."

On Barcelona, 1996.

"I always remember with a little smile that after I was upset after a defeat, he said, 'Don't be sad because in the other dressing-room, someone is bouncing around with happiness.'"

On Sir Bobby Robson's influence, 1996.

"Bring your sister along and we can find out if that's true."

On AS journalist Santi Jiménez's taunts that Mourinho was Sir Bobby Robson's boyfriend, 1996.

"It's no good scoring a wonder goal and then spending the other 89 minutes sleeping."

On Ronaldo's distaste of pressing for Barcelona, 1996.

"Today, tomorrow, always with Barcelona in my heart."

At Barcelona's civic celebration after their Copa del Rey win, 1997.

"When I spoke with van Gaal about going back to Portugal to be an assistant at Benfica, he said: 'No, don't go. Tell Benfica if they want a first-team coach you will go; if they want an assistant you will stay.'"

On rejecting Benfica's offer to assist Jupp Heynckes, 1999.

"I would only ever coach Real Madrid to destroy them: I will never stop being a culé."

Upon leaving Barcelona, 2000.

Appendix C

"I was nine or 10 years old and my father was sacked on Christmas Day. He was a manager, the results had not been good, he lost a game on December 22 or 23. On Christmas Day, the telephone rang and he was sacked in the middle of our lunch."

On understanding the ephemeral nature of football management, 2000.

"Don't doubt that sooner or later that I will go to a bigger club. And when I go, some of you are coming with me."

A prophetic opening statement to the União de Leiria squad, 2001.

"It was one of the worst Porto teams for decades"

Upon taking over at Porto, 2002.

"I'm sure that Porto will be champions at the end of my first full season."

Upon his unveiling at Porto, 2002.

"I made the point of walking on alone, before the team. I had never been a first-class player who could feel, for example, what Figo had felt upon returning to Barcelona. Upon hearing the whistles and jeers, I felt like the most important person in the world."

On returning to the Estádio da Luz as Porto manager, 2002.

"I don't shake hands with people I don't know."

On refusing to shake hands with Jaime Pacheco, Boavista's manager, 2003.

"Do you have a brother or cousin in Ivory Coast because I don't have the money to bring you to Porto!"

Upon meeting Didier Drogba for the first time, 2003.

"Pressure on the linesman, everybody!"

One of the suspended Mourinho's messages to the Porto bench from the stand during the UEFA Cup semi-final second-leg against Lazio, 2003.

"It was unforgettable...not unrepeatable".

On Porto's ground-breaking campaign, 2003.

"It is the first time that an injury so severe has happened to a player of mine since I'm coach and it is a very strange feeling. We cannot rely on the player for a long time and because it's César, the sadness is too big. We thought we'd found the player we wanted for the left flank. When he injured himself, I immediately thought that in terms of the team, we'd have to return to the 4-4-2 formation, as without César we couldn't play with three forwards. Together, we have to overcome this situation, but it's a shame what happened. It's a shame also for Portuguese football because, for sure, [Luiz Felipe] Scolari was already eyeing him."

On César Peixoto's anterior cruciate ligament injury, 2003.

"One of the most important things I learnt from Bobby Robson is that when you win, you shouldn't assume you are the team and when you lose, you shouldn't think you are rubbish."

On the fine line between victory and defeat, 2004.

"From my childhood, I had friends at the top of the social classes and friends who lived with great difficulties. This made me be prepared for everything in life and to know how to co-exist, to live and get along with everyone. It was a time of change in Portugal and for me, a very positive life experience that prepared me for a lifetime."

On growing up in a nation in flux, in 2004.

"You would be sad if your team gets as clearly dominated by opponents who have been built on 10 percent of the budget."

Taunting Sir Alex Ferguson after Porto defeated Manchester United 2-1 in the Champions League second-round first-leg, 2004.

"I don't think it's fair, really. It is not true that the Portuguese player is an actor. It's a result problem, I think."

On Sir Alex Ferguson's initial criticism of Roy Keane's sending off during the first-leg defeat to Porto, 2004.

"It's time for people to stop speaking about my past and start speaking about my recent past, because I did what almost nobody has done."

Upon winning the Champions League with Porto, 2004.

"Liverpool are a team that interests everyone and Chelsea does not interest me so much because it is a new project with lots of money invested in it. I think it is a project which, if the club fail to win everything, then Abramovich could retire and take the money out of the club. It's an uncertain project. It is interesting for a coach to have the money to hire quality players but you never know if a project like this will bring success."

On the initial choice between Liverpool and Chelsea, 2004.

"If I wanted to have an easy job, working with the big protection of what I have already done before, I would have stayed at Porto – beautiful blue chair, the UEFA Champions League trophy, God, and after God, me."

On seeking a new challenge, at Chelsea, 2004.

"Please don't call me arrogant, but I'm European champion and I think I'm a special one."

Mourinho's infamous declaration at his unveiling as Chelsea manager, 2004.

"I wanted to show them that I can be a sweetheart but at the same, can be very nasty: 'Hey, last two seasons, eleven matches – why? You play nothing, you don't work, you don't sleep, you are always injured. You say the manager was s***, racist and did not like you?'"

One off the record meeting with a member of the Chelsea squad, 2004.

"You are already a rich boy, you won a lot of money, you are still in a big contract. So no problem with your future about money, no problem about prestige in your home country. When you go back to Romania, you will be one of the kings. But five years after you leave football, nobody remembers you. Only if you do big things. This is what makes history."

On meeting Adrian Mutu for the first time, 2004.

"You have always to be there. If the plane is full from Argentina, come by bus. You can call. There's always a solution."

On Hernán Crespo arriving late for pre-season, 2004.

"Nobody in the club can tell me to buy a player. But they can say to me, you don't buy the player you want!"

Reminding the world just who handles transfer activity at Chelsea, 2004.

"If I did that they'd just laugh at me and think I was sick."

On Claudio Ranieri's use of Ridley Scott's *Gladiator* as a motivational technique, 2004.

"I have to defend what is mine and the Champions League is mine."

On the challenge of retaining the Champions League with a different club, in 2004.

"As we say in Portugal, they brought the bus and they left the bus in front of the goal. I would have been frustrated if I had been a supporter who paid £50 to watch this game because Spurs came to defend."

On Tottenham parking the bus, 2004.

"I think he has two faces: one beautiful and one that I don't like. He must keep one of them and change the other one."

On Joe Cole's goalscoring performance against Liverpool, 2004.

"It all depends on my wife. If I am at home, yes, I will see it. But maybe my wife would like to go somewhere. I would like to see it - I like to see football and it is a big game. But maybe I will have no permission."

On whether his wife, Tami, will let him watch Manchester United versus Arsenal, 2004.

"If they made a film of my life, I think they should get George Clooney to play me. He's a fantastic actor and my wife thinks he would be ideal."

On his Hollywood hopes, 2004.

"At the time, I was saying I was special because I was European champion two days before that so I arrived here with my ego this big. Now, it's even higher!"

On that opening press conference, 2005.

"Some clubs are treated as devils, some are treated as angels. I don't think we are so ugly that we should be seen as the devil and I don't think Arsène Wenger and David Dein are so beautiful that they should be viewed as angels."

On tapping-up Ashley Cole, 2005.

"In England, which club plays better than Chelsea? Arsenal? 10 points behind."

On the criticism of Chelsea's playing style, 2005.

"I want to give my congratulations to them because they won. But we were the best team."

On being knocked out of the League Cup by Charlton, 2005-06 season.

"My history as a manager cannot be compared with Frank Rijkaard's history. He has zero trophies and I have a lot of them."

On facing Frank Rijkaard, 2005.

"Do you want to know the team? I can say my team and the Barça team, and the referee. Referee: Frisk. Barcelona: Valdés, Belletti, Puyol, Márquez, Giovanni; Albertini, Deco, Xavi; Eto'o, Giuly, Ronaldinho. Chelsea: Petr Čech, Paulo, Ricardo, John Terry, Gallas at left back; Tiago, Makélelé, Frank Lampard, Joe Cole; Drogba and Gudjohnsen. It's a good finish."

Naming his, and Barcelona's, team before the 2005 Champions League second-round first-leg.

"The most difficult thing we did, in my opinion, was prove to ourselves and show Barcelona we can be better than them."

On losing 2-1 to Barcelona in the Champions League second-round first-leg, 2005.

"When I saw Rijkaard entering the referee's dressing room I couldn't believe it. When Didier Drogba was sent off, I wasn't surprised."

After that fateful night at the Nou Camp, 2005.

"I have to be very careful when talking about referees because Mr João Ferreira may also quit refereeing."

On the news that Anders Frisk had retired from refereeing, 2005.

"Why should I comment on Johan Cruyff? Who is Johan Cruyff in this game?"

On Johan Cruyff's criticism of Mourinho, 2005.

"What pressure? Pressure is poor people in the world trying to feed their families. There is no pressure in football."

On Chelsea's back-to-back defeats to Barcelona and Middlesbrough, 2005.

"I'm supposed to be a VIP, but I don't feel like one. Football is nothing compared to those who work for a better world."

On visiting the Peres Centre, 2005.

Appendix C

"I don't regret it. The only thing I have to understand is I'm in England, so maybe even when I think I am not wrong, I have to adapt to your country and I have to respect that. I have a lot of respect for Liverpool fans and what I did, the sign of silence - 'shut your mouth' - was not for them, it was for the English press."

On putting his finger to his lips during the League Cup final, 2005.

"You are the best player in the world."

Mourinho's words to Frank Lampard, 2005.

"I think he is one of those people who is a voyeur. He likes to watch other people. There are some guys who, when they are at home, have a big telescope to see what happens in other families."

On Arsène Wenger, 2005.

"We are on top at the moment but not because of the club's financial power. We are in contention for a lot of trophies because of my hard work."

Reminding the world just who is responsible for Chelsea's success, 2005.

"This could be the story of a donkey who worked for 30 years but never became a horse."

On Jesualdo Ferreira, 2005.

"During the afternoon it rained only in this stadium - our kit man saw it - they tried everything. There must be a microclimate here."

On a hard-fought victory against Blackburn, in 2005.

"After the game, after the press conference, we were together in my office. We laugh, we spoke, we speak, we drunk and, to be fair, when we go to Man United, I will bring a very good bottle of wine because the wine we drunk was very bad and he was complaining. So, because when we go there it's my birthday, I will go with a beautiful bottle of Portuguese wine to enjoy with him at the end of the game. I have a lot of respect for the big man. I call him 'boss' because he's our [the other managers'] boss. He's the top man, a really nice person and he deserves to be the boss. Maybe when I am 60 the kids will call me the same."

On facing Sir Alex Ferguson in the second-leg of the League Cup semi-final, 2005.

"Why drive an Aston Martin all the time, when I have a Ferrari and Porsche as well? That would just be stupid."

On rotating Arjen Robben, Joe Cole, and Damien Duff, 2005.

"Everybody was waiting for Chelsea not to win every game and one day when we lose there will be a holiday in the country. But we are ready for that."

On becoming the team everyone wanted to beat, 2005.

"You cannot lose the game. I am not putting pressure on you with 'we have to win' – I don't like that kind of pressure – but we cannot lose. We cannot lose."

Mourinho's team talk on the eve of sealing the title against Bolton, 2005.

"We've played in rain, sun and snow, in heat and cold, in north and in south, at home and away. We've played 3,060 minutes. With these next 90 minutes, we can become champions. Go out there, play as a team, win the game! I want this dressing-room to be celebrating when the game is over!"

Mourinho's team talk before the game against Bolton, 2005.

"What you saw was more than a hug – it was trust."

On hugging Frank Lampard after the 2-0 victory against Bolton, 2005.

"I think it's time to stop criticising Bolton for playing direct football, because Liverpool play more direct than Bolton."

On Liverpool's tactics following the Champions League semi-final first-leg 0-0 draw, 2005.

Appendix C

"I felt the power of Anfield, it was magnificent. I felt it didn't interfere with my players but maybe it interfered with other people and maybe it interfered with the result. I went through many experiences in football in difficult atmospheres. I never found cannibals in the stands, only noisy people. I saw a stadium where the crowd scored the goal. You should ask the linesman why he gave a goal. Because, to give a goal, the ball must be 100% in and he must be 100% sure that the ball is in."

On Luis García's infamous ghost goal against Chelsea in the Champions League semi-final second-leg, 2005.

"The best team lost. After they scored only one team played, the other one just defended for the whole game."

On Liverpool, supposedly, defending their 1-0 lead for 86 minutes in the same match, 2005.

"I saw their players and manager go for a lap of honour after losing to us in their last home game. In Portugal, if you do this, they throw bottles at you."

On Manchester United's lap of honour, 2005.

"If Roman Abramovich helped me out in training we would be bottom of the league and if I had to work in his world of big business, we would be bankrupt!"

Reminding the world who's boss at Chelsea, in 2005.

"Ricardo Carvalho seems to have problems understanding things, maybe he should have an IQ test, or go to a mental hospital or something."

On Ricardo Carvalho's criticism after being dropped, 2005.

"We have eight matches and eight victories, with 16 goals, but people say we cannot play, that we are a group of clowns. This is not right."

After defeating Liverpool 1-4, 2005.

"What do you have to do to beat Manchester United this weekend? We score more goals than them."

On facing Manchester United, 2005.

"Barcelona have a great club. But in 200 years of history they have won the European Cup only once. I have been managing for a few years and I have already won the same amount."

On facing Barcelona, 2006.

"Sometimes you see beautiful people with no brains. Sometimes you have ugly people who are intelligent, like scientists."

On Barcelona's criticism of the Stamford Bridge pitch ahead of the sides' Champions League second-round first-leg match, 2006.

"Barcelona is a cultural city with many great theatres and this boy has learned very well. He's learned play-acting."

On Lionel Messi after a collision with Asier del Horno in the first-leg of the sides' Champions League second-round first-leg, 2006.

"We have played against them in four matches in two seasons. 11 against 11, they never beat us. That is the reality."

After facing Barcelona with 11 men in the 1-1 draw in the Champions League second-round second-leg, 2006.

"For me, pressure is bird flu. I'm feeling a lot of pressure with the problem in Scotland. It's not fun and I'm more scared of it than football."

On the pressures of retaining the title, 2006.

"Who were Lampard, Terry, and Drogba two years ago? They were certainly not world stars. And in this moment who are they?"

On elevating the careers of Chelsea's key players, 2006.

"She is the real manager of family life. You are the star outside, here you are not a star."

On his wife, Tami, 2006.

Appendix C

"Today is a day when the dream became reality – Andriy has always been my first choice for Chelsea since I arrived."

On signing Andriy Shevchenko, 2006.

"As you know Gallas had an unbelievable holiday. I hope he enjoyed it very much in Guadeloupe, which I think is a fantastic place to be on holiday, so he wanted to stay there for a long time."

On William Gallas missing the opening days of the pre-season tour to the U.S., 2006.

"Look at my haircut. I am ready for the war. I did it because I want to push my son to do the same. I also did it because I want to push the young players on my team to have a proper haircut, not the Rastafarian or the others they have."

On shaving his head, 2006.

"We don't have second-line players like we have had in the last few seasons. Scott Parker, Eidur Gudjohnsen, Tiago, Damien Duff and Glen Johnson have left, meaning a different way to approach the season and prepare for the future. The doors are open for Salomon Kalou and Mikel John Obi. Are they ready like Gudjohnsen and Duff? We will see. They have to be ready to play for 90 minutes. We cannot lose the qualities that made us champions."

On a changing transfer policy, 2006.

"It's a pleasure to become the first Portuguese person to be inducted in such an important museum."

On being inducted into Madame Tussauds, 2006.

"I think Makélelé is not a football player. Makélelé is a slave. He doesn't want to go but he has to go. In the national team of France they do not have the word liberté."

On Claude Makélelé being selected by France despite announcing his international retirement, 2006.

"Maybe the guy drank red wine or beer with breakfast instead of milk."

On Frank Lampard being hit by a bottle at Brammal Lane, 2006.

"A brilliant reaction. I hate it when players just walk off."

On Arjen Robben storming down the tunnel after being substituted against Aston Villa, 2006.

"After that he turned, came back and was laughing right in front of us. He was motivating his people but gave not one single sign that he was worried about the situation."

On Stephen Hunt after the winger's collision with Petr Čech, 2006.

"A player from Man City showed half of his ass for two seconds and it was a big nightmare. But this is a real nightmare."

Comparing Joey Barton's antics with Petr Čech's head injury, 2006.

"Many great managers have never won the Champions League - a big example is not far from us."

On Arsène Wenger, 2006.

"I wouldn't change the squad and I wouldn't change the journalists in the room."

On the English media, 2007

"Barcelona wants to be the best team on the pitch. Chelsea wants to be the best team on the pitch. I hope the referee wants to be the best team on the pitch."

On facing Barcelona in the Champions League group stage, 2007.

"If you're not a big club, you choose one competition and you fight in that competition and forget the others. Big clubs - we cannot do this."

On Chelsea's quadruple difficulties in comparison to Liverpool, 2007.

Appendix C

"This is the only time we have had to play before United and that's because we control the fixtures. Just imagine if we didn't control them!"

On fixture scheduling, 2007.

"Which manager I wouldn't like to fight? Big Sam – he'd kill me!"

On which Premier League manager Mourinho feared the most, 2007.

"I am happy to be six points behind. In my opinion, Manchester United did not take advantage of our bad moments."

On Chelsea's perceived difficult position, 2007.

"It's not even a game between me and him. It's a game where a kid made some statements not showing maturity and respect. Maybe [it's his] education, difficult childhood, no education, maybe [it is] the consequence of that."

On Cristiano Ronaldo, then of Manchester United, 2007.

"Liverpool are favourites because in the year 2007 we've played 27 matches and Liverpool play three or four."

Ahead of facing Liverpool in the Champions League semi-finals, 2007.

"Three years without a Premiership title? I don't think I would still be in a job."

On Rafa Benítez, 2007.

"My wife is in Portugal with the dog. The dog is with my wife so the city of London is safe, the big threat is away."

On the quarantine of his Yorkshire Terrier, 2007.

"If you ask me if I jump with happiness when I know Mr Poll is our referee? No."

On Graham Poll, 2007.

"We all want to play great music all the time, but if that is not possible, you have to hit as many right notes as you can."

On Chelsea, 2007.

"Are you ready to enjoy us playing with 16-year-olds and 17-year-olds, and still be chasing prizes?"

On Roman Abramovich cutting costs, 2007.

"Young players are a little bit like melons. Only when you open and taste the melon are you 100 per cent sure that the melon is good. Sometimes you have beautiful melons but they don't taste very good and some other melons are a bit ugly and when you open them, the taste is fantastic! One thing is youth football, one thing is professional football. The bridge is a difficult one to cross and they have to play with us and train with us for us to taste the melon. For example, Scott Sinclair, the way he played against Arsenal and Man United. We know the melon we have."

On his young players, 2007.

"I would love an Aston Martin but if you ask me one million pounds for an Aston Martin, I tell you, you are crazy because they cost 250,000 pounds."

On the difficulties of landing a defender for Chelsea, 2007.

"Shevchenko was treated like a prince at Milan."

On Andriy Shevchenko's application in training, 2007.

"It is like having a blanket that is too small for the bed. You pull the blanket up to keep your chest warm and your feet stick out. I cannot buy a bigger blanket because the supermarket is closed. But I am content because the blanket is cashmere. It is no ordinary blanket."

On Chelsea's injury crisis, 2007.

"If the club decide to sack me because of bad results, that's part of the game. If it happens I will be a millionaire and get another club a couple of months later."

On the dangers of being sacked at Chelsea, 2007.

Appendix C

"Porto in the last year were a better team from the tactical point of view because it was my third year with them. They knew everything I knew. They knew how to adapt. I could start the game with 4-3-3, switch to 4-4-2, change back to 4-3-3. When we get to my third or fourth year, we can say that this will be my best Chelsea team."

On his high hopes for Chelsea, 2007.

"Entertaining? Too much!"

Upon defeating Birmingham City 3-2, 2007.

"I think I have a naive team. They are naive because they are pure and they are clean. We don't have divers, we don't have violent people."

On the fall-out of Florent Malouda winning a controversial penalty against Liverpool, 2007.

"I could feel immediately the movement. To somebody that understands the game and feels the football, smells the situation, it was obvious."

On an incorrectly disallowed goal for Chelsea against Blackburn, 2007.

"The style of how we play is very important. But it is omelettes and eggs. No eggs – no omelettes! It depends on the quality of the eggs. In the supermarket you have class one, two or class three eggs and some are more expensive than others and some give you better omelettes. So when the class one eggs are in Waitrose and you cannot go there, you have a problem."

His final pre-match press conference in his first spell at Chelsea, 2007.

"They are the laws of football."

On departing Chelsea, 2007.

"I was hours away – I almost signed. But at the last minute I began thinking, 'I am going to coach a national side, there will be one match a month and the rest of the time I will be in my office or overseeing matches.'"

On turning down the England national team, 2007.

"It was the biggest regret of my career."

On not leaving Chelsea after the 2007 FA Cup final, 2008.

"I always wanted to coach a big club in Italy. The job at Inter is a big challenge for me. And I do believe it could be very entertaining for the journalists."

On taking over at Internazionale, 2008.

"The president gave me a beautiful book about Inter's history, but we need to write a new book. I like to win and forget the past. I have arrived at a special club and I believe I am a great coach but I don't want to be special. I am Mourinho – that's all."

Upon taking over at Internazionale, 2008.

"Ranieri? He's actually right – I am very demanding with myself and I need to win to be sure of things. For that reason, I have won so many trophies in my career. He, on the other hand, has the mentality of one who does not need to win and, at almost 70 years of age, has won a Super Cup and another small cup. He is too old to change his mentality."

On Claudio Ranieri, 2008.

"Boredom by Ranieri? Is it like Sartre's 'Nausea', which I used to study."

After Claudio Ranieri criticised his Internazionale team for being boring, 2008.

"Frank is in my heart for everything we have done together. But I'm left with a bitter taste in the mouth. He said to me 'I will go with you to Inter, if it's not possible now, then in a year we will be together'. Afterwards he changed his mind. What would have disillusioned me is if he had gone to another club. He renewed with Chelsea. Okay, friends as before."

On Frank Lampard rejecting Internazionale, 2008.

Appendix C

"I am no longer Chelsea coach and I do not have to defend them anymore, so I think it is correct if I say Drogba is a diver."

On Didier Drogba, 2008.

"I could have played in goal and we still would have won."

On defeating Catania 3-1, 2008.

"As for Lo Monaco I do not know who he is. With the name Monaco I have heard of Bayern Monaco and the Monaco GP, the Tibetan Monaco, and the Principality of Monaco. I have never heard of any others."

Upon hearing Catania's managing director, Pietro Lo Monaco, wanted to 'smack him in the mouth', 2008.

"Ronaldo is a good player but he is certainly not the best. He deserved the Golden Ball award because his team won the Champions League and the Premier League. But, for me, Ibrahimović is the best."

Paying tribute to Zlatan Ibrahimović, 2008

"Muntari had some problems related to Ramadan, perhaps with this heat it's not good for him to be doing this [fasting]. Ramadan has not arrived at the ideal moment for a player to play a football match."

On Sulley Muntari fasting for Ramadan, 2009.

"Why have Chelsea suffered so much since I left? Because I left."

Following Luiz Felipe Scolari's sacking, 2009.

"Three of the four Champions League finalists – Arsenal were the exception – were simply stronger than us. Yet if we managed to sign those three or four players that we are chasing then we can be as strong as them."

On challenging for the Champions League with Internazionale, 2009.

"I hadn't spoken to him in the last two months because it was hard for me because I didn't want to think that he was dying. That wasn't the image I wanted to keep with me forever...that wasn't the voice I wanted to hear."

On Sir Bobby Robson's death, 2009.

"Cannavaro is still a player, but he talks like a coach, director of sport and president."

On Fabio Cannavaro urging Davide Santon to leave Inter, 2009.

"Wesley, you look tired, take some days off, go to the sun with your wife and daughter."

On giving Wesley Sneijder time off, 2010.

"It was a strange game. I think we all understand that it was no coincidence that he showed the red card to Sneijder. I have realised that they are not going to allow us to wrap this title up. But we were perfect. We would have won this game even with seven men. Maybe with six we would have struggled, but we would have won with seven."

On nine-man Inter's 2-0 win over AC Milan, 2010.

"I don't stick my head in the sand, I know there is only one team [in Italy] that has a penalty area 25 metres long."

On Serie A referees supposedly favouring Juventus, 2010.

"You can take me away, arrest me, but my team is strong and will win anyway, even if we are reduced to nine men."

On the referee, Paolo Tagliavento, and his performance against Sampdoria, 2010.

"The warm-up is the warm-up they did in our time. The way they defend set-pieces is exactly the same. Sometimes they play a 4-4-2 diamond, sometimes they play 4-3-3, which are exactly the systems we worked when there. Chelsea have suffered in the last two years, and it's no coincidence that their decline happened after I left."

On facing Chelsea at Stamford Bridge, 2010.

"Everything was done today to try and prevent Inter from winning, but my squad is strong and we will win the Scudetto. But I will leave it at that. This is your country and your league. I am just a foreigner working here. One day, I will go and leave this problem with you."'

On the difficulties of life at Internazionale, 2010.

"I am very happy at Inter. I am not happy in Italian football - because I don't like it and they don't like me. Simple."

On Italian football, 2010.

"For Barcelona it's an obsession. Our dream is more pure than obsession. A dream is about pride. Our players will be proud to reach the final in Madrid. It's an obsession you can see and feel. I was here in 1997 and I lived a Spanish Cup final at the Bernabéu between Real Betis and Barça. It seemed like we won the World Cup. To have a Catalan flag in the Bernabéu is an obsession. It's anti-Madridismo."

On Barcelona's 'obsession' with reaching the Champions League final at the Santiago Bernabéu, 2010.

"The way they are, tomorrow we will probably read I am to blame for the volcano. Maybe I have a friend in the volcano and I am responsible for that."

On Barcelona's lament that the Eyjafjallajökull volcano affected their preparations for the Champions League semi-final first leg at the San Siro, 2010.

"It is always difficult to lose, especially for those who are not used to it."

On Barcelona's 3-1 Champions League semi-final first-leg defeat to Internazionale, 2010.

"In five years I have never had a match where my team has had less possession than the opponents."

Pre-empting the Champions League semi-final second-leg against Barcelona, 2010.

"We did not park the bus, we parked the plane."

On ten-man Internazionale's defensive heroics in the Champions League semi-final second leg at the Nou Camp, 2010.

"Do you really want me to compete for possession with them and lose? If you have a Ferrari and I have some small car, I have to puncture your tyres or put sugar in your petrol tank."

On Internazionale's 24% possession against Barcelona in the Champions League semi-final second-leg, 2010.

"I won UEFA Cup final, I won Champions League final, I won big matches. I had great moments in my career. This one is the best one."

On defeating Barcelona 3-2 on aggregate in the Champions League semi-final, 2010.

"We had a really special rapport. He showed faith, gave me confidence and responsibility It's been 12-13 years but I never forget those times and that person who was fantastic for me. But when my friend, Louis van Gaal, says he wouldn't have celebrated the same way as I did in Barcelona, he couldn't anyway because he is too slow. He can't run the way I can. I'm fast like a lion! Voom! Did you see that run!"

On Louis van Gaal, 2010.

"Whoever arrives will be lucky because they will get the chance to play in three finals, the Italian Super Cup, European Super Cup and World Club tournament, a present I have left."

Throwing down the gauntlet for Rafa Benítez, 2010.

Appendix C

"I don't need photos to make those around me love me. They carry me in their hearts."

On Rafa Benítez reportedly taking down photographs of Mourinho's Champions League triumph, 2010.

"I am prepared. The more pressure there is, the stronger I am. In Portugal, we say the bigger the ship, the stronger the storm. Fortunately for me, I have always been in big ships. FC Porto was a very big ship in Portugal, Chelsea was also a big ship in England and Inter was a great ship in Italy. Now I'm at Real Madrid, which is considered the biggest ship on the planet."

On taking over at Real Madrid, 2010.

"I only won my last one ten days ago and I already miss it!"

After Florentino Pérez showed Mourinho Madrid's nine European Cups, 2010.

"If I am hated at Barcelona, it is their problem but not mine. Fear is not a word in my football dictionary."

On taking over at Barcelona's bitter rivals, Real Madrid, 2010.

"I am José Mourinho and I don't change. I arrive with all my qualities and my defects."

Upon being unveiled as Real Madrid manager, 2010.

"Look, I'm a coach, I'm not Harry Potter. He is magical, but in reality there is no magic. Magic is fiction and football is real."

On the pressures of managing Real Madrid, 2010.

"This is the first time I have ever been beaten 5–0. It is a historically bad result for us. It is not a humiliation, but I am very disappointed. It is sad for us, but it is not difficult for me to swallow. What's difficult to swallow is when you lose a game because you have hit the post or the referee has been bad. I have left here in that state before with Chelsea and Inter Milan but that was not the case tonight. It is easy for me to take because it is fair. We played very, very badly and they were fantastic. We gifted them two goals that were bordering on the ridiculous. It is our own fault."

On Madrid's 5-0 defeat to Barcelona, 2010.

"Second place is just the first loser. If Madrid were to fire me, I wouldn't go to Malaga. I'd go to a top-level team in Italy or England."

On his predecessor, Manuel Pellegrini, 2010.

"I live and work in a world where you can't say what you think, can never say the truth. Not being a hypocrite, a diplomat and a coward is my biggest defect."

On his outspoken style, 2011.

"I would rather play with 10 men than wait for a player who is late for the bus."

Laying down the law at Real Madrid, 2011.

"You are traitors. I asked you not to leak information about the line-up and you have betrayed me! It's obvious you are not on my side! The only friend I have in this room is Granero, but I can hardly trust him! You have left me alone. You are the most treacherous squad I've had in my life!"

On his tactics being leaked ahead of Real Madrid's 1-1 draw with Barcelona, 2011.

Appendix C

"A new era has begun. Until now, there were two groups of coaches. One very, very small group of coaches who don't speak about refs and then a big group of coaches, of which I am part, who criticise the refs when they make mistakes – people like me who don't control their frustrations but also people who are happy to value a great job from a ref. Now there is a third group, which is only Pep, that criticises referees when they get decisions right! In his first season, [Guardiola] lived the scandal of Stamford Bridge, last year he played against a ten-man Inter. Now, he is not happy with refs getting it right. I'm not asking the referee to help my team. If the referee is good, everyone will be happy – except Guardiola. He wants them to get it wrong."

On Pep Guardiola lamenting Pedro's correctly disallowed goal in the Copa del Rey final, 2011.

"I have to train with 10 men, how to play with 10 men, because I go there with Chelsea, I finish with 10, I go there with Inter, I finish with 10 and I have to train to play with 10 men because it can happen again."

On facing Barcelona at the Nou Camp, 2011.

"If I tell UEFA what I really think and feel, my career would end now. Instead, I will just ask a question to which I hope one day to get a response: Why? Why? Why Øvrebo? Why Busacca? Why De Bleeckere? Why Stark? Why? Because every semi-final the same things happen. The question is why? I don't know if it is the Unicef sponsorship or if it is because they are nice guys. They have power and we have no chance."

On Real Madrid's 0-2 defeat to Barcelona in the first-leg of the Champions League semi-final, 2011.

"Josep Guardiola is a fantastic coach, but I have won two Champions Leagues. He has won one Champions League and that is one that would embarrass me. I would be ashamed to have won it with the scandal of Stamford Bridge and if he wins it this year, it will be the scandal of the Bernabéu. I hope that one day he can win a proper Champions League. Deep down, if they are good people, it cannot taste right for them. I hope one day Guardiola has the chance of winning a brilliant, clean championship with no scandal."

On the same defeat, 2011.

"You can't win the treble every season. But I've done it twice and I think twice is quite a lot."

Paying self-tribute, 2011.

"What I'm about to say is not a criticism, I'm just stating a fact: there were no ball-boys in the second half, which is something typical of small teams in difficulty. We intended to play like men and not fall on the ground at the slightest touch."

On Real Madrid's Supercopa de España second-leg defeat to Barcelona, 2011.

"Quality, unity, passion, work methods: there is not just one or two reasons. When I go to a club, I wear the shirt; I feel the shirt like it's my first one or my last one. There are a lot of factors and they must work in unison."

On his ingredients for success, 2012.

"As you Spanish are world champions, your friends in the press protect you... like the goalkeeper."

Criticising Sergio Ramos and Iker Casillas, 2012.

"I'm not bothered by the whistles at me. It's not a problem. It's the first time it's ever happened to me. There's a first time for practically everything. Zidane was whistled at here. Ronaldo has been whistled at here. Cristiano, who is the latest Golden Boot winner, has also been whistled at. Why can't I? Zidane responded with his football, the same as Ronaldo and Cristiano. I work hard to be able to respond like they did some day, but there may come a day when the fans are sad."

On being booed at the Santiago Bernabéu, 2012.

"I should not have done what I did. The person who messed up there was me. I work a lot with my players precisely on this: control the emotions, only think about playing, and work well. The key thing is the negative image. As Tito said a few weeks ago, the footage will be there forever. There are no problems between him and me. The story is over and what needs to be done now is to make sure nothing similar happens again."

Eventually apologising for poking Tito Vilanova in the eye, 2012.

"Messi scored 50 goals that were worth nothing, in the same way that, last season, Cristiano scored 42 that didn't achieve anything."

On Lionel Messi's record-breaking year, 2012.

"Cristiano Ronaldo is fantastic. I will not compare him with Messi, we're talking about two great players. I will say this year Cristiano Ronaldo has been better."

On the Ronaldo/Messi rivalry, 2012.

"If Messi is the best on the planet, Ronaldo is the best in the universe."

On Cristiano Ronaldo's battle with Lionel Messi for the Ballon d'Or, 2012.

"I'm not even the boss at home – that's my wife – so how am I supposed to run my club!"

On family life, 2012.

"He's a six-out-of-ten player."

On Alvaro Arbeloa's consistency, 2012.

"When I say forever, I mean forever. I can't say that the players I had at Chelsea, Porto and Inter are my ex-players, they continue to be my players. And they don't talk about their former boss, they say: 'You are the boss'. They are ties forever."

On the close bonds with his players, 2012.

"They talk about the national team and Barcelona but there are also five players from Real Madrid. I don't understand why they mix them because they are two distinct things. Spain isn't Barcelona. Barcelona were the champions of Spain. And I repeat, were the champions because now they are not."

On Spain's win at the European Championships, 2012.

"Like me or not, I am the only one who won the world's three most important leagues. So, maybe instead of the 'Special One', people should start calling me the 'Only One'."

On becoming the only manager in history to win titles in England, Spain, and Italy, 2012.

"I am José Mário dos Santos Mourinho Félix and I am manager of Real Madrid. I never once witnessed any demonstration of racism or racial abuse or behaviour. I am certain that John Terry is not a racist."

Mourinho's character witness statement for John Terry's racism trial, 2012.

"I made two changes at half-time; I could have made seven. There are very few whose heads are focused on football. Right now, I do not have a team."

On the 1-0 defeat to Sevilla, 2012.

"What position is my wife in? Eighth at least."

On being ranked the ninth most influential man in the world by AskMen, 2013.

"One, two or three people called me to tell me they had voted for me, but another person's name had appeared in their votes."

On Vicente del Bosque winning the FIFA Coach of the Year Award, 2013.

"I would love to be the national team coach one day. I think the Portuguese people are waiting for that to happen."

On managing Portugal, 2013.

"Has he deliberately chosen a league I am not involved in? I don't know."

On Pep Guardiola's decision to manage Bayern Munich, 2013.

"I want to be where people love me, in England I am loved by the fans and the media who treat me in a fair way. I know in Spain it is different because some people hate me."

A come-and-get-me plea to Chelsea after Real Madrid are knocked out in the Champions League semi-final by Borussia Dortmund, 2013.

"I damaged Spanish football by breaking Barcelona's dominance."

Responding to Andrés Iniesta's criticism, 2013.

"I am one of you."

To Chelsea's fans, 2013.

"When I was managing for the first time, I thought I knew everything. After 13 years, you realise you knew nothing and you have to learn every day."

On developing as a manager, 2013.

"If I have to describe myself, I would describe myself as a very happy person because it's the first time I arrive in a club where I already love the club."

On becoming the Happy One upon returning to Chelsea, 2013.

"Now we are back together and we are getting together at a great moment for us both, so I think we are ready to marry again and be happy and successful. I had to prepare myself not to be too emotional but, obviously, I am very happy. I love it here."

On reuniting with Roman Abramovich, 2013.

"I don't want to win the Europa League. It would be a big disappointment for me. I don't want my players to feel the Europa League is our competition."

On Rafa Benítez's continental achievement with Chelsea, 2013.

"I don't love this, but it's part of my job. I have to try and do it. I try to give what you want, but I can't always give you a good line. I try to be honest and try and give you what you're expecting from me at this moment. But what I want to do is work."

On reuniting with the English media, 2013.

"I have some white hairs but in my case that's a good sign. It means I am better now than before."

On a different look compared to his first spell at Chelsea, 2013.

"Any player that wants to go to the World Cup... if they are second choice in their club they are in trouble."

On Wayne Rooney's predicament at Manchester United, 2013.

"I had a chance to meet him much, much better when I left England and I started meeting him in UEFA [coaching meetings], at the Euros, the World Cup. I think I met him a few times, we had dinner and so on. And when you are not in the same league and when you are not playing against each other, it is easier to get to know people, it is easier to go deeper. It is easy to speak about football. He's a very nice guy. I wouldn't bet for one single problem between us."

On building bridges with Arsène Wenger, 2013.

"Maybe I am going to be The Godfather."

On becoming one of the Premier League's most experienced managers, 2013.

"I look forward to the salt and pepper of football, the unpredictability of every game, every result."

On returning to the Premier League, 2013.

"At the end of my contract - which is quite a long one - I will try for the club to be happy with me so we both want to keep together."

On staying at Chelsea beyond 2017.

"I like the stadium, I like the opponent, I like the difficulty of the game. I like it very, very much."

On facing Manchester United again, with Chelsea, at Old Trafford, 2013.

"'In this moment, I would say Tito Vilanova to recover from his problem, [Nelson] Mandela to recover from his problem, and everybody in the world that is suffering from similar problems to recover from them."

On what he would do with three wishes, 2013.

"I'm a very, very, very big fan of Bryan Adams."

On his music taste, 2013.

"I think he already made his decision. That's the danger of medicals before contracts."

On beating Tottenham to the signing of Willian from Shakhtar Donetsk, 2013.

"It's not about me and Pep, it's about Chelsea and Bayern Munich. Pep is not European champion and I'm not Europa League champion. We are just coaches here now, so it's not about us."'

On facing Pep Guardiola, again, in the European Super Cup, 2013.

"I think, with climate change, winter becomes summer and summer becomes winter, so maybe not a problem."

On the 2022 World Cup being held in Qatar, 2013.

"We are not unbeatable. This is a different profile [to 2004]. This is a different team."

After the 2-1 defeat to Everton, 2013.

"Beautiful, young eggs. Eggs that need a mum or, in this case, a dad to take care of them, to keep them warm during the winter, to bring the blanket and work and improve them. One day the moment will arrive when the weather changes, the sun rises, you break the eggs and the eggs are ready to go for life at the top level."

On Chelsea's young squad, 2013.

"Of course [it hurts], but I think the team probably is not a team with such maturity and personality to face the difficult moments of the game,"

On Chelsea's first home defeat in the Champions League group stages in ten years, 2013.

"If anyone tells me Oscar has not been Chelsea's best player this season, I'd have to disagree. I have to prove to the fans that I am good. Now [Mata] must do the same."

On Juan Mata, 2013.

"I don't like the way Chelsea were playing the last couple of years; the club doesn't like it and we want to change," he said. "We want to play a different style. The past is history – even my past."

On the task ahead, 2013.

"I'm not a kid [here] to discuss relationships with the media. It's a personal thing. I don't care what he says. I'm not interested. If I have something to discuss with someone, we go upstairs, have lunch and speak about it. I don't do it in front of you."

On André Villas-Boas, 2013.

"He's a special guy because three days ago he left the Aston Villa striker naked – and it was not a penalty or a yellow card."

On Tottenham's Jan Vertonghen not receiving a red card, 2013.

"With Kevin I didn't like the match he played against Swindon and I didn't like the way he was training. But you only ask about the guys who were not selected. Thank you."

On Kevin de Bruyne's omission from Chelsea's Champions League game against Steaua Bucureşti, 2013.

"One thing is to play for Everton, another is to play for Chelsea."

On Romelu Lukaku's form with Everton, 2013.

"[It's] better to win seven [games] 1-0 than one 7-0 and lose points in others."

On shifting Chelsea's mentality, 2013.

"I smell things, and when that easy goal [from Demba Ba] was missed, I had a smell that they would score a goal. That is why I had Eden [Hazard] warming up at 1-0 because I smelled that."

On his trademark double substitution, of Eden Hazard and Willian, in the 1-3 victory over Norwich City, 2013.

"If Chelsea fans at Norwich are singing: 'José Mourinho', and the other guys sing: 'F*** off Mourinho', I don't think it's aggressive hostility. It's better than them ignoring me."

On English football's unique atmosphere, 2013.

"He's recovering his self-esteem."

On John Terry's renewed form, 2013.

"Ideally it's not just about having British players either, but having players who are made in Chelsea. In three or four years' time, if we don't have other Englishmen to replace this nucleus of players – when Lamps is 39, John [Terry] is 36 – I will be very sad. Every club needs that."

On the importance of having a nucleus of players from the nation he is working in, 2013.

"He has shown good dedication and work during this period, almost all day every day, so he's back."

On Fernando Torres, 2013.

"Samuel [Eto'o] did an intelligent action. When I arrived home the first thing I told my kid who likes to play goalkeeper was, 'See the goal and don't do that, eh?'"

On Cardiff City's goalkeeper, David Marshall, 2013.

"Who is more important? The billions of people who love football, or the few thousand who behave disgracefully."

On the racist abuse Yaya Touré received against CSKA Moscow, 2013.

Appendix C

"You didn't let me read the book! You write about it so much. It seems you don't want people to buy the book."

On Sir Alex Ferguson's autobiography, 2013.

"The Clásico? I don't care. I'll be having dinner with my family tomorrow but if you ask me who I'd prefer to win, I'd say Madrid."

On the first El Clásico without Mourinho for three years, 2013.

"I don't look back. Somebody told me I have 65 matches unbeaten at home. I don't have 65, I have 5. The past is the past."

On a new era, 2013.

"I promise that I went for him [José Jr]. But this is the drama of the last minute."

On leaping into the crowd after Fernando Torres' last minute winner against Manchester City, 2013.

"If they want Arsenal to win a trophy, that's a help. If they want a big game between two big teams in London they should put the game on Wednesday and not on Tuesday."

On facing Arsenal in the League Cup just two days after defeating Manchester City, 2013.

"I feel I made 11 mistakes."

After the 2-0 defeat to Newcastle United, 2013.

"They were competing more in training sessions than they were in that game [against Newcastle]."

On the same defeat, 2013.

Bibliography

Books

Carlo Ancelotti, *The Beautiful Games of an Ordinary Genius: My Autobiography*, (Rizzoli International Publications, 2010).

Rob Bagchi, *The Unforgiven: The Story of Don Revie's Leeds United*, (Aurum Press Ltd, 2009).

Phil Ball, *Morbo: The Story of Spanish Football*, (WSC Books, 2001).
White Storm: The Story of Real Madrid, (Mainstream Publishing, 2003).

Guillem Balague, *Pep Guardiola: Another Way of Winning*, (Orion, 2012).

Patrick Barclay, *Further Anatomy of a Winner*, (Orion, 2011).
Football – Bloody Hell!: The Biography of Sir Alex Ferguson, (Yellow Jersey, 2011).

Rafael Benítez, *Champions League Dreams*, (Headline, 2013).

Jimmy Burns, *Barça: A People's Passion*, (Bloomsbury Publishing, 1999).
The Real Deal: A History of Real Madrid, (Endeavour Press, 2012).

Mike Carson, *The Manager: Inside the Mind of Football's Leaders*, (Bloomsbury, 2013).

Michael Derrick, *The Portugal of Salazar*, (Nabu Press, 2011).

Didier Drogba, *Didier Drogba: The Autobiography*, (Aurum Press Ltd, 2008).

Jerzy Dudek, *Under Pressure*, (Sport and Profit, 2012).

Bibliography

Sir Alex Ferguson, *Alex Ferguson: My Autobiography*, (Hodder & Stoughton, 2013).

Richard Fitzpatrick, *El Clásico: Barcelona vs Real Madrid: Football's Greatest Rivalry*, (Bloomsbury Publishing, 2012).

David Goldblatt, *The Ball Is Round: A Global History of Football*, (Penguin Books, 2007).

The Guardian, *I am the Secret Footballer: Lifting the Lid on the Beautiful Game*, (Guardian Books, 2012).

Mark Halsey, *Added time: Surviving cancer, death threats and the Premier League*, (Floodlit Dreams Ltd, 2013).

Bob Harris, *Sir Bobby Robson: A Life in Football*, (W&N, 2009).

Duncan Hamilton, *Provided You Don't Kiss Me: 20 Years With Brian Clough*, (Harper Perennial, 2008).

Graham Hunter, *Barça: The Making of the Greatest Team in the World*, (BackPage Press, 2012).

Zlatan Ibrahimović, *I am Zlatan Ibrahimović*, (Albert Bonniers Forlag, 2011).

John Foot, Calcio: *A History of Italian Football*, (Harper Perennial, 2007).

Henry Kormelink, *The Coaching Philosophies of Louis van Gaal and the Ajax Coaches*, (Reedswain Corporated, 2003).

Simon Kuper, *Football Against the Enemy*, (Orion, 2003).

The Football Men: Up Close With the Giants of the Game, (Simon & Schuster, 2012).

Why England Lose & Other Curious Football Phenomena Explained, (HarperSport, 2010).

Frank Lampard, *Totally Frank: The Autobiography of Frank Lampard*, (Harpersport, 2010).

Luís Carlos Lourenço, *José Mourinho: Made in Portugal*, (Dewi Lewis Media Ltd, 2004).

Sid Lowe, *Fear and Loathing in La Liga: Real Madrid vs Barcelona*, (Yellow Jersey, 2013).

Niccolò Machiavelli, *The Prince*, (Penguin Classics, 2003).

Claude Makélelé, *Claude Makélelé:Tout Simplement*, (Editions Prolongations, 2009).

Gabriele Marcotti, *Capello: Portrait of a Winner*, (Bantam Press, 2008).
The Italian Job, (Bantam, 2007).

Dominic Midgeley, *Abramovich: The Billionaire From Nowhere*, (Willow, 2004).

Desmond Morris, *The Soccer Tribe*, (Jonathan Cape, 1981).

Luis Miguel Pereira, *André Villas-Boas: Special Too*, (Dewi Lewis Media, 2011).

Keir Radnedge, *50 Years of the European Cup and Champions League*, (Carlton Books Ltd, 2007).

Bibliography

Claudio Ranieri, *Proud Man Walking: My Chelsea Diary*, (Willow, 2004).

Ronald Reng, *A Life Too Short: The Tragedy of Robert Enke*, (Yellow Jersey, 2012).

Sir Bobby Robson, *My Autobiography: An Englishman Abroad*, (Pan Books, 1999).
Farewell But Not Goodbye - The Autobiography, (Hodder Paperbacks, 2006).

Jonathan Wilson, *Inverting the Pyramid*, (Orion Books Ltd, 2009).
Nobody Ever Says Thank You, (Orion, 2012).

Newspapers and Magazines

AS (Spanish)

Dez Record (Portuguese)

El Mundo Deportivo (Catalan)

Four Four Two

Marca (Spanish)

The Blizzard

The Guardian

The Independent

The Observer

The Sunday Times

The Times

The Telegraph

When Saturday Comes

World Soccer

Film

Blue Revolution, Prod. Marianne Wall, (EMI Catalogue, 2007).

Football's Greatest Managers, Prod. Ian Brackley, (Pitch International, 2011).

Mourinho, Prod. Jay Gill, (ITV, 2012).

The Special One, Prod. Pete Andrews, (BBC, 2005).

Index

Index

Index

Index

Index

Index

Some Other Bennion Kearny Football Titles:

Soccer Tough by Dan Abrahams

"Take a minute to slip into the mind of one of the world's greatest soccer players and imagine a stadium around you. Picture a performance under the lights and mentally play the perfect game."

Technique, speed and tactical execution are crucial components of winning soccer, but it is mental toughness that marks out the very best players – the ability to play when pressure is highest, the opposition is strongest, and fear is greatest.

Soccer Tough demystifies this crucial side of the game and offers practical techniques that will enable soccer players of all abilities to actively develop focus, energy, and confidence. Soccer Tough will help banish the fear, mistakes, and mental limits that holds players back.

Small Time: A Life in the Football Wilderness by Justin Bryant

In 1988, 23-year-old American goalkeeper Justin Bryant thought a glorious career in professional football awaited him. He had just saved two penalties for his American club - the Orlando Lions - against Scotland's Dunfermline Athletic, to help claim the first piece of silverware in their history. He was young, strong, healthy, and confident.

Small Time is the story of a life spent mostly in the backwaters of the game. As Justin negotiated the Non-League pitches of the Vauxhall-Opel League, and the many failed professional leagues of the U.S. in the 1980s and 90s - Football, he learned, is 95% blood, sweat, and tears; but if you love it enough, the other 5% makes up for it.

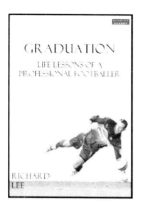

Graduation: Life Lessons of a Professional Footballer by Richard Lee

The 2010/11 season will go down as a memorable one for Goalkeeper Richard Lee. Cup wins, penalty saves, hypnotherapy and injury would follow, but these things only tell a small part of the tale. Filled with anecdotes, insights, humour and honesty - Graduation uncovers Richard's campaign to take back the number one spot, save a lot of penalties, and overcome new challenges. What we see is a transformation - beautifully encapsulated in this extraordinary season.

Saturday Afternoon Fever: A Year On The Road For Soccer Saturday by Johnny Phillips

You might already know Johnny Phillips. He is a football reporter for Sky Sports' Soccer Saturday programme and a man who gets beamed into the homes of fans across the country every weekend.

For the 2012/13 season, Johnny decided to do something different. He wanted to look beneath the veneer of household-name superstars and back-page glamour to chronicle a different side to our national sport. As Johnny travelled the country, he found a game that he loved even more, where unheralded stars were driven by a desire to succeed, often telling stories of bravery and overcoming adversity. People who were plucked from obscurity, placed in the spotlight and, sometimes, dropped back into obscurity again. Football stories that rarely see the limelight but which have a value all fans can readily identify with.

The Way Forward: Solutions to England's Football Failings by Matthew Whitehouse

English football is in a state of crisis. It has been almost 50 years since England made the final of a major championship and the national sides, at all levels, continue to disappoint and underperform. Yet no-one appears to know how to improve the situation.

In his acclaimed book, The Way Forward, football coach Matthew Whitehouse examines the causes of English football's decline and offers a number of areas where change and improvement need to be implemented immediately. With a keen focus and passion for youth development and improved coaching he explains that no single fix can overcome current difficulties and that a multi-pronged strategy is needed. If we wish to improve the standards of players in England then we must address the issues in schools, the grassroots, and academies, as well as looking at the constraints of the Premier League and English FA.

The Modern Soccer Coach 2014: A Four Dimensional Approach by Gary Curneen

The modern player is technically more capable, physically faster and stronger, and has access to more coaching and sports science resources than ever before. Aimed at Soccer coaches of all levels and with players of all ages and abilities The Modern Soccer Coach 2014 identifies the areas that must be targeted by coaches who want to maximize a team's potential – the Technical, Tactical, Physical, and Mental sides to the game.

Written by UEFA 'A' and NSCAA Premier licensed coach Gary Curneen – The Modern Soccer Coach 2014 offers contemporary, focused, and distilled insight into what soccer coaches need to do, and how!

Lightning Source UK Ltd.
Milton Keynes UK
UKOW04f2137281014

240751UK00001BA/87/P